Something in the Wind

Politics After Chernobyl

EDITED BY LOUIS MACKAY and MARK THOMPSON

PLUTO PRESS

European Nuclear Disarmament (END) in
collaboration with the Transnational Institute (TNI)

First published in 1988 by Pluto Publishing Ltd
11–21 Northdown Street
London N1 9BN

Distributed in the USA by Allen & Unwin Inc.
8 Winchester Place
Winchester
MA 01890, USA

Typesetting: Ransom Typesetting Services, Woburn Sands, Bucks

Printed and bound in the United Kingdom by Billing & Sons Ltd,
Worcester

British Library Cataloguing in Publication Data

Something in the Wind: politics after Chernobyl
1. Nuclear power. Political aspects
I. Mackay, Louis II. Thompson, Mark
333.79'–24

ISBN 0–7453–0257–2
ISBN 0–7453–0258–6–Pbk

Contents

List of Maps and Diagrams

Acknowledgements

The editors wish to thank: the Save the Earth Trust in New York, for a grant which made this project possible; the authors, for their enthusiasm and punctuality; Mary Kaldor, Kate Soper and Taggart Deike, for many helpful suggestions; Roger van Zwanenberg and all at Pluto Press; and – for support and assistance of various kinds – Paul Anderson, Hugh Baldwin, Patrick Burke, Bernard Dréano, Peter Findlay, Renata Ingrao, Martin Jacobson, Lynne Jones, Gerhard Jordan, Nikki Kortkelyessy, Jakob Lagerkrantz, Tim Lang, Hugo Maldonado, Bob McGlynn, Kim Mills, Sara Parkin, Walt Patterson, Mario Pianta, Mr Pospiesalki, John F. Potter, Editor of *The Environmentalist*, Brendan Prendiville, Sybla Schoene, Taeko Miura of the Tokyo Citizens' Nuclear Information Centre, the Ukranian Peace Committee, Fiona Weir, Professor Peter Worsley.

Preface

MARY KALDOR

In 1986, six weeks before the Chernobyl explosion, I visited Bhopal in India. There, in 1983, a cloud of poisonous gas (methyl isocyanate) leaked from the Union Carbide chemical plant. Ten thousand people or thereabouts – no one knows how many – were killed, and others are still dying. Some 200,000 were severely incapacitated, mostly by eye and lung injuries. There were psychological effects, too – the incalculable sense of loss. Something about Bhopal – an uneasy quietness, a look on people's faces in the streets – reminded me of nothing so much as the pictures I had seen of survivors of Hiroshima and Nagasaki: a blank, hopeless expression of emptiness.

Hiroshima, Nagasaki, Bhopal, Chernobyl: all were man-made catastrophes, unprecedented in their enormity. And yet, precisely because of their enormity, they are hard to comprehend. We try not to think about them. Hiroshima and Nagasaki took place over 40 years ago. Bhopal is far away. In the case of Chernobyl all of us, in Europe especially, were in a certain sense victims. Invisible and insidious, the radiation passed over the Northern hemisphere enveloping us all, socialist and capitalist, neutral and aligned, rich and poor. It irradiated the food which was offloaded in the Southern hemisphere. For many years to come it will claim cancer patients, but we will never know for sure whether the cancers were caused by the cloud.

'Civil' nuclear energy is the offspring of nuclear weapons. It originated with the Manhattan Project in the United States. Zhores Medvedev points out in the first chapter of this book that the Soviet Union was the first country to adapt a nuclear reactor to generate electricity, at Obninsk in 1954, and that the reactor was part of an 'empire of military atomic installations and research centres'. The first British 'civil' reactor at Windscale was designed to produce weapons-grade plutonium. The link with nuclear weapons continues to be important, especially in relation to the spread of nuclear facilities to the Third World.

Nuclear energy has never fulfilled the dreams of its promoters. Although it clearly had some economic attractions, it has never been either safe or cheap. It turned out to be technically very difficult, and involved expensive arrangements for security. In recent years particularly, it has generated considerable public unease and has been a source of x Something in the Wind

continuing domestic conflict and tension. After Chernobyl, Soviet demonstrators handing out petitions which demanded a reassessment of nuclear energy were arrested and eventually expelled to the West. In Britain, the Minister of the Environment explained that the only problem with nuclear energy was convincing the public of its safety.

Nuclear energy survived and continues to survive because of the support of the state – and this is true East and West, North and South. State support is greatest where there is a parallel commitment to national nuclear weapons, as in France. It is the nuclear establishment – the scientists and engineers, the enterprises which constructed the plants – that have been the most enthusiastic advocates of nuclear energy. 'Atoms for peace', as it was called in the 1950s, provided a rationale for their work.

The development of both nuclear weapons and nuclear energy has been shrouded in secrecy and virtually removed from public and parliamentary control. The secrecy is justified in the name of national security and the Cold War. It is the continued East–West confrontation which legitimises this state within a state – legitimises the kind of political behaviour that, at least in Western democracies, is normally warranted only in wartime.

Right from the beginning, the nuclear programme was linked to the Cold War. The decision to keep the technology a secret, even though scientists warned that the secret could not be kept for long, precipitated an almost mystical paranoia about communist subversives in the US in the late 1940s and early 1950s. The Atomic Energy Act, passed in 1946, contained severe penalties, including the death sentence, for anyone giving away atomic information to foreign nationals. And when the USSR exploded its first device in 1949 the witch-hunt for spies was on, even though the scientists pointed out many times that the passing of information could not accelerate the development of a Soviet bomb (or a British bomb, for that matter) by more than a few months.

It is worth noting that the only country which had, before Chernobyl, taken a decision to phase out nuclear power is Sweden (though many other 'developed' countries, including Australia and New Zealand, have never initiated nuclear power programmes). Sweden stands outside the Cold War and has a history of openness in government and responsiveness to public concern.

It was because of our conviction that Chernobyl was, above all, an expression of the deeper underlying structures of the Cold War that we in European Nuclear Disarmament decided to take up the issue. We have always argued that the Cold War is both a conflict and a kind of collusion between the superpowers, a way of maintaining a permanent wartime atmosphere without the danger and unpredictability of war, in order to preserve social hierarchy and political cohesion within the respective spheres of influence. It is an ideological collusion as well; the last two chapters of this book both point out that what appears to be a fundamental opposition between liberalism and Marxism – the ideologies of Cold War – is based on a shared Northern premise of modernity which dates back to the Enlightenment. That premise includes the notion that science and technology inevitably bring human progress and that a Newtonian rationality can be imposed on both nature and society. The belief in pure rationality is also a universalist claim. If there is one logic to be discovered in society and nature, then there is also one correct solution to human problems, which cannot tolerate other 'solutions'. Fundamental antagonism and totalitarian technologies, like nuclear power, are an inevitable corollary to this way of thinking. And these ideological assumptions are built into the institutions of Cold War.

In END, our strategy is to excavate Cold War assumptions and challenge the institutions founded on them. We do not propose yet more solutions or certainties, though we do not reject rational thinking. Rather, we hope that the dialogue between a variety of movements which cross the East–West and North–South divides can help to change political processes and cultural attitudes. Communication and sharing of experience is both a form of enlightenment and a way of creating a space for alternative thinking in different societies.

In various chapters of this book, we use terms like 'civil society', 'antipolitics' or 'autonomy', which have been learned or relearned from our friends in Eastern Europe. These terms have to do fundamentally with democracy. 'Civil society' means the establishment of social institutions which are independent or 'autonomous' from the state, and therefore able to influence the state. The term 'antipolitics', used by George Konrád in Hungary and Václav Havel in Czechoslovakia, is really a political concept. It is about our own responsibility for constructing social relationships to which the state has to respond, rather than the other way round. In the realm of state and party politics, which extends through the whole of society in Eastern Europe, the only options are 'with us' or 'against us'. No middle way is permitted. The Cold War antagonism is reproduced inside each individual. In the realm of antipolitics, variety and experiment are tolerated and indeed encouraged. There are, of course, practical political and technological proposals to be argued for and against. But there are no once-and-for-all answers and so, one hopes, no big mistakes like Chernobyl.

If Chernobyl was a turning point, it is perhaps because it facilitated this dialogue. It heightened our awareness of the common European, indeed global, predicament. Chernobyl was equivalent to a small nuclear explosion. It helped us to realise that we have to live together on this overcrowded continent and in this world, which is all we have. And learning to live together is a much more difficult and painful process than simply forswearing nuclear war. For those of us in the West, Chernobyl offered some glimpses into the workings of authoritarian non-democratic societies; we learned a little bit more about the difficulty of questioning technological assumptions in a society where one is not allowed to question. Especially on the Left, Eastern Europe has been one of those problems we did not want to think about; Chernobyl forced us to think, and to realise some of the connections between their problems and ours.

In the East, Chernobyl aroused a new consciousness of nuclear weapons and nuclear power. Earlier, our obsessions with the nuclear issue had proved a barrier to communication between Western peace groups and peace, civil liberties, and green groups in the East. Just as many activists in the Third World argue that worrying about nuclear war is the luxury of those who don't have to worry about their next meal, so in the East, our counterparts argued that dying in a nuclear war was not as bad as the living death of a Stalinist society. Moreover, nuclear power seemed preferable to the fearful environmental and human cost of giant hydroelectric plants or dirty fossil fuel plants. Chernobyl introduced the hazards of radiation to Eastern European citizens. And more importantly, it may have helped our Eastern friends to understand our concerns about democracy a little better. Although we in the West are free to speak, organise and publish, the nuclear state does threaten to infringe and erode Western democracy.

Not all this was due, of course, simply to Chernobyl. Chernobyl brought to the surface existing concerns in our societies. It was a kind of proof, if proof were needed, of warnings and worries already expressed. Chernobyl had less visible impact in France, for instance, than in Britain; not just because of governmental deceit, but because French public opinion had not been prepared by recent debate on nuclear issues. Indeed, there is a danger that by focusing on the accident, or on the horrors of nuclear war, we lose sight of the deeper anxieties about the continuing arms race and the environment. Our concern is with the denial of civil liberties, with being poisoned, with poverty. Disasters like Chernobyl or Bhopal draw our attention to the continuing consequences of a technocracy which is subject only to the dictates of military priority or profit, beyond democratic accountability.

The impact of Chernobyl was different from previous nuclear accidents: different from Three Mile Island in 1979 and different from Windscale in 1957, which most of us did not even know about. It was different not so much because of the accident itself as because the growth of peace and green movements, the loss of post-war optimism, and the growing diffidence about progress in East and West shaped a different kind of reaction. If Chernobyl marks a turning point, it is because the world has begun to query the certainties of a generation.

Since Chernobyl, *perestroika* and *glasnost* have been announced in the USSR. The possibility of space for social movements in Eastern Europe or of troop withdrawals is no longer ruled out. Since Chernobyl, the INF treaty has been signed and nuclear disarmament has been put on a realistic agenda for the coming years; it is no longer just the aspiration of utopian mass protest. What Chernobyl taught those of us preoccupied with disarmament is that if we are to dismantle the structures of Cold War, our thinking has to encompass other concerns, to weave the problems of disarmament, the environment or poverty into new forms of democratic politics.

This book intends to show the connections between peace, green and civil liberties issues, as revealed by Chernobyl. In the first chapter, Zhores Medvedev provides a remarkable account of the Soviet nuclear power programme. Richard Erskine and Philip Webber establish the connections between nuclear power and nuclear weapons in the second chapter, and in Chapter 3 Martin Ince considers the role of special interest groups, and of secrecy, in nuclear power decision-making. The next two chapters, by the editors, are based on END's own experience of East–West and North–South dialogues between social movements, and how Chernobyl opened new possibilities to develop these dialogues.

In the book's final section, we put forward some thoughts about alternative possibilities. Gordon MacKerron shows in very concrete terms the immediate ways in which the world could reduce its reliance on nuclear energy. Praful Bidwai proposes alternative ways of thinking about economic and social/political development in the Third World. And in the concluding chapter, Kate Soper and Martin Ryle develop the philosophical thrust of our argument: how to move away from the technocratic assumptions of Cold War towards an international democratic politics. They explore the kinds of contradictions, difficulties and objections involved in this process of thinking beyond the narrow limitations defined by the market and the centralised state, by consumerism and by militarism – beyond the technological delirium of the post-Second World War period.

On a wall in Bhopal someone had painted, in English, 'No Bhopal! No Hiroshima! Down with the superpowers! Smash multinationals!' I was struck that in this poverty-stricken city in the middle of India, someone had been able to see their situation in a global perspective. Now, I keep wondering whether they have added: 'No Chernobyl!'

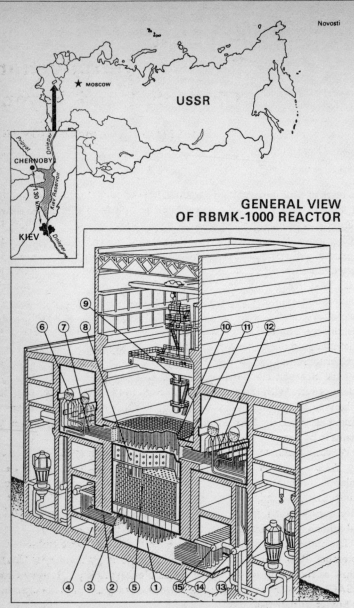

USSR

★ MOSCOW

CHERNOBYL

KIEV

Pripyat

Dniepr

Kiev Reservoir

30 Km

Dniepr

GENERAL VIEW OF RBMK-1000 REACTOR

1—support metalwork; 2—individual water pipes; 3—bottom metalwork; 4—side biological shield; 5—graphite pile; 6—drum-separator; 7—individual steam-and-water pipes; 8—top metal-work; 9—charge and discharge machine; 10—top central floor; 11—top side floor; 12—fuel element can tightness check system; 13—master circulating pump; 14—suction manifold; 15—header manifold.

Introduction:
Chernobyl and Beyond

LOUIS MACKAY and MARK THOMPSON

This book was germinated by Chernobyl, but our subject is much wider than that single catastrophe, and wider than the dangers of nuclear power generation, on which the accident has focused much-needed attention. For us, Chernobyl offers a lens through which to examine the broader political context in which nuclear technology exists – a context formed by the interwoven threads of energy and development policy, the ecological crisis, East–West and North–South relations, military and security considerations, and the political problems of achieving democratic control over policy-making, with freedom of information and expression. These questions were around long before 26 April 1986, when the No. 4 unit of the Soviet plant ran out of control, and they remain with us.

Chernobyl was only one environmental disaster among many, and only one – the most serious to date – of a catalogue of accidents in the history of nuclear power. With the number of reactors in the world still rising, it is unlikely to be the last. Whether or not it will prove to have been the moment at which the tide began at last to turn against nuclear power still remains to be seen.

We see no need to rehearse in detail the sequence of events of April and May 1986; much has been written about them elsewhere, and is easily available. But because Chernobyl is our starting-point we think it would be useful, before going on to consider the background to the accident and the wider questions it raises, to summarise what actually happened, and its local human and environmental effects, so far as they are known.

The most authoritative account of the accident was published in September 1986 by the International Atomic Energy Agency (IAEA) in Vienna as the report of the International Nuclear Safety Advisory Group (INSAG) which investigated the circumstances with the cooperation of the Soviet authorities.

It was in the course of what was intended to be a special electrical systems test, begun on 25 April, shortly before the unit was due to be shut down for scheduled maintenance, that the accident occurred. The test was supposed to demonstrate improvements in the capacity of the plant's turbine generators, running only on their own inertia, to keep the reactor's

1

'emergency core cooling system' operating during the brief interval between shutting off the normal steam supply and starting up the emergency diesel generators. This test was initiated by electrical engineers, rather than nuclear experts, and the presumption was that it would have no effect on the reactor's safety systems. Consequently, INSAG reported, 'procedures were poorly prepared in respect of safety', and the authority to go ahead with the experiment was given 'without the necessary formal approval by the station safety technology group'. Subsequent events, according to INSAG's assessment, were primarily the product of a series of further 'wilful violations of procedure', stemming from over-confidence and compounded by certain characteristics of the RBMK reactor design.

Like all nuclear power reactors, the RBMK (decribed in more detail by Zhores Medvedev in Chapter 1) is designed to generate steam with the heat of a controlled nuclear chain-reaction; the steam drives the turbines which generate electricity. The chain reaction is the multiplying effect of neutrons hitting the nuclei of uranium atoms, causing them to undergo fission – to split and emit a greater number of new neutrons, which in turn strike other uranium nuclei with the same result, releasing a great deal of energy in the process. The reaction depends on the presence of a certain 'critical' mass of the uranium fuel within a confined space. In a power reactor, this reaction takes place in the reactor 'core' (which houses the fuel elements), where it is controlled with the aid of a 'moderator' (material which slows down the neutrons and improves their chances of hitting a nucleus – all reactor types except 'fast breeders' have some kind of moderator), a 'coolant' (liquid or gas which conducts heat away from the fuel elements in the core), and a control system – often consisting, as it does in RBMK reactors, of rods of neutron-absorbing material which can be inserted into the core to slow or stop the reaction. In the RBMK system the moderator is graphite and the coolant, water. A somewhat unusual feature of this Soviet system is the use of the same water as coolant and as the source of the steam which drives the turbine-generators. The system has other idiosyncrasies, which we shall return to shortly.

At the start of the test at Chernobyl, safety procedures were immediately violated when the emergency cooling system was isolated in order to forestall the possibility of triggering it and aborting the experiment (Soviet experts later said that the test could in fact have been conducted without isolating the cooling system). The power being generated by the reactor was then gradually run down according to plan, but the operator neglected to enter the command which would have held it at the required level of 700 megawatts of thermal power (700 MWt). As a result, the power was allowed to drop right down to 30 MWt. The loss of 'reactivity' (the rate of the nuclear fission reaction) was aggravated by the presence of xenon gas (a normal product of the fission) which absorbs neutrons to a degree which is described as 'poisoning' the system. To compensate for this, the similarly neutron-absorbing 'manual' control rods were withdrawn from the reactor core. This allowed the reactivity, and thus the power level, to rise again; but this was only achieved with some difficulty. After a time the power was stabilised at 200 MWt – still well below the minimum permissible level, where the required reserve reactivity was lacking.

It is in this condition of low power, with the control rods withdrawn, that a characteristic feature of the RBMK reactor becomes problematic – its 'positive void coefficient'. What this means is that increased boiling (which reduces the 'coolant density' by creating greater 'voids' of steam in the water cooling the reactor core) increases the reactivity and the power, while reduced boiling has the reverse effect. In normal operating conditions at high power levels, the positive void coefficient is offset by a 'negative fuel temperature coefficient' (that is, the reactivity declines as the temperature of the fuel rises). At low power, however, the positive void coefficient becomes dominant in this particular system, which then also becomes unstable and difficult to control as a consequence of volatile relationships between power, steam volume and steam mass.

With the reactor in this unstable condition, and in order to simulate the load normally provided to the generators by the emergency cooling system pump (now disconnected), the operators switched in some additional cooling pumps. This further reduced the reactivity (and the reserve margin) and more control rods were withdrawn to compensate. The coolant-flow rate was also boosted beyond the permitted limits, which led to serious difficulties in handling the cooling system. To keep the test going, the operators blocked a further set of automatic shutdown signals operated by steam pressure.

Over the next few minutes, there were a number of other fatal mistakes and procedural violations, including the further withdrawal of control rods to the point where the operators should have recognised that it was imperative to shut down the reactor. According to INSAG, however, the reactor (and the lives lost) might still have been saved until 23 minutes and four seconds past one a.m. on 26 April when, in order to allow a repeat of the test, the operators disabled yet another safety system – a trip activated by the loss of one of the generators which would have shut the reactor down automatically – and closed off an emergency stop valve on the turbine itself. The steam pressure began to rise, and with it, the reactivity and the power. But in the reactor's highly unstable state, the control rods were no longer able to balance the power surge. Barely half a minute after blocking the last automatic trip, the station foreman ordered a shutdown. But it was now too late. It is estimated that within the next four seconds, the power level rose to 100 times the reactor's maximum rating.

The containment structure housing the reactor was covered by a concrete plate weighing 1,000 tonnes. An explosion of steam blew it off like the lid of a saucepan.

Two or three seconds later, with the control rods now blown out and the cooling system pipes ruptured, there was a second explosion in which the core largely disintegrated. The operators pumped water into the remains of the reactor, but it was now exposed to the air. Steam was seen escaping during the first day. By the second day, there was smoke. The fire burned for ten days, until 5 May, consuming at least 10 per cent of the graphite from the reactor core, and probably much more.

During those ten days strenuous efforts were made to control the fire. First, some 5,000 tons of sand, clay, lead and dolomite were dropped on the burning plant from the air. This actually caused the temperature in the remains of the reactor core to rise further, to about 3,000°C, which led ultimately to a meltdown in the individual fuel channels. What finally put the fire out was probably the liquid nitrogen injected in massive quantities beneath the reactor, to solidify the underlying soil and thus prevent the meltdown from penetrating the foundations and reaching the groundwater.

These changing conditions led to major variations in the pattern of radionuclides released into the atmosphere during this period. Not counting the inert radioactive gases, xenon and krypton (which escaped in large quantities but are not considered a major environmental hazard), the total radioactivity released from an array of different isotopes is estimated to have amounted to about 50 megacuries (a megacurie (MCi) is a million Curies; a Curie (Ci), the radioactivity of one gram of radium, is equal to 37 thousand million Becquerels (Bq), or radioactive emissions per second). The final day of the fire alone accounted for the discharge of some 8 MCi. The following day, when the situation was reported finally to be 'under control', a mere 150,000 Ci were released – still more than the total during the 1957 Windscale fire. The scale of the emissions gradually declined, but even at the end of May more radioactive material was still being released each *day* from Chernobyl (20–50 Ci) than the total from the Three Mile Island accident. Not until October, when the reactor was finally entombed in its 'sarcophagus' – 400,000 tons of reinforced concrete – did it cease to be a source of airborne fallout.[1]

Detectable fallout from Chernobyl eventually reached most parts of the northern hemisphere. In several European countries it seriously affected agriculture and livestock husbandry, bringing substantial economic losses as well as some danger to health. But only in the Soviet Union did the radiological contamination reach the levels officially considered incompatible with human habitation, necessitating the resettlement of some 130,000 people and a massive decontamination programme.

The most thorough independent study published so far of the environmental impact of the accident within the USSR, by Zhores

Medvedev, appeared in the Autumn 1987 number of *The Environmentalist* magazine. To date, only one scientific paper dealing with the environmental and medical consequences has been published in the USSR, so Medvedev's analysis is based largely on information submitted to the IAEA by the Soviet delegation, and on some general reports in the Soviet media, backed up by the author's own knowledge and experience – both of radiobiological studies in the Soviet Union (in which he participated directly for 20 years up until 1972), and of previous analysis of the ecological aspects of a Soviet nuclear disaster.[2] It is with the permission of the author, and the editor of *The Environmentalist*, that we summarise and paraphrase some of the main points in the article.

The original 'exclusion zone' around the stricken reactor, announced on 27 April, was only 10 km in radius. Extended to 30 km on 2 May, this zone included many of the most heavily contaminated areas, though others were found outside the zone, as far as 60 km to the north and north-west of Chernobyl, near the small towns of Bragino and Elsk. Areas relatively close to the reactor site also accounted for much of the most dangerous contamination by heavy and long-lived radionuclides, such as strontium-90 and several isotopes of plutonium. Little if any of these was carried to more distant parts of Europe, where more volatile caesium isotopes were the main long-term contaminants.

Within the 30 km zone, the level of ground contamination was high enough to produce such obvious ecological effects as visible damage to rodents and plants. One Soviet press report in July said that 'people could see with their own eyes how pine trees turned yellow and died.'[3]

During the first ten days after the accident, 72 villages near Chernobyl were evacuated and abandoned for good. The decontamination measures carried out during the summer and autumn included the removal of topsoil from the most seriously affected areas, both inside and outside the exclusion zone; what was done with the topsoil is not known. Bush land was cleared, but there was no means of decontaminating the marshes and swamps which are common to this region on the border between the Ukraine and Byelorussia – known in English as the Pripet Marshes, and in Russian as *Polesye* ('the Woodlands'). This forested wetland will remain contaminated for decades with radioactive caesium, which is quickly absorbed into plant tissues. The 'Working Document' submitted by the Soviet authorities to the IAEA's Post-Accident Review Meeting in Vienna considered 100,000 sq km of the Polesye region to be the most seriously in danger from fallout. But outside the exclusion zone, its human population (about 6 million) was not considered to be at risk. The Soviet figure for the amount of caesium-137 released, incidentally, is regarded as a serious underestimate by Harwell scientists, whose own estimate is almost twice as high, corresponding to 25 per cent of what had been in the reactor core.

The Polesye region would also have received a substantial dose of strontium-90, also likely to remain dangerous for several decades. Occasional reports in the Soviet press have indicated some of the measures taken in an attempt to deal with strontium contamination on agricultural land, including the distribution of lime, whose calcium has the property of fixing strontium, and extra deep ploughing, to bury the original topsoil. How effective these measures will have been is open to question. Other reports suggested that surface contamination was to be reduced over an area of 200 km radius as a result of collecting mown grass and fallen leaves, and burying them as nuclear waste. This would have had some effect in the case of caesium, but less in the case of strontium and plutonium.

The 30 km exclusion zone encompassed a number of aquatic ecosystems (which would have been subjected to significant radioactive contamination even from the normal operation of the Chernobyl plant, with its relatively 'dirty' RBMK system), including a section of the Pripyat river and the northern part of the 1,000 sq km Kiev reservoir behind the Kiev–Dniepr dam.

The Chernobyl cooling ponds, whose water already contained substantial concentrations of radionuclides, would have received severe additional contamination as a result of the accident – not only from fallout, but also from reactor debris, broken pipes, the emergency cooling system and the water with which the fire brigade flooded the reactor in an effort to cool it, over a period of some 12 hours, at a rate of 200–300 tons per hour. The decontamination teams spared no efforts to prevent this accumulated water entering the nearby reservoirs and river systems – a particular danger during the spring thaw. By April 1987 they had erected some 80 km of protective dams and underground walls with this purpose, including a 2 km diameter 'saucepan in the earth' around the plant site – a wall extending 34 metres below the surface so as to reach the layer of impermeable clay and isolate the site hydrologically. The 22 sq km cooling pond next to the plant, though, was beyond salvation. Soviet experts acknowledge that the fish population in this lake will be badly damaged (and fish are ten times more resistant to radiation than mammals). Some injection of caesium salts from ground water into the surrounding water systems during the spring run-off is also inevitable.

The impact of the accident on Soviet agriculture was much more far reaching than its direct impact on ecological systems. Restrictions on the consumption of various foodstuffs were imposed in 15 regions of the Soviet Union, where they affected 75 million people. The levels of radioactive iodine and caesium contamination allowed by Soviet emergency regulations, however, are much higher than those laid down by the World Health Organisation. A blanket ban on the sale of dairy products (except through regulated state shops) was imposed in many regions. This provided only partial protection for people in the affected areas. The scale of the contamination, and the shortage of equipment and qualified personnel, made it impossible to monitor the contamination in most villages outside the exclusion zone. The rural population (about 30–40 per cent of the total in the Ukraine and Byelorussia) is still largely self-sufficient in milk, meat and vegetables, and the state had few alternative supplies with which to replace, even temporarily, these staples in people's daily diet.

Livestock farming in the Polesye region was most seriously affected. In addition to the 72 villages pemanently abandoned, a further 180 were temporarily evacuated, with the expectation that they would be repopulated after the completion of decontamination work. By April 1987, only 16 of these had been repopulated.

Contamination of milk by iodine-131 was well above the Soviet 'action level' throughout the central Ukraine, the whole of Byelorussia, parts of Moldavia and several regions in Russia proper, including Kaluga, only 100 km from Moscow. In many regions, 30–50 per cent of meat and milk was judged unfit for human consumption. Instead of destroying contaminated milk, however, the Soviet authorities, always concerned about shortages, recommended that it be used to make cheese and butter, which could be kept in long-term storage while the radioactivity declined. Contaminated grain was to be used as animal fodder, but not within two months of slaughter, so the meat would be 'clean' by the time it was killed. It is unclear what became of contaminated meat. Two years after the accident, much else concerning its effects on agriculture remains classified.

The official death toll from the accident presently stands at 31; two people were killed in the accident itself and 29 died later in hospitals in Moscow and Kiev. Among them were courageous members of the emergency services who must have known, as they fought to control the fire, that they were cutting short their own lives. According to a recent report in *Sovyetskaya Rossiya*, other casualties included 238 cases of acute radiation sickness (seven more than previously admitted).[4] Of these, 209 are said to be 'out of danger', although 24 are 'invalids of the first or second category' – permanently and severely disabled. The same article put the total cost of the tragedy at 8 million roubles.

The information provided by the Soviet Union to the 1986 IAEA symposium following the accident was generally regarded as very inadequate. At the end of September 1987, a second report was delivered to the Agency's International Conference on Nuclear Power Performance and Safety in Vienna, which revealed further details both of the scale of the contamination and of the measures taken to mitigate its impact.[5] This document mentions the decontamination of 600 population centres with measures which included, besides the stripping and burial of topsoil, 'the suppression of dust over large areas' and 'the asphalting or covering of

contaminated sectors with gravel, chippings, sand or fresh earth.'
Initially, the main concern was with iodine-131, which accumulates in the
thyroid gland. In all, 5.4 million people, including 1.7 million children,
were given prophylactic iodine in order to inhibit the intake of the
radioactive isotope.

The report concedes that the average overall per capita radiation
dose from Chernobyl – which added about 2 per cent to the natural
background radiation – was two to three times higher than the additional
dose received in other countries affected by the fallout. (The Soviet
average dose includes, of course, regions such as the Soviet far east,
extremely remote from Chernobyl, where the fallout was scarcely
significant.) But the general drift of this latest report is to emphasise the
success of the measures taken, and the minimal character of the injury
inflicted on the health of Soviet citizens. The birthrate in the
contaminated regions has not been affected, and no 'teratogenic' effects
(resulting from irradiation of a foetus) have been observed in any child
born. Nor, for that matter, have the Soviet authorities observed any
statistical increase in deficiencies of the auto-immune system, allergies,
congenital heart disorders, pneumonias, infectious diseases or cancers: 'not
one case of leukaemia was recorded among the children exposed in
1986–87'.

The highest doses of radioactive caesium (50 milli-Sieverts, or 5
rems), which affected fewer than 1 per cent of those examined, are said to
have been ingested as a consequence of disregarding bans on consumption of
farm produce in severely affected areas. As for the 'psychoneurological
disease rate', again, no increase was noticeable. Some people did
complain, however, of 'mental and physical sluggishness and vegetative
disorders'. In this respect, the authors note a rise in the level of anxiety
concerning health risks to children and the disruption of normal life in
areas bordering on the 30 km exclusion zone. This stress, they continue, was
causing 'radiation phobia syndrome', which, in the current situation,
might 'pose an even greater threat to health than exposure to radiation
itself'.

It is with this threat in mind, no doubt, that the Soviet authorities
refrain from publishing any cancer case projections, while being very
critical of the projections that have been made elsewhere. It is true, of
course, that projections made in respect of a given dose of radiation vary
widely – from WHO's 100 additional cancer deaths per million per rem of
increased radiation, to the several thousand deaths predicted for the
same circumstances by some US scientists.[6] It seems unlikely, however,
that many oncologists would be impressed by the absence of any increase in
cancer deaths during the immediate aftermath of Chernobyl, since most
cancers resulting from radiation exposure take 20–30 years to manifest
themselves – and even leukaemias (of which 'not one case was recorded')

typically take 2–7 years. Over such a period, though, a study of the incidence of leukaemia in fallout areas would be informative – the more so since the underlying incidence of these and other cancers is relatively low in rural parts of the Soviet Union.

Outside the conference hall, the 1987 Soviet report to the IAEA found a somewhat sceptical response. Much critical comment centred on the presentation of the statistics, particularly the use of averages, applying to the entirety of a vast country (much of it untouched by any serious contamination), or to whole administrative regions, in a way which appeared designed to downplay the gravity of the effects in the more severely irradiated districts; or – as the authors infelicitously put it in a phrase which perhaps said more than it was intended to – 'to eliminate the consequences'.

Within the conference, however, the report encountered little criticism. This was scarcely surprising. For one thing, it probably contained more information than had been expected. But its tone of confidence and optimism could only have been welcome to the representatives of other countries' nuclear establishments, which share wholeheartedly the concern of the Soviet authorities to protect people from such grave threats to health as 'radiation phobia syndrome'.

Notes

1. Zhores A. Medvedev, 'The Environmental Impact of Chernobyl in the Soviet Union', *The Environmentalist*, vol.7, no. 3, Autumn 1987.
2. Zhores A. Medvedev, *Nuclear Disaster in the Urals*, W.W. Norton, USA, 1979.
3. *Nedeliya*, 17–20 July 1986.
4. *Sovyetskaya Rossiya*, 31 January 1988.
5. L.A. Ilyin and O.A. Pavlovsky, *Radiological Consequences of the Chernobyl Accident in the Soviet Union and Measures taken to Mitigate their Impact*, Institute of Biophysics, USSR Ministry of Public Health, Moscow, 1987.
6. See, for instance, Manusco et al. Source: *Chernobyl: the Aftermath*, BEUC, Brussels, 1986.

Part I
The Facts

1

The Soviet Nuclear Energy Programme: The Road to Chernobyl

ZHORES MEDVEDEV

Introduction

The Soviet Union was the first country to adapt nuclear reactors for the production of electricity. Soviet nuclear scientists, therefore, proudly consider this apparent achievement as the beginning of a new era of peaceful atomic energy use. An experimental nuclear power station, known now as the Obninsk Atomic Energy Station (AES), started to generate electricity on 27 June 1954. This plant was an integral part of the Physico-Power Institute, now the largest centre of reactor technology in the Soviet Union and responsible for the development and design of many subsequent types of reactor, including the pressurised water reactors for ships and submarines, and the fast breeders.

> The city of Obninsk, where this Institute is located, is now well-known not only to the Soviet people, but to the whole civilised world. It was here that the world's first nuclear power station was built. It was here that the triumphant procession of nuclear power generation started. It was here that the problem of controlling the fission reaction of uranium was solved, for the production of electric power, so necessary to mankind.[1]

This opinion, expressed by N. Petrosyants, Chairman of the Soviet Committee for Atomic Energy, and commonplace in the Soviet Union, is disputed by many experts in the West, however, as the Obninsk AES was experimental and very small – only about 5 MWe (megawatts of electric power) – and therefore had no commercial value. Its own electrical needs (for water pumps and other systems and controls) probably required more than 5 MW and drew on the general grid of the Moscow energy network.

Western authors normally take the Calder Hall 50 MWe reactor as the first real nuclear power station. This plant was an order of magnitude larger than Obninsk AES. It was switched into the British national grid on 17 October 1956 by Her Majesty Queen Elizabeth II, amid much international publicity. This high public profile made Calder Hall's claims for priority defensible, as Walter Patterson has noted, 'by default, if not by common consent' and 'because the general public heard little about the first US and Soviet power reactors'.[2] (The first US power reactor was tested for military submarines and was a secret project.) Petrosyants's statement that Obninsk is well known to the 'whole civilised world' is, of course, an optimistic exaggeration. Even now, in 1988, Obninsk is closed to foreigners. In 1954 it was not even a town in the conventional sense, but a kind of secret prison-camp research facility, where prominent Soviet scientists worked alongside German physicists who were prisoners of war. A prison labour camp was attached to the research centre, and the construction and other work on the site were largely carried out by its inmates. The settlement – still with no name in 1954, only a 'PO Box' with a number – was part of a vast empire of military atomic installations and research centres headed by Igor Kurchatov, a father of the Soviet atomic bomb and a legendary figure in Soviet science.

One of Kurchatov's biographers has described how public excursions were organised to the first AES after its existence was officially announced.[3] Officials were probably familiar with Obninsk, but the public knew very little about it and even its location was kept secret. The announcement by the USSR Council of Ministers 'Concerning the Inauguration in the USSR of the First Industrial Power Station using Atomic Energy' was published in all Moscow newspapers on 1 July 1954; but it was very brief, indicating only the date, the power produced, and the claim that its electricity would be used by industry and agriculture in surrounding districts. The location of the plant was not given, and no further details were released for nearly a year. Even the photo of the building, now reproduced in every Soviet book on nuclear energy, was not made available in 1954. That the event did not become an international sensation is not, therefore, surprising.

Igor Kurchatov was also a chief designer of the first Soviet experimental reactor, tested in a northern suburb of Moscow on 25 December 1946. (The site now belongs to the Kurchatov Institute of Atomic Energy.) He was also in charge of the first Soviet military reactor designed and built – in the Kyshtym district of the Chelyabinsk region in the Urals – to produce plutonium for the first atomic bomb test, carried out on 23 September 1949. Kurchatov's biographers indicate that his proposal for the first power reactor was submitted in 1949 and that within a year he had already received governmental approval to start work.[4] Kurchatov picked D. I. Blokhintsev, who directed the 'Obninsk Institute', to head the project, though Kurchatov himself often visited the site and examined everything, particularly the emergency shutdown mechanisms. The scientific team responsible for the first AES also included Nikolai A. Dollezhal and Anatoly A. Alexandrov.[5] Dollezhal – an expert on power stations, not an atomic physicist – completed the blueprints for the power turbine, while Kurchatov chaired discussions concerning the best choice of reactor model. The alternatives included the gas-cooled system. It was Kurchatov himself, according to his biographers, who finally chose the graphite-moderated, water-cooled model, apparently because it had already been successfully tested for military purposes. During this period, plutonium production was the most important economic consideration, and designers naturally favoured the models which would yield the most.

The 'dawning of a new era' with the inauguration of the 'first AES' on 27 June 1954 was not a public event: no journalists were present. It was not described in detail until 1967, seven years after Kurchatov's death, by his biographers.[6] The prison research centre at the place which is now Obninsk was dismantled in 1955, when all the remaining German prisoners of war and deportees were released and returned to Germany – a condition for the establishment of diplomatic relations between the USSR and the Federal Republic of Germany. The participation of German scientists in the Soviet nuclear programme was known in the West, but only acknowledged in the Soviet Union with D. A. Granin's 1987 biography of N.W. Timofeeff-Ressovsky, a prominent Soviet radiation geneticist who lived and worked in Germany from 1926 to 1945.[7] Granin describes the work of a research team of German scientists in the Ural nuclear–military centre, where they were attached to the plutonium producing facilities. In 1955 the 'laboratory was closed and the Germans were allowed to return home. This surprised them very much: they had expected to have to work much longer for the victorious power.'[8] The most prominent of these German scientists were Professors A. G. Zimmer and N. Riehl. Riehl was also closely involved in Germany's own nuclear project in 1941–5. (The US Institute of Information *Citation Index* shows a gap in Riehl's obtainable publications between 1941 and 1956.)

The secret research facilities in Kaluga were only given the status of a town, and named Obninsk, in 1958 – that, at least, was the year when Obninsk first appeared on Soviet maps. Several more research institutes were established here, including the Research Institute of Medical Radiology in 1962. That same year, I was invited to the Institute to establish the laboratory of molecular radiobiology. I lived in Obninsk for nearly ten years (1963–73), and it was then, and probably still is, a very pleasant town. Everybody who lives and works in an 'atomic' centre like Obninsk acquires a more than superficial knowledge of the details of atomic energy, although local officials are very concerned with preserving the secrecy of everything linked to atomic research.

Between 1974 and 1980, while based in Britain, I was able to visit the United States' principal nuclear research centres – the Argonne, Brookhaven, Oak Ridge and Los Alamos National Laboratories. At none of these did I see such elaborate security systems as those at Obninsk, where more than a battalion of professional military guards, with dogs, patrol a system of multiple fences and electrified wires separated by strips of freshly ploughed ground. Obninsk scientists played a very active role in the repair work at Chernobyl and helped to bring the other three units there back into operation. However, when *Sarcophagus* – a play about Chernobyl by V. Gubarev, science editor of *Pravda*, published in Moscow at the end of 1986[9] and staged in Tambov and other towns and cities (and in London in 1987) – was rehearsed by an amateur dramatic group in Obninsk, the local party committee banned the production. The Obninsk party secretary, A. V. Kamaev, explained that it would be insensitive to stage such a play in the 'centre of Soviet atomic science'.[10]

The 'world's first' AES at Obninsk was the only known AES in the Soviet Union for nearly a decade. The road from experimental power reactor to economically viable, commercial nuclear power station proved to be a long one. In the 1950s the USSR had more than enough non-nuclear sources of cheap energy, and the government prioritised the construction of military plutonium-producing reactors (graphite-moderated), and power reactors for ships and submarines (pressurised water reactors, which have the same output and are more compact). In March 1956 Kurchatov strongly advocated the rapid development of nuclear power stations. In addition to the two models already tested (later known as RBMK and VVER reactors), he was enthusiastic about small reactors which might be used by locomotives and even by aeroplanes. He also wanted fast breeders to be developed as the most promising future source of energy. When the Soviet nuclear energy programme was finally approved by the government sometime in 1956 or 1957, scientists were able to get all three reactor types (graphite-moderated, pressurised water and fast-breeder) included as valid for commercial development. It was not so much considerations of economic efficiency, safety or institutional support which later gave priority to the RBMK system; in the late 1950s and the 1960s, it was simply easier for the Soviet industry to manage this less sophisticated design. The dictat of producers over consumers, which is now pinpointed by *glasnost* as the main weakness of the Soviet economy, was important in giving a technically obsolete model a new lease of life for decades. The Ministry of Electric Power Stations, responsible for running nuclear power stations, was given no choice; it was permitted to decide design and construction questions affecting turbines, but not reactors. There were also political reasons for giving priority to the RBMK system: it was the only *otechestvennaya* ('conceived and made in the fatherland') system, designed and used entirely in the USSR. Other designs would have entailed copying or imitating Western models. The RBMK system therefore satisfied national pride.

High-powered, Channel-type Boiling Uranium-graphite Reactors (RBMK)

The acronym RBMK stands for 'reactor, high power, channel-type' (or 'pressure-tube') in Russian. Obninsk's 'first' reactor was not an RBMK because it was not a 'high-power' model; the acronym only appeared with the first 1000 MWe reactors in 1973. The RBMK-1000 was the first Soviet standard-type reactor. All pre-RBMK graphite-moderated reactors had been designed individually, with different characteristics and power-ratings. They represent stages in the development of the standard RBMK-1000 model.

The immediate successor to the Obninsk 5 MWe was completed near Troitsk in Siberia, in 1958. It was intended to provide both plutonium and electricity for a separate plutonium-producing and reprocessing plant. It was essentially a military project (and still is, in its modernised 600 MWe six-unit version), and as authorised commentators make clear, 'the principal expenses of this power station are covered by the cost of plutonium produced.'[11] Neither Obninsk nor the Siberian nuclear plants produced cheap electricity; it was at least ten times more expensive per unit than coal or hydroelectric energy. This did not make Soviet planners very enthusiastic about the nuclear energy options. Kurchatov's biographers admit that he had numerous high-level critics who disputed his insistence on the necessity of building more and more nuclear power stations. Khrushchev, who was generally very enthusiastic about nuclear energy for ships and submarines, was rather sceptical about the need for nuclear-generated electricity for civilian projects, and this scepticism was grounded in economic considerations.

But atomic scientists were a very powerful lobby in the USSR in the 1950s. Khrushchev describes in his memoirs how Kurchatov wanted to be appointed as special scientific adviser to the Chairman of the Council of Ministers, and to be an offical spokesman for Soviet scientists.[12] There was no such position in the Soviet government structure, and Khrushchev's chief scientific adviser at that time was Academician Vladimir A. Kirillin, Chairman of the Department of Science and Technology of the Central Committee of the CPSU (Communist Party of the Soviet Union), which was the main link between the Party and the scientific community. A prominent thermophysicist and expert on thermodynamics and power engineering, Kirillin was not a great supporter of nuclear dreams. Soviet uranium resources, moreover, had not then been properly investigated, and inevitably the military lobby argued that they should be used for strategic rather than routine electricity-generating purposes.

The Soviet nuclear energy programme really dates from 1958, when construction began on the first commercial (but not yet economic) atomic power station at Beloyarsk, near Sverdlovsk. With a design power of only

100 MWe, this AES was also semi-experimental and for dual use (military and civilian). The key Soviet energy project at that time was the Bratsk hydro power station on the Angara river in Siberia, which was expected to produce 4,500 MWe when completed. It was only one of four hydro stations in the Angara cascade. The Bratsk hydroelectric station and the Beloyarsk nuclear power station were completed almost simultaneously six years later. The hydroelectric design was comparatively simple and seemed more durable. Forty-five nuclear power stations of the Beloyarsk type would be necessary to produce the electricity generated by the Bratsk hydroelectric station alone. It was therefore understandable that Khrushchev's government considered it more important to build additional hydro stations, rather than accelerate the nuclear programme.

Beloyarsk became operational on 26 April 1964, and was immediately named after Kurchatov, who had died at the age of only 57. The reactor at the Beloyarsk Kurchatov station was a modernised version of a smaller reactor in Obninsk. However, as is now clear, the modernisation's economic improvement (bringing a better ratio between the output of heat and electric energy) was achieved at the expense of safety. The Obninsk design (duplicated at the Siberian station) generated the superheated steam for the turbines in a separate circuit, uncontaminated by radionuclides. But this necessitated a special 'heat exchanger', and some heat was lost in the process. The uranium fuel elements often leaked, but no contamination reached the turbines; small quantities of contaminated water had to be disposed of periodically. Obninsk AES was considered so safe that it had no 'sanitar' health-protection zone around it; only a small square separated it from the apartment blocks of Lenin Prospect, the town's main street. The system's main disadvantage was the high ratio between thermal and electric output (6:1). For every 30 MWt (megawatts of thermal power), only 4.8 MWe was produced (the ratio in modern RBMK reactors is 3:1). To prevent accidents, the steam pressure in the pressure tubes was also very low – 12 atm (atmospheres). For the next generation of reactors, the quality of pressure tubes and pipes was improved, which allowed higher pressure and the introduction of a single circuit system.

At Beloyarsk, steam for the turbines was produced directly in the reactor core (nuclear superheating), which was considered a technical advance. This design gave a much better ratio between thermal power (285 MW) and electrical capacity (100 MW).[13] The station was also more economical with the uranium fuel. But the circulation of the same water first through the reactor core and then as steam through the turbine hall made the contamination of much larger quantities of water inevitable. The production of superheated steam directly inside the reactor core fuel channels was also a high-risk 'solution' – a source of that 'positive void coefficient' which was the main cause of the Chernobyl disaster (see the Editors' Introduction). The Beloyarsk 100 MW reactor had fuel channels of a unique type; 730 of them were evaporative channels for the generation of steam, and 268 were for superheating the steam. The temperature of the outlet steam (mixed with water) was 340°C, but its temperature on leaving the superheating channels was 500°C. This is much higher than the maximum steam temperature of 284°C in the RBMK-1000 reactors. The steam pressure in the Beloyarsk reactors also reached the much higher level of 150 atm, compared to 83 atm in the RBMK-1000.

Despite these very high pressures, the Beloyarsk reactor was built without protective containment. The reactor vault was designed to accommodate only a single coolant channel failure. (This inadequate safety margin was to remain the major liability in all future Soviet graphite-moderated channel reactors.) But the absence of both a containment structure and the single strong pressure vessel usual for PWRs was often presented as an advantage, not as a liability. Soviet industry in the 1960s was not capable of manufacturing large steel pressure vessels, and scientists had no choice but to pretend that they had found a simpler solution. They did realise, however, that having hundreds of fuel assemblies in separate pressure channels, each individually controlled, was making the system too complex. The official history of the Soviet nuclear programme insists that the engineers succeeded in overcoming the problem:

> Nuclear superheating effected directly in the reactor is associated with the well-known difficulties of controlling the process and particularly of monitoring its course, with the required operating accuracy of very many instruments, the presence of a large number of tubes of different dimensions under high pressure, etc. However, all these difficulties are obvious to the scientists and engineers, and they have worked successfully to overcome them.[14]

This, however, was untrue; the subsequent increase in reactor size and power has made them even more complex. Each reactor behaves like several independent reactors, and operators need to observe signals from each individual pressure channel. In the early 1960s, computer control of the system was at a rudimentary level. The unit cost of electricity in the first Beloyarsk reactor was also too high – much higher than at the conventional thermal power stations around Sverdlovsk. The Ural region was rich in cheap coal deposits, and the nuclear power stations there were not justifiable on the basis of energy needs alone. The main Soviet military reprocessing facilities were situated between Sverdlovsk and Chelyabinsk, in the Kyshtym and Kasly districts. After the Kyshtym nuclear accident, and the heavy contamination of a very large area with nuclear waste radionuclides,[15] it was probably thought necessary to site new reactors farther apart, but not too far, or spent fuel rods would have had to be transported over long distances. This probably explains why the second graphite-moderated reactor with a capacity of 200 MWe was already under construction on the same site well before the first was tested in operation. This second unit was of a different design; scientists were experimenting and comparing the different models. It was scheduled to be operational in October 1967, just in time for the fiftieth anniversary of the October Revolution.

The second reactor at Beloyarsk was already simplified. Two-stage overheating was eliminated and the steam for the turbines was generated directly in the first circuit. Only one assembly of channels in the reactor core was needed to produce superheated steam of about 510–520°C. However, the high steam temperature was a serious disadvantage and this second unit in turn came to be considered as transitional, not as a basic design. In 1967 the 200 MW reactor was considered a great success, but later its main drawback was acknowledged:

> The increase of the working temperature in the reactor core leads to the necessity of using temperature-resistant materials which, in the majority of cases, is less favourable from the neutron-physics aspect and leads to a reduction of the overall utilisation efficiency of the nuclear fuel. This is the major objection against the use of steam superheating in the reactor.[16]

This was the end of the Beloyarsk model. In 1968 the fast-breeder reactor was already under construction in Beloyarsk, where it was intended to operate alongside the old reactors. On the whole, the economic performance of the Beloyarsk reactors was very poor. The attempt to work at very high steam temperatures can only be explained by the need to use the existing turbines, designed and built for coal or oil thermal stations which normally work at these levels of steam temperature and pressure. Nuclear energy was not yet separate from the military structure, and not yet able to design and manufacture turbines which could be adapted to the most rational reactor models. It was also calculated that in order to produce nuclear-generated electricity at acceptable cost, the power of individual units had to be raised to 1,000 MWe. Reactors of this power had already been licensed for operation in the United States, but they were either pressurised water reactors (PWR) or boiling water reactors (BWR), with massive, welded steel pressure vessels which Soviet heavy industry could not yet manufacture.

In the early 1960s the US nuclear energy industry was forecasting a growing need for nuclear energy to supplement fossil fuels and predicting that by the 1970s, nuclear-produced electricity would cost less than electricity from conventional sources. These projections stimulated many orders for large nuclear plants, and the PWR was the most popular model.

By the late 1950s the US was already well ahead in nuclear production of electricity, and by 1962 it had 18 reactors on stream, as well as 13 large reactors producing plutonium. It was expected that by 1971 the US would have a combined nuclear-electric capacity of over 8,000 MW. In Britain, a high-power gas-cooled graphite reactor (1,180 MWe) was under construction in the late 1960s. In fact, at the end of 1960s the Soviet Union was well behind not only the US, but France, West Germany and Britain too, which each had 10 to 15 reactors operating or in the final stages of construction.[17]

These were the circumstances in which Soviet atomic industry experts decided to design a high-power version of the pressure tube model – the unit now known as the RBMK-1000. The disadvantages of the graphite-moderated channel-type reactor were already obvious; but it represented the only genuine Soviet design, which had very strong institutional support as well as its own industrial base. Anatoly Alexandrov, a member of Kurchatov's original team, was now an academician and a director of the Kurchatov Institute of Atomic Energy. Nikolai Dollezhal, also now a full member of the Academy, was a director of the Power Engineering Institute of the State Committee for the Utilization of Atomic Energy. The USSR's independent programme of pressurised water reactors was represented at the time by a different network of research, design and industrial facilities, but their leading experts were not so well decorated or influential.

It is not clear exactly when construction of the Leningrad nuclear power station, consisting of two RBMK-1000 reactors, was started. Apparently the project was under preparation in 1964–5 when it became clear that the system with superheated steam (or 'supercritical coolant parameters') could not serve as a basic model. A different solution was required in order to improve the ratio between thermal and electric energy; and it was found in the use of fire-resistant zirconium alloys. These alloys, replacing steel or aluminium alloys in the fuel element claddings of uranium-graphite reactors, improved the fuel cycle parameters by reducing the neutron absorption of the cladding. However, this innovation, which might have been justified by physics, is now not considered by US experts as reliable from an engineering point of view. The US study of Chernobyl indicates that the zirconium-to-steel transition welds are weak points in the RBMK piping system, prone to rupture (and so cause an accident) with a rapid rise of temperature. There are no comparable weld joints in the US PWRs or BWRs.[18]

With the introduction of zirconium alloys, the reactor core had to be redesigned. The size of individual channels (or pressure tubes) was enlarged and their number increased in order to reach 1,000 MWe, with 3,200 MWt – the same ratio as in the US PRWs. Alexandrov, Dollezhal and Petrosyants headed the project and they presented a very optimistic view of prospects for the RBMK models in their report (called 'Leningrad Power Station and the Prospects for Channel Boiling Reactors') to the Fourth International Conference on the Peaceful Uses of Atomic Energy in Geneva in 1971, more than two years before the first such reactor was tested. The designers' and scientists' confidence in this model was so high that construction of a second unit was begun almost simultaneously, and several more followed. The Chernobyl nuclear plant was under construction from 1970, when the foundations for two reactors practically identical to the Leningrad station were laid down. Designs for the RBMK-1500 and RBMK-2000 – the most powerful reactors in the world – were also completed well before the Leningrad power station went operational.

The first reactor in the Leningrad plant was tested in September 1973. But it took more than a year to put the RBMK-1000 Unit One into operation: only in October 1974 did the first unit reach its projected power. The second unit went on stream at the end of 1975. The plant was declared a historic success, and with 2 million kilowatts of electric power it was the biggest in Europe at that time. It was therefore named after Lenin. (When the record passed to Chernobyl a few years later, that was given the name of Lenin too, so two plants in different parts of the USSR became 'Lenin stations'.) The RBMK model seemed to be heading squarely for success and winning the competition with the Soviet-made PWRs (known as VVERs).

The electricity generated by the RBMK-1000 was calculated to be cheaper than that produced by the already-operational VVER-440 models. The absence of the massive steel pressure vessel for the reactor core and the absence of the containment structure contributed greatly to the cost-effectiveness. These controversial design features, which can now be seen as liabilities, were declared to be the main advantages of the RBMK model. They were unnecessary: this particular Soviet design was completely safe without them – so the argument went. The existing protection was expected to hold if one of the 1,600 fuel channels ruptured, or even, in the worst case imaginable, if two were to burst. Nobody ever ventured to suggest the possibility of a more general core explosion.

The designers of the RBMK-1000 (and -1500 and -2000) models greatly reduced the temperature (280°C) and the steam pressure (65 kg/sq cm before turbines) without losing efficiency. (The corresponding figures for the Beloyarsk station were 500°C and 90 kg/sq cm.) The serious drawback of the RBMK-1000 was the size of the core, which was such that too much water in the first circuit was needed to cool it. The use of low-pressure saturated steam for the turbines also means more water being involved in the process. The 'complex and bulky coolant circulation circuits and a large number of auxiliary systems' are actually listed as the RBMK system's major handicap in the Soviet textbook on the construction of nuclear power plants.[19] Each RBMK-1000 has four main pumps circulating 37,600 metric tons of water per hour in the first circuit, not to mention several other, smaller pumping systems. This is less than the total volume of water circulating in the VVER system with the same power output. But in the VVER system most of the cooling water circulates in the second circuit. In the VVER-1000 reactor, where it is separate, the steam output is 1,469 tons per hour, while the RBMK-1000 reactor produces 5,800 tons of steam per hour.[20]

This significant difference created the problem of circulation of contaminated water. In most Western nuclear power stations, circulation water is normally cooled (recirculated) in tall cooling towers – now a familiar feature of nuclear power plant. This is more expensive than the direct-flow water supply system, standard in the first military graphite reactors in the Hanford reservation in Washington state (where the water was taken directly from the Columbia river) and probably in the first Soviet-made reactors in the Urals as well. Environmental considerations, however, made the use of natural reservoirs for nuclear power plants impossible; water which circulates through the reactor core is always slightly radioactive, and the heating under pressure kills all water-borne biological life. Moreover, the water's radioactivity is constantly increasing.

At the same time the use of closed cooling tower circuits for RBMK systems would have raised the price of electricity and made them less competitive (or frankly uncompetitive) in comparison with VVER-1000 models. Therefore the designers decided in favour of a very controversial simplification – a direct-flow water supply, not from natural bodies of water (rivers or lakes) but from reservoirs purpose-built near the reactor site and isolated from the nearest water system. These reservoirs act as biological deactivators of radioactive water; the radionuclides precipitate to the bottom and are absorbed by silt. The calculations showed that such cooling through artificial pools, and active decontamination, needs very large reservoirs indeed. To cool one RBMK-1000 the pool may be shallow (about 4 metres) but must be at least 5 or 6 sq km in size. The Leningrad power plant needed a 10 sq km pool, and the Chernobyl pool was about 22 sq km to compensate for the warmer climate in the Kiev region.

Officially, land in the Soviet Union is nationalised and therefore without price, and the area occupied by the pool did not add much to the cost of the station – nobody pays for this land anyway. There was, of course, the trouble and expense of resettling the local inhabitants, but this was not the designers' problem. The construction of plants of this sort which require the sacrifice of so much land would hardly be possible in the more densely populated countries of Western or Eastern Europe, where in general land has commercial value and a high price. (In Japan, this factor has led to the new policy whereby nuclear power plants are built on rock, away from from population centres.)

The RBMK-1000's direct-flow water supply system is considered simpler than the recirculation system, and it costs nearly 25 per cent less.[21] It was of course necessary to introduce certain environmental standards (e.g. waste water should not raise the water temperature in the reservoir above a certain limit; the volume of radioactivity discharged into the reservoir should not be higher than a certain level, so allowing the silt to fix most radionuclides reasonably quickly). It is also necessary to keep the reservoir water in motion with a natural water supply, such as a river, in order to compensate for evaporation and to prevent an increase in salinity. In this way a certain amount of radioactive material from the reactor core passes into the environment, and it is one of the tasks of radiological services is keep this within permissible limits.

Despite the insistence on the total safety of the RBMK-1000 reactors, the absence of pressure and containment vessels and the comparative fragility of individual channels (the danger of rupture is higher during the initial launch when all 1,600 channels have to be tested simultaneously, or in one half of the reactor) made it necessary to have a protection zone around the reactor much larger than for PWR or VVER systems. The RBMK-1000 'health protection zone' from which all settlements have to be removed and agricultural use of the land halted, has a radius of 2.5 km. The whole system thus needs a lot of space, and planners suggested that the land allocated for such reactors should be of little or no agricultural use. This requirement could probably be met in the Leningrad region where agriculture is difficult anyway. But in the rich *chernozem* (rich black soil) region of the Ukraine it is difficult to find such waste land. The Ukraine, which for centuries was the granary of Russia and later of the whole USSR, could ill afford to sacrifice land, particularly along the rivers. There is nothing more precious than *chernozem* soil in the Russian and Ukrainian environment. However, it was in the Ukraine that nuclear power station construction received the highest priority. The RBMK-1000 became the most important type of reactor in the Soviet nuclear power industry. At the time of the Chernobyl accident, there were 14 RBMK plants across the country (at Leningrad, Kursk, Smolensk, Chernobyl), providing about half the Soviet nuclear electric generating capacity. Several more were under construction. More powerful RBMK-1500 plant was also in operation at Ignalina, with a second one under construction on the same site.

The RBMK-1500 differs very little from the RBMK-1000, yet has a 50 per cent higher power level. The core of the RBMK-1500 has the same dimensions as the core of the RBMK-1000 and the same number of channels. An increased thermal capacity – 4,800 MWt – became possible with the introduction of a new system of heat transfer from the fuel channels and a simplification of the circulation loop. Other technical innovations made it possible to increase the steam volume. The increase of power with the same number of standard channels and the same load of uranium fuel (2 per cent enrichment) made the electricity produced by the RBMK-1500 potentially cheaper than that generated by the RBMK-1000 or the VVER-1000. Construction of the RBMK-2000 and 2400 reactors has not yet started, despite the existence of ready projects with some advanced features. The RBMK-2400 reactors were planned as a new generation with a much larger core.[22] They are projected to achieve a better thermal/electric power ratio, by superheating up to 450°C. The construction of such reactors, however, first needs the creation of a new industrial base.

The Ignalina plant was expected to be the most economic of Soviet nuclear plants when fully operational. Until 1986, however, the most economic was Chernobyl – with its four RBMK-1000 reactors, the largest nuclear plant in the USSR. The two additional reactors of the same type, which were under construction, would make Chernobyl the biggest plant in the world. But the designers were not yet entirely satisfied, and a project to develop RBMK reactors with an electric output of 2,000 MWe, without any modifications in the channels, was also undertaken in order to make use of the existing industrial base more efficiently. The increased power was to be achieved simply by increasing the number of channels and the diameter of the reactor core.

Thus there has been some evolution in design but without the introduction of any new technology: the whole family of RBMK reactors derives directly from the early experimental and plutonium-producing reactors of the early 1950s. The main arguments in favour of the RBMK system, which was technologically obsolete, were always linked to its relative cheapness and its good safety features. (The attitude to safety at this time was notably anxious.) The RBMK reactors were certainly recognised as being accident-prone, but these accidents were never expected to amount to more than minor problems with individual pressure tubes – easy to repair or cover up. The VVER pressurised water systems were, in principle, less vulnerable to accidents, but any accidents were potentially more dangerous; they could involve the whole core, in which case they could be classified as disasters, economically if not environmentally. The Three Mile Island accident in 1979 was taken as confirmation of this assessment and further strengthened Soviet commitment to continuing and modernising the RBMK system.

The Second Line: Pressurised Water Reactors (VVER)

Pressurised water-cooled and water-moderated reactors, PWRs or VVERS, were initially developed for nuclear submarines. (The acronym VVER comes from the Russian for 'water-water power reactors'.) Tested on 30 March 1953, the first small 2.4 MWe US PWR was used the next year for the USS *Nautilus*, the first nuclear-powered submarine. A reactor with this purpose has to fit into a very small space, so the engineers needed a design with a core of high power density (heat output per unit volume) and which was easy to operate. The solution was simple – to use ordinary, 'light' water both as the neutron moderator (instead of graphite) and as the coolant for the fuel elements. (Heavy water – with deuterium – is a much better moderator, but is expensive and its manufacture demands too much energy.) The reactor consisted of uranium fuel elements immersed in water in a strong steel pressure tank or vessel. It was necessary to keep the water under pressure to prevent it from boiling. Steam for the turbines was generated in a boiler in a separate circuit, linked to the primary high-pressure circuit through a heat exchange system. Its simplicity of design has made this the most popular system, and it now dominates the world reactor market.

The Soviet Union also needed reactors with a much higher power density than that provided by the graphite-moderated models. The inexorable logic of military competition meant that as soon as the US started to build nuclear submarines, the USSR had to follow. It is not known when the first Soviet-made PWR was tested, but it was probably in 1954, very soon after the first US test. Construction of the atomic ice-breaker *Lenin* began in 1956, and this ship needed much larger reactors than the *Nautilus*. The Soviet steel industry was able to manufacture steel pressure vessels for ships' reactors, but the construction of larger and heavier pressure vessels for power stations was a problem. Such pressure vessels entail very complex engineering and consist of many parts (main vessel, removable vessel cover, coolant outlet nozzles, control assembly shroud, etc.). Small vessels of welded steel for the first Soviet VVER station were made in Leningrad and shipped to the site at Voronezh. But technical problems kept larger vessels for more economic reactors (VVER-440 and VVER-1000) at the project stage for many years.

The first nuclear power station with a VVER reactor (VVER-210) was started up in September 1964 about 50 km from Voronezh. The site was named Novovoronezh. The project was completed well behind schedule. (The Five Year Plan adopted in 1959 at the Twenty-first Party Congress included a more ambitious nuclear energy programme.) Because the design of PWRs and VVERs is less relevant to the subject in hand than the RMBK design, I will not give a technical description of the model, which can be found elsewhere.[23] But it will be useful to review the Soviet VVER programme's part in the overall Soviet nuclear power programme.

VVER reactors were necessary for export, primarily to Comecon countries. The Soviet Union had an obligation to provide these countries with energy, but it was important to reduce oil and coal exports to Eastern Europe and Cuba in order to sell more of these resources for hard currency. But RBMK-1000s were not suitable for export, and plants of this particular design would never have been licensed for operation in the US or any other

Western countries because of their poor safety features, the absence of containment structures, and the radioactive contamination of the environment by discharges of radioactive water into cooling pools. The VVER-210 reactor at Novovoronezh was connected to closed circulation towers and did not discharge contaminated water into open reservoirs (the Don river was the nearest water source). The VVER-210's economic performance was rather poor. During its first full year of operation (1965), the 'power for use' factor – i.e. the proportion of projected output actually realised – was 54 per cent, and the unit cost of electricity was nearly double the average production cost of electricity from thermal power stations in the European parts of the USSR.[24] In 1967 and 1968 the plant performed better, but its electricity still cost more than the average.

In December 1969 the second, modified and more powerful unit was brought into operation on the same site: VVER-365. The electricity it generated was already cheaper and more comparable with that from thermal stations. The main problem with the VVER and PWR is recharging (one-third of the fuel elements need to be replaced annually, involving a complete shutdown of the reactor). The cooling period is rather long (waiting for the short-lived isotopes to decay). Each recharging takes some 30 days, or longer if the vessel is found to need repair.[25]

In 1970 when the Soviet Union already had two RBMK-1000s under construction, the prospect of building VVERs with the same power was still remote, owing to the problems of industrial base. RBMK-1000 reactors could be assembled from smaller parts, whereas the VVER-1000 needed a single large, heavy, solid steel structure which Soviet industry could not manufacture. In order to give the VVER system a lease of life for large power reactors, it was decided to create a supergiant 'plant of plants', *Atommash* (an abbreviation of 'atom machinery'), to manufacture pressure vessels and other components for the VVER system, at first for the VVER-440 but later for the VVER-1000 as well.

The first two VVER-440s went operational in 1971 and 1972, well before the *Atommash* plant was completed. Their pressure vessels and other components were manufactured at the modernised Izhorsky works in Leningrad. New reactors at Novovoronezh were provided with containment structures in the form of reinforced concrete cells, 42 metres by 39 metres. The first VVER-1000 was planned for 1978 and its parts had to be manufactured at *Atommash*. The components were too heavy to be transported from Leningrad, and *Atommash* was in the Rostov region up-river from Voronezh. The pressure vessels can weigh 500–800 metric tons each, and it was easier to transport them by barge than rail.

Atommash was a key project in the Soviet energy programme. A special site in the Rostov region was selected for the plant and the workers' settlement. The 'strategic' decision to 'accelerate' nuclear power had been made in 1974, prompted by the sharp rise in the international price of oil and by the new export demands. Planners and builders were in a hurry and nobody made a proper geological survey of the site. The Rostov regional party boss (*obkom* secretary) Ivan Bondarenko was a close friend of Brezhnev. The siting of *Atommash* was a favour bestowed by his patron – important development projects give *obkom* secretaries a much higher profile and greater influence in Moscow.

It was hoped that *Atommash* would make it possible to inaugurate the first VVER-1000 in 1978. This was under construction in Novovoronezh – the fifth reactor there. But construction of *Atommash* and the VVER-1000 proved to be more difficult than expected. In 1974 the US and Western Europe also escalated their nuclear energy programmes, in response to the oil embargo imposed after the Arab–Israel war in October 1973. By 1979 about 130 US-made PWRs were operational in the US and many other countries, while the USSR was experiencing difficulties with its domestic reactors and its export obligations (export of Soviet VVER-440 reactors to Comecon countries went in tandem with domestic construction, but plans for the export of the VVER-1000 were delayed). After 1974, oil became the main source of foreign exchange for the USSR, and the large imports of grain and food necessitated by poor harvests made hard currency earnings and the replacement of oil by nuclear energy a priority. Nuclear energy now appealed to the Soviet Union not because it was expected to be cheap, but because it would help to increase foreign trade. In 1979, however, the Soviet Union's nuclear-generated capacity was only 4,500 MW, or 2 per cent of the total Soviet production of electricity – too low to make much difference. Several more VVER-1000 plants were under construction (in the Kalinin region, and in the south and west Ukraine) with many more on the drawing board.

The first VVER-1000 was finally tested in May 1980, two years behind schedule. *Atommash* was officially opened in 1978, but only part of the plant was in operation. Wholly unexpected problems were covered up at first, but they did not disappear; time made things worse when the inevitable happened.

The site for *Atommash* and the new town of Volgodonsk had been badly chosen. It was just behind the hydroelectric dam across the Don which had created the Tsimplyanskoye reservoir of nearly 2,000 sq km. The *chernozem* soil was poor protection against the pressure of the water mass above the level of the town site, and the area around Volgodonsk was gradually becoming a swamp. This was quite a common problem with many Soviet hydroelectric projects: the designers simply took no account of the environmental consequences of their projects. The hydroelectric construction was done rather quickly, while raising the level of rivers and transforming them into huge reservoirs had only a gradual effect, over 10 or 15 years or more, on the level of the surrounding water-table. It is possible that in the early 1970s, when the geological survey for the *Atommash* site was hastily carried out, the water-table was still well below the surface. But by the time the project was nearing completion, the problem was already obvious and a hindrance to the construction. But it was too late: Volgodonsk was already a city of more than 100,000 people. In the usual way, the problem was simply covered up.

According to the original plan, *Atommash* should have produced eight pressure vessels by 1980, as well as components for the primary circuits; but this soon became entirely unrealistic. Only one or two vessels had been completed by 1983, when one of the plant's huge walls suddenly collapsed as a result of the sinking foundations. There were casualties, and the accident was so serious that it was reported in the Soviet press (without details) on 20 July 1983, and a commission set up to investigate the causes and consequences.[26] The matter was eventually discussed by the Politburo, and Ignaty Novikov, Chairman of the State Construction Committee, was held responsible and dismissed. The new chairman – an experienced construction engineer[27] – could not solve the problem; and Volgodonsk, now with 134,000 inhabitants, could not be transferred to a safer place, at least not in the near future. But the plans for the construction of *Atommash* were apparently modified and scaled down.

This accident called into question the whole programme of rapid development of VVER-1000 nuclear plants. *Atommash* was regarded as the key to the accelerated development of nuclear energy, and the plans for manufacturing and installing reactors of the VVER-1000 type were now well behind schedule for both the 1981–5 and the 1986–90 Five Year plans. *Atommash* is thought to have delivered its fourth pressurised vessel by August 1985.[28] *Atommash* also had a programme for manufacturing giant steam generators, each weighing 320 metric tons.

To compensate for the problems with *Atommash*, the manufacture of smaller pressurised reactor vessels (for VVER-440 models) was continued at the Izhorsky works and also contracted out to Czechoslovakia's Skoda works. The VVER-440 became a commercial model for Eastern Europe.

Compared to the RBMK-1000 reactor, the core of the VVER-1000 reactor is smaller – only about one-eighth the size. The water flow-rate through the reactor is over twice that of the RBMK-1000, and it therefore needs much more powerful pumps. This larger volume of water is necessary because of the much higher power density in the core. Open reservoirs to cool so much water would have to be enormous, and closed circuits through cooling towers were necessary to save land. This more active cooling of circulating water makes the production of electricity more expensive, and the reactor itself consumes a larger part of the electrical energy it produces.

Pressure in the primary circuit is higher in the VVER-1000 (160 atm) than in the RBMK-1000. Because of their much higher density of heat production, VVER-1000 reactors are considered to be more prone to interruption of cooling water flow by pipe rupture, pump breakdowns, 'blackouts', etc. – in which event the stand-by diesel generators and emergency cooling would have to be started up very fast to avoid a serious accident. It was calculated that if the water pumps were stopped by a blackout, the RBMK-1000 reactors would not reach the point of 'meltdown' because the natural circulation of water would be enough to prevent the accident and also any damage to the core – as long as the control rods are moved down and the heating is caused only by accumulated fission products and not by a chain reaction with generation of neutrons.[29] In the event of similar problems with water pumps in VVER-1000 reactors, the 'natural circulation' is certainly not enough to prevent accidents, and the immediate switching over to the emergency cooling system is essential.

These and other features led Soviet designers to believe that the VVER system was potentially more dangerous; so it was provided with an appropriate containment structure as well as the strong steel pressure vessel to house the reactor core itself. In the VVER-1000 the whole reactor section is separated from other buildings and enclosed in a steel-lined containment structure of prestressed reinforced concrete, in the form of a vertical cylinder topped with an elliptical dome. This is made to withstand the 'worst case' of an explosion in which flying metal fragments might destroy the lining or depressurise the containment. To avoid this, the circuit section is also protected by a reinforced concrete shield which usually serves as the interior wall as well.[30] In the Chernobyl RBMK-1000 reactor Unit Four, the accident happened not because of heating and meltdown from accumulated fission radionuclides, as at Three Mile Island, but because of failure to stop the unexpected power increase from the chain reaction by immediately lowering the control rods. Because the reactor core of the VVER-1000 model is much smaller, it would take less time to put down the control rods in the event of trouble. The VVER-1000 reactors also have less complex controls and do not need so many operators.

But a sudden loss of coolant is considered less dangerous for the VVER than for the RBMK. Nuclear chain reactions can continue only in the presence of moderator, and coolant (water) is also a moderator in the VVER systems. If coolant is lost the nuclear chain reaction is also halted immediately. Meltdown of fuel elements can still happen because of the presence of fission radionuclides which produce heat, particularly at the end of the reactor fuel cycle. But core meltdown is not yet an explosion. In the RBMK, a sudden loss of coolant does not stop the nuclear chain reaction in uranium-235 because moderator (graphite) remains. The reaction should and could be stopped only by neutron-absorbing control rods.

Despite this, the RBMK designers have always argued that it is safer than PWR or VVER systems, that each system has its advantages and disadvantages, and that both, therefore, should be refined and developed.

This approach has been adopted. In 1986 the number of VVER-1000 reactors in operation was smaller than the number of the RBMK-1000s, but the gap was narrowing. Six or seven VVER-1000s were in operation and about 25 more were either under construction or planned on 13 sites, half of which were in the Ukraine.[31] The smaller VVER-440 was considered a success, and 27 of them were operating in the Soviet Union, in Comecon countries and in Finland. A VVER-500 was also designed, which shared standard parts and components with VVER-1000. (There was no standardisation between the VVER-440 and -1000, and the smaller model was expected to be phased out and replaced by the VVER-500.)

Soviet energy experts, however, like many of their foreign colleagues, were well aware that global deposits of uranium are not unlimited. Their hopes were pinned on the fast-breeder reactors. In this field, at least, the Soviet Union was far in advance of the US, where the construction of fast reactors was delayed by economic and safety considerations.

Soviet Fast-breeder Reactors

The most common reactors use uranium as fuel and the first reactors were designed to use natural uranium which consists of a mixture of stable uranium-238 and fissile uranium-235. Only uranium-235 is a fuel material, but in raw uranium deposits this lighter uranium represents only 0.7 per cent of the mixture. Modern reactors normally use enriched uranium which is produced by special enrichment plants. Although the process is complex and costly, it makes it possible to load more fuel material into the reactor core and to use fuel elements for longer. The RBMK-1000 reactors normally use only slightly enriched uranium in which the content of uranium-235 is about 2 per cent. VVER and PWR reactors use more highly enriched uranium (between 3 and 4 per cent of uranium-235) which makes it possible to reduce the total amount of the uranium charge (66 tons in the VVER-1000 instead of 170 tons in the RBMK-1000). Fission of uranium-235 produces slow and fast neutrons, and when some of the fast neutrons hit and fuse with uranium-238 nuclei, they generate reactions which release energy and also form a new 'synthetic' element – plutonium-239. Plutonium was the principal product of the first military reactors. The first atomic bomb dropped over Hiroshima in August 1945 was made from uranium-235, whereas the second bomb dropped over Nagasaki was made of plutonium-239, which has certain advantages as fissile material, and much smaller 'critical mass' for explosion. With each fission, plutonium produces about 2.9 neutrons, whereas each fission of uranium-235 produces only 2.3 neutrons.

When uranium-235 mixed with uranium-238 is used as a nuclear fuel, some of the neutrons transform or 'breed' uranium-238 into plutonium. However, the ratio between disappearing uranium-235 and accumulating plutonium-239 is less than one. Different conditions in the fission process can increase or reduce this ratio, but the best conversion ratio ever achieved in this system was about 0.7 (in graphite-moderated reactors, which made them so popular for military purposes). If plutonium mixed with uranium-238 is used as fuel product, the conversion ratio can be higher than one, meaning that new plutonium is bred in larger quantities than have been spent.

Uranium-238 is very cheap, compared with plutonium. This is why the system in which fuel plutonium converts uranium-238 in the process into larger amounts of plutonium was so attractive to nuclear physicists. Because the natural deposits of uranium are limited and high-grade uranium ores have already been worked out, plutonium fast-breeder reactors were advocated as the most promising future replacement for ordinary nuclear reactors. In ordinary reactors, fast neutrons are slowed down by the moderator (graphite or water) in order to make better use of their energy. In plutonium reactors which use fast neutrons, no moderator is needed, and this is why they are known as 'fast-breeder reactors', or simply as 'fast reactors'. The first fast-breeder reactors were designed in the US at the end of the 1940s and the first small, experimental prototype was tested in 1951 in Idaho. In the Soviet Union, the development of fast-breeder reactors was initiated by Kurchatov in 1950.[32] Similar experimental reactors were being developed in Britain and France. The first fast reactors intended as prototypes for larger commercial reactors were built in Britain in 1959 (Dounreay) and in the US in 1963 (Detroit, Edison-Enrico Fermi–1). The Detroit reactor later achieved notoriety when a frightening accident forced a permanent shutdown.

Very little is known about the first experimental fast-breeder reactors in the Soviet Union; as a rule, they were secret projects. The first 'official' Soviet fast neutron (BN in Russian) reactor, with a capacity of 60 MWt and 12 MWe, was built in Dmitrovgrad in the Ulyanovsk region in 1965. It was experimental, used as a prototype for larger commercial fast breeders. Because fast-breeder technology was not considered entirely safe, the first Soviet commercial fast reactor with an electrical capacity of 350 MW was built a long way from large population centres, near Shevchenko on the eastern shore of the Caspian Sea. It is a semi-desert area with no fresh water supplies. The BN-350 reactor was intended to generate power for the distillation of sea-water into fresh water for the new town of Shevchenko.

In fast reactors, the fuel used is plutonium produced at a reprocessing plant. Because no moderator is necessary and fast neutrons are more efficient in a very compact core, fast breeders must have a very high density of heat energy generation in a very small core. The cylindrical core of the BN-350 in Shevchenko is at least ten times smaller than the core of the VVER-365 reactor at Novovoronezh, and at least 50 times smaller than the 285 MWe Beloyarsk graphite-moderated channel reactor. It is obvious that if about the same amount of thermal energy (about 1,000 MWt) is released in the compact space of the BN-350, neither ordinary nor heavy water will be able to remove such intense heat, even if the flow is very rapid. It is also technically impossible to circulate tens of thousands of tons of water per hour through the very small core of fast reactors. Only molten metal has a thermal conductivity high enough to serve as a coolant in fast reactors. Liquid sodium was selected for this purpose.

However, molten sodium as a coolant creates its own engineering problems. Any system in which thousands of tons of liquid sodium and water are circulating must be entirely leak-proof, because any contact between sodium and water produces explosion and fire. Leakages of water from cooling circuits are common occurrences, and the rupture of even a small pipe is a serious accident demanding immediate shutdown of the reactor. But leaked water does not present a serious danger itself (apart from some radioactivity in the RBMK systems), whereas leakage of sodium is more serious: rupture of a pipe holding molten sodium could lead to disaster. That said, sodium has some advantages as a coolant. One is its very high boiling temperature (990°C), which allows its use as a coolant under normal pressure and reduces the danger of pipes rupturing. However, sodium reacts instantly and violently not only with water but with many other substances as well. It also solidifies into a metal below its melting point (97.5°C), making it necessary to keep huge amounts of sodium coolant in a hot state even when the reactor is shut down.

Fast reactors pose many other challenging technical problems which make the electricity they generate very expensive. Their main advantage – the fact that they produce more plutonium than they consume – is itself not without drawbacks. The higher yields of newly-bred plutonium accumulate only after the reactor has been in operation for many years, and both loaded plutonium and bred plutonium can only be extracted by reprocessing spent fuel through very complex and expensive methods and with by-products in the form of millions of gallons of highly radioactive liquid waste ('radwaste') which must somehow be disposed of in such a way as to guarantee safety for centuries.

Even Soviet authors do not consider the Shevchenko plant a success. Many of its problems were due to the poor quality of pipes and tubes. Leaks were common and the plant remained shut down for most of the first few years. Although it was literally started up in 1972, there were four years of improvements, repairs and replacements before the plant was considered operational in 1976.[33] The cost of its energy was very high. The projected productivity of the plant was about 100,000 tons of distilled water per day. But with six loops of the primary cooling circuit needing nearly 20,000 cubic meters of sodium per hour (and with six more sodium cooling loops in the second circuit), and similar quantities of water in the third circuit, as well as a lot of other problems, the production cost of distilled water was certainly too high.

The second Soviet commercial fast reactor had been under construction since 1968, well before the Shevchenko plant was in operation. The site for a new fast reactor at Beloyarsk, where two graphite reactors had already been built, was chosen largely on practical grounds – to re-employ many thousands of qualified construction workers and engineers who already lived here and would be jobless without a new project. The design was not a repetition of the Shevchenko project, but more modern: the reactor was more powerful (1,470 MWt and 600 MWe) and categorised as BN-600. But again, as in Shevchenko, construction proved more difficult than expected and was beset with many problems. The BN-600 plant took 12 years to complete and started commercial operations only on 20 April 1980. (The government pressed hard to get this reactor on stream on this particular date – to coincide with V.I. Lenin's 110th birthday.)[34] At that time it was the largest commercial fast reactor in the world, and its unveiling was hailed as a great achievement for Soviet technology, opening the future to unlimited energy supplies. There is no information about the cost of electricity produced by BN-600, but it is apparently much higher than for the RBMK and VVER reactors.

The main liability of Soviet fast reactors is the very short operational time before the reactor core needs recharging: only 50 days for BN-350 and 150 days for BN-600. The replacement of fuel elements is the most hazardous operation in the reactor cycle and takes several weeks each time. The sodium temperature in the first circuit is also very high – 500°C – and the combination of the high temperature with the very intensive bombardment by fast neutrons produces rapid corrosion of pipes, valves and many other parts of the system.[35] Under the influence of intense bombardment by fast neutrons, some molecules of stable sodium absorb neutrons and convert into sodium-24, which is a radioactive gamma emitter. This is why the second circuit of sodium is necessary, with a heat exchange system between the two and an inevitable loss of energy in the process. Eventually a heat exchanger between the hot sodium and the water (for the steam generator) is also necessary and this requires a very sophisticated design to prevent any direct contact between the sodium and the water. Breeding new plutonium is a slow process. It takes about 20 years to double the original load, with many spent-fuel reprocessing operations. Soviet authors claim that the breeding factor of BN-600 is better than in French or British reactors, but that 'improvement' is only possible by increasing the power density in the core, which in turn creates more safety problems.

However, as with other reactors, the designers thought that the more powerful fast reactors could be made commercially more viable. New BN-800 and BN-1600 projects were ordered, but their realisation was seriously delayed. Sverdlovsk regional leaders lobbied strongly in 1979–80 for construction to begin on the new BN-800 at the same Beloyarsk site in order to keep the large work force and design bureau employed; for they had become redundant as soon as BN-600 was completed. Polemical articles in national newspapers, written by local party officials arguing in favour of new fast reactors in Beloyarsk,[36] clearly signalled that there were reservations in government planning circles about the rationale for expensive new fast reactors which provided no economic benefits. However, the new Five Year Plan for 1981-5 called for the construction of new BN-800 and BN-1600 reactors. But as usual, nuclear planning was over-optimistic: not a single new Soviet fast reactor has yet been built. The new BN-800 was finally approved for the Beloyarsk site, but the technical project was only completed in 1984,[37] because better solutions were needed than those found for the BN-600. The actual construction work only started in 1985, the last year of the Five Year Plan. Judging by previous experience, it may take eight to ten years before this reactor becomes operational.

Nothing is known about the construction of the BN-1600, despite the provision in the new, 1986-90 Five Year Plan for accelerated construction of fast breeders. The BN-1600 model is considered an 'improved design'. But even the most modern and highly advanced new French fast reactor, the 'Superphénix', produces electricity twice as expensive as that from thermal nuclear reactors. In the US, where the construction of reactors is based on purely economic considerations, not a single fast breeder is being built. It is very likely that the ambitious Soviet fast-breeder programme will be adversely affected by the Chernobyl accident.

So far, Soviet nuclear technology and Soviet industry have certainly not attained the high quality needed to deal with the more complex problems of fast reactors. The liquid metal fast breeders require new, very high quality steels, and other materials. Breeder technology is based on higher temperatures, much higher neutron density levels, and plutonium fuel assemblies. The history of fast-breeder reactors in other countries is far from trouble-free, and some accidents have been very serious or potentially disastrous. This makes a cautious approach inevitable in the USSR.

Fast breeders everywhere have one other big problem – they need plutonium as their fuel. Plutonium is nuclear weapons material, and complex safeguards will be needed before any country except the main 'nuclear powers' and their closest military allies are given a chance to buy and operate fast-breeder nuclear stations.

Nuclear Central Heating

The use of nuclear reactors to produce electricity is now more or less common in many countries. However, where the Soviet Union apparently has a leading position is in the construction of reactors exclusively for centrally heating big cities. The idea was, in theory, always attractive: nuclear-generated electricity is widely used for heating in Europe and the US anyway. But only a small fraction of the total thermal energy from nuclear fission was actually being used. The proportion of thermal energy to electrical energy in most reactors is 3:1, which is less efficient than in coal power stations, where it can reach 2:1.

The VVER reactors were considered more suitable for central heating because the location of reactors close to big cities requires reliable containment structures. It was at first considered economic to use the same reactor to produce both electricity and heat; but this idea was later given up, except for industrial heating systems where high-temperature steam could be used directly. For central heating in cities, heating reactors only were selected as a safer option. They were expected to operate with reduced pressure in the primary circuit (up to 50 kg/sq cm) and with the addition of a third heating circuit which would guarantee that no leaked radioactivity could reach domestic heating networks. The idea of nuclear heating was presented by Soviet experts at the Fourth UN Conference on Peaceful Use of Atomic Energy in Geneva in 1971.

Because of the rapid loss of heat in steam or water circuits, heating reactors need to be as close to their end-users as possible. But this requirement made the idea unpopular in Western Europe and in the US where anti-nuclear lobbies are strong, climates are mild, and the economic advantages of nuclear heating might be wiped out by the reduction in property values as a result of popular reluctance to live too close to nuclear reactors. In the Soviet Union these problems do not exist because the government owns all houses and heating is free. As such, the government rather than the customer is interested in reducing the heating bill. The cold climate of most of the country also makes a great deal of difference. It is, therefore, natural that nuclear heating stations were initially tested in the remotest and coldest Arctic locations. The first such station was built in the early 1970s at Bilibino, in the Soviet far north-east. It was designed to provide central heating and electricity to a mining settlement and is a very small plant producing 48 MWt. This would be uneconomic for the European USSR, but in distant Arctic regions the production cost of electricity from diesel-electric stations is 8 to 16 kopecks per kilowatt – nearly ten times the Soviet average. It is also very difficult to transport diesel fuel to such remote areas. Sweden is the second country which has tried to use one of its small reactors (60 MW of thermal power) both for generating electricity and to produce heat for central heating through the third water circuit.

In the Soviet Union, coal and oil power stations are often used for dual purposes – as thermoelectric stations. It was thus predictable that the possibility of using reactors, in order to save oil or coal fuel, would be discussed sooner or later. Rapid urbanisation, together with the shortages of oil and coal for domestic use (because of transportation and pollution problems) have finally compelled the planners to use this alternative. But it was decided that special, purely thermal reactors of the 500 MWt size should be built for this purpose – the transportation of hot water from existing large nuclear power stations, which as a rule are situated 50–100 km from major population centres, being impossible. 'Heat-only' reactors of this sort, producing temperatures of around 150°C, were developed in the Soviet Union in the early 1980s. It was considered safe to locate them only 2 km or so from city boundaries. The first two reactors of this type (based on the VVER mode) were near completion in 1986, and their construction did not seem to be seriously affected by the Chernobyl accident. However, the public attitude has certainly changed. The construction work is behind schedule – two thermal reactors were originally expected to come on stream at the end of 1985. But delays in nuclear construction projects are routine. The whole project of heat-only nuclear stations was born out of an assumption that such reactors were completely safe and could therefore be located very close to large population centres. This 'absolutely safe' argument is no longer valid.

The construction of heat-only nuclear stations was included not only in Soviet plans for economic development, but also in the plan for technical and scientific progress of Comecon countries (1985–2000). The USSR is desperate to reduce both its own domestic oil consumption and oil exports to Comecon countries. The export of nuclear reactors is seen as the only real alternative.

Fourteen more such heat-only reactors were also at the planning or construction stage. But it now seems that the programme might be open to reconsideration, at least in certain details. Because the first such plants were designed with very low pressure in the primary circuits, they were also designed without high-quality steel pressure vessels. Some reactor vessels were to be made with a wall thickness of only 2 cm.[38] This design would scarcely be acceptable in any other country and it is unlikely that this cost-cutting approach to safety will remain the same after Chernobyl. The designers of some of the new heat-only reactors were concerned that the third water circuit, which circulates heat through houses, should be completely safe from any radioactive contamination. Despite the low pressure, leaks are still possible. The problem was tackled in a very original way, by making the pressure in the second circuit (3 atm) higher than in the first (1.5 atm), and the pressure in the third circulating circuit even higher (6 atm). This would make it impossible for leaks from the first or second circuits to penetrate the third, because of the higher pressure in it. However, such a system of increasing pressures with decreasing temperatures is not possible with water in all three circuits. Therefore, the thermal layout of these reactors uses organic liquids in the first two circuits and water only in the third. Organic coolants which were tested (such as hydrostabilised gas-oil) 'later proved not to be the best',[39] but the study of other organic liquids is continuing. But it is also possible that inflammable substances of this sort will be unpopular after the Chernobyl fire.

Soviet nuclear research institutes have come up with several other ideas for heat-only reactors able to generate much higher temperatures for different chemical industries. The Comecon plan for technical cooperation calls for the development of 'nuclear energy-technological stations with multi-purpose utilisation'.[40] But this remains an idea without an experimental prototype. Its realisation would require high-temperature gas-cooled reactors, and some experiments concerning the design of such reactors are underway. The current Five Year Plan calls for accelerated research in this field.

Debates on Nuclear Power

In some countries, debates, public hearings, inquiries and open discussions among experts on various aspects of nuclear power, such as siting, safety, disposal of nuclear waste and so on, are quite common. They are conducted by independent organisations like Friends of the Earth or Critical Mass, and by government bodies and parliamentary commissions. They are published in newspapers and journals, and as special proceedings. In my own library, I have more than 30 volumes documenting debates which have taken place in the US and the UK since 1973 – and this is only a random collection. There has never been open discussion of this sort in the Soviet Union, and issues such as safety, radwaste disposal and transport, economic records, uranium mining, occupational health statistics and so on are all classified. Nobody consults the public over the reasonable siting of nuclear power stations. The Chernobyl accident finally cancelled this *carte blanche* for government bureaucracy and technocracy, and ended the period of public apathy and silence. In the Ukraine this new mood was also mixed with strong local nationalism. A group of Ukrainian writers decided to set up an international 'Chernobyl Forum' to discuss the problems of nuclear power and to stop the proliferation of atomic power stations in densely populated regions. The prominent Ukrainian writer Oles Gonchar publicly tested *glasnost* with his angry questions:

Why did these atomic power stations sprout on our soil, one after another, almost back-to-back? Rovenskaya, Khmelnitskaya on the Dniepr river, Zaporozhe, and not far away, the South Ukraine station. Why do these dig great holes in our land, displacing villages, laying waste our meadows? And why are they now starting work on another at Chigirinsk, which has not yet been officially approved? We cannot see any end to this madness. A reactor is being built at Palesnya on the

Crimean steppes, and there's a plan to build another plant on the upper reaches of the Disna river, the last Ukrainian river not yet poisoned by industrial waste, in the area which till now we always associated with the epic of Prince Igor. It is not the custom in our country to ask people whether or not they want their city to be renamed, or what they think of the power station in this region so precious to us. And of course, why should they ask?[41]

The Soviet Union is not, of course, alone in this secrecy. France is the most obvious Western example of a similar attitude: the French government imposed a massive nuclear programme on the country without proper public consent. When asked about this, the director of Electricité de France, M. Remy Carle, made his now-notorious remark: 'You don't tell the frogs when you are draining the marsh.'[42]

But even after Chernobyl, no real debate was possible in the USSR; only a few mildly critical articles appeared in the mass media, with complaints by some editors that neither nuclear power nor space research were subject to *glasnost*. Inside the nuclear establishment, however, disputes probably did occur from time to time, particularly after the Three Mile Island accident in March 1979. But very little about these disputes reached the public.

In 1979 the Soviet Union was about to launch its most ambitious nuclear energy programme yet, as part of the eleventh Five Year Plan (1981–5), and the problem of siting large nuclear power stations became the focus of a disagreement. One group of scientists, headed by the President of the Soviet Academy of Sciences, Anatoly Alexandrov, and most likely supported by the Brezhnev leadership, favoured siting the AESs in the European USSR, close to population and industrial centres. Their recommendations were based on the 'absolute safety' principle and on economic advantages. The second group, clearly represented by Academician Dollezhal and supported by an unknown but influential group in the government and the party, tried to argue the necessity of siting clusters of nuclear power stations in remote, sparsely populated areas of Siberia and the arctic regions of the European USSR. This group did not question safety standards, but used environmental and ecological arguments, and also cast doubt on the wisdom of losing so much good agricultural land.

This dispute became explicit when a well-argued, detailed article by Dollezhal and Y. Koriakin on the future of nuclear energy was published in *Kommunist*.[43]

Publication in *Kommunist* normally indicates that the author's position is supported by very influential senior party officials. The article attracted much attention abroad, exactly because it was the first sign of dissent on Soviet nuclear energy strategy. Of course, the authors did not challenge the general policy of rapid development of nuclear power. They predicted that the rate of growth of nuclear power in the USSR will reach 5–8 million KW per annum by the end of the 1980s, and more than 10 million KW by the end of the century, and also that the main proportion of the increase of electric power would be nuclear-generated. They also expected nuclear power to account for nearly 50 per cent of global power production in the year 2000, and more than 60 per cent in 2020.

They approved in principle the current practice of building nuclear power stations in the European part of the USSR, despite the higher construction cost. The benefits of this practice, they explained, were indirect, through savings on coal transport and reduced pollution. The authors also praised the RBMK reactor as allowing the maximal power of up to 2,400 MW per unit. They also insisted that the development of the new VVER reactors was only to supplement the RBMK systems and that the three-way approach (which includes fast reactors as well) made Soviet nuclear energy options very flexible. However, they also argued that the future of nuclear energy in the USSR, and in many other countries too, must be envisaged in terms of the fast-breeder reactors because they generate more nuclear fuel than they consume. Up to this point, the authors did not dissent from the established official view.

The authors then acknowledge, however, that fast-breeder technology was proving much more problematic than expected. The construction of economic and powerful fast breeders was not feasible for the 1980s, as planned. Fast breeders might reduce the demand for uranium-235, which was already difficult to extract, but they also needed very large nuclear processing facilities in order to produce plutonium from spent nuclear fuel (from all types of reactors). Nuclear reprocessing for the regeneration of plutonium made it necessary to operate with enormous amounts of radioactive material, and in conditions which could lead to potentially unforeseeable side effects (i.e. accidents, leaks, etc.). They also generated huge quantities of liquid radwaste which had to be disposed of safely – a very costly operation. Big new reprocessing plants could not be located near population centres. However, if they were built in distant parts of Siberia or European Russia, this would inevitably create the problem of transporting spent fuel safely over long distances. It would be uneconomic and dangerous to separate the AESs from the reprocessing facilities by such distances, over country which did not have well-developed rail and road networks. This problem indicated the merits of creating giant complexes with reprocessing plants and power stations – in fact, the entire nuclear fuel cycle – on the same site, making it necessary only to transport electricity.

Dollezhal and Koryakin advanced several further arguments in favour of locating new nuclear power stations in Siberia, the Arctic or the Soviet far east: abundance of water, saving fertile land in the European USSR, and saving water through evaporation in the cooling processes (by 1979, evaporation from nuclear-generated heat was already at the level of 2 cubic km per year).

Thus far, the authors' arguments were very simple. Nuclear stations were safe but nuclear reprocessing, the piecemeal transportation of spent fuel, and the burial of nuclear waste were not safe and could not really be made safe. The achievement of complete safety in these operations would involve very large investments which were not economic. But the authors' solution also seemed very problematic. The best option, they suggested, was the construction of supercomplexes with large clusters of AESs on the same site as reprocessing plant. Each such complex could produce 30 to 40 million KW or more. Even with the most powerful 2,000 MW reactors, this project needed 15 to 20 reactors on each site.

This article, which at first glance looks like a project for fusion energy in the distant future, was, however, taken as a criticism of the current siting of AESs near the population centres in the European USSR. The suggestion that at least some parts of the nuclear fuel cycle might not be wholly safe was also too bold for the establishment. The arguments concerning the loss of too much valuable land and water to nuclear power were also seen as criticisms of current practice, and as support for the agrarian anti-nuclear and anti-hydro lobby. Each AES with RBMK-1000 reactors includes an artificial cooling reservoir of some 20–25 sq km for each 4,000 MW generated, a *sanitar* zone of 2.5 km radius, and land for the plant itself, for workers' quarters and other facilities. Situated near rivers, such plants take a great deal of good agricultural land out of service, and require the resettlement of at least 100 villages and dozens of collective farms. The Chernobyl plant, for instance, took more than 4,000 hectares out of agricultural use. There was strong resistance to the resettlement plans from the agricultural sector. Dollezhal and Koryakin calculated that the land required by the project to build 50 nuclear power plants in the European USSR would be enough to produce food for several million people.

The authors' position was quickly challenged. Alexandrov, Director of the Kurchatov Institute of Atomic Energy as well as President of the Academy, called an unprecedented open press conference in order to refute publicly the case made by Dollezhal and Koryakin. This demonstrated that there were disagreements in senior scientific circles and also worries among the general public. Alexandrov stated that atomic energy was among the safest industrial technologies and posed no threat either to the environment or to the population.[44] He was particularly critical of Dollezhal's and Koryakin's comments on the safety aspects of the reprocessing and burial of liquid nuclear waste. He emphasised that Dollezhal was an expert on reactor design, Koryakin was an economist, and that neither was well acquainted with the broader aspects of nuclear technique. Many diplomats and foreign jounalists were invited to this press conference – which indicated that it had been given top-level approval.

Alexandrov also dismissed suggestions that there were any problems with fast breeders. He claimed that towards the end of the century about a third of nuclear-generated electricity in the USSR (or more than 10 per cent of total electricity output) would come from fast breeders. This prediction, which would mean at least ten BN-1600 reactors in operation, now looks wildly optimistic.

Alexandrov also ridiculed Academician Peter Kapitsa's suggestion (probably made at one of the Academy's meetings) that nuclear power stations should be sited on remote islands.

To foreign journalists, the article and the rebuff appeared to indicate the beginning of a genuine public debate over nuclear power in the USSR. In fact, it was the end of an abortive attempt at debate. From 1980 until the Chernobyl accident, there was not a single article in the Soviet academic or popular press which in any way contested the official nuclear programme. V.A. Legasov, Alexandrov's deputy in the Kurchatov Institute, was particularly active in asserting the complete safety of nuclear energy and trying to suppress any effort to resume the debate even among scientists. The main Soviet academic journal in this field, *Atomnaya Energiya*, whose editorial policy was rigidly controlled by Alexandrov and Legasov, rejected all papers which touched on safety problems in any way. Soviet experts on nuclear safety simply had no forum in which to exchange views and discuss important issues. It was no accident that Legasov headed both the scientific team sent to investigate the causes of the Chernobyl disaster, and the Soviet delegation to the IAEA Post-Accident Meeting in Vienna; he was supremely qualified to present the 'official' view on the Soviet nuclear safety record.

The suppression of scientific debate over the future of nuclear energy was closely linked to the suppression of anti-nuclear opinion among the general public. No anti-nuclear movement has ever been tolerated and anti-nuclear power campaigns in the West (as distinct from the anti-nuclear weapon campaigns, which were welcomed) were presented as the tools of oil or coal companies anxious to preserve their positions in the market.

The absence of any open debate about nuclear power problems allowed planners, scientists, designers, constructors and operators to remain entirely insulated from criticism and to cover up both minor and major accidents. This was the road to Chernobyl, a catastrophe born of secrecy. The only known debate on nuclear safety took place in July and August of 1987, during the two-week trial – by the special Collegium of the Supreme Court of the USSR – of the former director of the Chernobyl plant, Brukhanov, chief engineer Fomin, and four other defendants, on charges of 'criminal negligence'. But this trial, which took place at the former workers' club in Chernobyl town, inside the exclusion zone, some 15 km from the destroyed reactor, was held in camera. All proceedings, except the opening session and the final 'sentencing', were closed. The judgement implicated many senior officials and various authorities, but only a few short extracts were ever published.[45] Public pressure against the nuclear power programme is, however, increasing, and has been acknowledged as largely responsible for the recent cancellations of three nuclear projects already under construction – the Kuban power station in Krasnodar Krai, and thermal nuclear stations at Minsk and Odessa.

Conclusion

It is clear that the secrecy which has protected all Soviet nuclear power programmes since the start of the first small AES project in 1954 was the main contributory factor in the Chernobyl accident. There had been several previous accidents, but these were covered up at all levels. Small mishaps were concealed from their superiors by operators and local engineers and often not even recorded in the operational logs. More serious accidents and shutdowns were covered up by the nuclear plant administrators, because all their bonuses and rewards depended upon good records. Construction and design faults were covered up by the ministerial and atomic energy bureaucracies, which had vested interests in the good image of the nuclear industry. Really major accidents, like the Kyshtym nuclear disaster in the Urals in 1958, which created a contaminated exclusion zone as large as that at Chernobyl, or the 1983 *Atommash* accident, were covered up by the government. Not a single plan for the development of nuclear energy has ever been fulfilled on time.

Even the new Five Year Plan approved by the Supreme Soviet in June 1986 – after Chernobyl – was not realistic. This plan calls for the addition of 41,000 MW of electric power from new nuclear plants. This would mean nearly 40 new reactors, of the RBMK-1000 or VVER-1000 type, in operation in 1990.[46] But only 20 reactors were under construction in 1987, and each reactor, even when it stays on schedule, takes more than 5 years to build. In the previous (1981–5) Five Year Plan, instead of the planned 25 MWe of new nuclear power, only 15 MWe were actually added. The acceleration during 1986–90 was necessary if the targets of the more general 'Energy Programme of the USSR', introduced in 1983, were to be attained. But this planning bore no relation to real possibilities.

The latest statement of accounts from the January 1988 Politburo meeting puts the economic cost of the Chernobyl accident at 8 billion roubles,[47] which is the projected construction cost of 16 Chernobyl-type power reactors. But this is only a fraction of the real costs and losses resulting from Chernobyl, which will continue to accumulate for several decades to come. Even the estimated loss of 8 billion roubles up to the end of 1987 is clearly an underestimate, because this figure does not include many indirect losses and expenses. The methods by which the reported costs of the accident were calculated have not yet been disclosed, analysed or discussed. It is unclear, for example, whether they take account of the expensive modernisation of the safety systems in existing reactors, or the necessary changes in the design of reactors under construction and in the project stage. If the true costs were properly calculated, they might well come close to the total investment in the Soviet nuclear power industry since 1954. In this situation, no one can insist any longer on the economic benefits of nuclear power in the Soviet Union.

Notes

1. A.M. Petrosyants, *Problems of Nuclear Science and Technology. The Soviet Union as a World Nuclear Power*, fourth edition, revised and enlarged, Pergamon Press, Oxford and New York, 1981, p. 343.
2. W. Patterson, *Nuclear Power*, second edition, Penguin Books, Harmondsworth, 1983, p. 47.
3. P. Astashenkov, *Kurchatov*, Molodaya Gvardija, Moscow, 1967, p. 167.
4. I.N. Golovin, *I.V. Kurchatov*, Atomizdat, Moscow, 1967, p. 77.
5. Ibid., p. 84.
6. Ibid., pp. 84–5; Astashenkov, *Kurchatov*, p. 167.
7. D.A. Granin, *Zubr, Novy Mir*, Moscow, no. 2, pp. 7–92, 1987.
8. Ibid., p. 46.
9. Vladimir Gubarev, *Sargophag, Zhamya*, Moscow, 1986. English translation by Michael Glenny: *Sarcophagus*, Penguin Books, Harmondsworth, 1987.
10. Vladimir Gubarev, 'None v Obninske', *Sovietskaya Kul'tura* (Moscow), 28 May 1987, p. 3.
11. Petrosyants, *Problems of Nuclear Science*, pp. 103–4.
12. *Khrushchev Remembers. The Last Testament*, translated and edited by S. Talbott, Little, Brown & Co, Boston, 1974, p. 60.
13. Petrosyants, *Problems of Nuclear Science*, p. 109.
14. Ibid., p. 105.
15. Zhores A. Medvedev, *Nuclear Disaster in the Urals*, W.W. Norton, New York, 1979.
16. Petrosyants, *Problems of Nuclear Science*, p. 107.
17. 'Nuclear reactor development', *Encyclopaedia Britannica*, vol. 13, 1982, p. 321.
18. *Report of the US Department of Energy's Team Analysis of the Chernobyl Atomic Energy Station Accident Sequence*, November 1986, US Department of Energy, Washington, DC 20585, p. C-7.
19. V. Dubrovsky (ed), *Construction of Nuclear Power Plants*, Mir Publishers, Moscow, 1981, p. 92.
20. Petrosyants, *Problems of Nuclear Science*, p. 118; p. 146.

21. Dubrovsky, *Construction*, p. 37.
22. Petrosyants, *Problems of Nuclear Science*, p. 118.
23. Petrosyants, ibid.; Dubrovsky, *Construction*.
24. Petrosyants, *Problems of Nuclear Science*, pp. 130–1.
25. Ibid., p. 132.
26. *Pravda*, 20 July 1983.
27. *Pravda*, 31 July 1983.
28. G. Greenhalph, 'Soviet drive to nuclear power', *New Scientist*, vol. 110, no. 1507, 8 May 1986, p. 198.
29. Soviet Working Document, *The Accident at the Chernobyl Nuclear Power Plant and its Consequences*, Annex 2, Information compiled for the IAEA Expert Meeting, 25–9 August 1986, Vienna.
30. Dubrovsky, *Construction*, p. 85.
31. D.R. Marples, *Chernobyl and Nuclear Power in the USSR*, Macmillan, London, 1986.
32. Petrosyants, *Problems of Nuclear Science*, p. 153.
33. Ibid., p. 162.
34. *Pravda*, 25 April 1980.
35. Petrosyants, *Problems of Nuclear Science*, p. 153.
36. *Izvestiya*, 14 December 1979.
37. *Ekonomicheskaya Gazeta*, no. 52, December 1983.
38. Petrosyants, *Problems of Nuclear Science*, p. 231.
39. Ibid., p. 232.
40. *Izvestia*, 19 July 1985.
41. Oles Gonchar, 'Otkuda yavilas "Zvezda Polyn"', *Literaturnaya Gazeta*, 9 December 1987.
42. G. Lean and R. Smith, 'The menace on our doorsteps', *Observer* Magazine, 11 October 1987.
43. N. Dollezhal and Y. Koryakin, 'Yadernaya energetika. Dotizheniya i problemy', *Kommunist*, no. 14, 1979, pp. 19–28.
44. *The Times*, 20 December 1979.
45. *Moscow News*, 9 August 1987.
46. *Moscow News*, 10 January 1988.
47. *Pravda*, 16 January 1988.

2

Accidents, Risks and Consequences

RICHARD ERSKINE and PHILIP WEBBER

When asked for his immediate reaction to the news of the Chernobyl accident, Tony Benn, a former British Secretary of State for Energy, said: 'it was Hiroshima all over again.' A Soviet spokesman characterised it as the 'worst accident in the world', a description which seems to have stuck. These descriptions were both overstatements and understatements. At Bhopal, for example, 2,000 people died in the immediate aftermath, and there will be a continuing death toll amongst the 100,000 affected. In comparison, 31 people had died by August 1986 as a direct result of radiation sickness induced by the Chernobyl disaster. At least 6,500 premature deaths due to cancer are expected in the Soviet Union. Tens of thousands will die prematurely from radiation-induced cancers over the next 30 to 40 years in the Soviet Union and Europe. But Chernobyl could have been much worse; there are potentially far more serious reactor accidents that could occur. It would be profoundly mistaken, however, to conclude that, as we have survived Chernobyl and are still here, maybe radiation is not so bad after all. The point is that Chernobyl is the worst *nuclear reactor* accident *so far*.

Chernobyl Compared to a Nuclear Weapon

The first, and obvious, point of comparison is that even a very small nuclear weapon would have caused far more casualties than the Chernobyl disaster. However, the actual radioactive release from the reactor core was equivalent to roughly the level of radiation that would have been created by a ten kiloton nuclear weapon (about the same size as the weapon which destroyed Hiroshima), one hour after detonation.

Further away, the levels of radiation measured in Sweden 24 hours after the accident were equivalent to those that would have been produced by a nuclear weapon of about one kiloton detonated in the vicinity of Chernobyl (assuming a constant wind direction). The 24-hour figure of one kiloton is lower than the ten kiloton figure because the radiation was not carried on a constant wind but was spread in a quite complex way by the winds. A one kiloton weapon is termed a 'tactical' nuclear weapon. In the event of a non-nuclear attack in Europe, NATO threatens to use nuclear weapons of up to 1,000 times this size in its 'first-use' policy.

A more serious possibility in the event of nuclear war is a nuclear weapon hitting a nuclear reactor. This would mean the lethal combination of short-term deaths from the bomb – far exceeding those that could occur from a nuclear reactor meltdown – plus long-term denial of land for farming or other activities, resulting from the fact that the bomb's fireball would break and vapourise the reactor core completely and then suck up the radioactive material and spread it over a large area.

The contents of the reactor core would be mixed with the radioactive elements created by the bomb. For a one megaton bomb, the radioactivity would initially be 50 times that contained in a one Gigawatt reactor, such as that at Chernobyl (one Gigawatt is a power output sufficient to operate 1,000 million single-bar electric heaters). The radioactivity from the bomb would decay away faster than that from the reactor; after four days the radiation contributions from the two sources would be the same. After one year, the radiation contribution from the reactor would be 100 times that of the bomb.

The Chernobyl Fallout

In Europe, the quantity of radioactivity (caesium-137) deposited by Chernobyl was 400 times more than the peak levels released by all the open-air nuclear weapons tests up to 1963, when public outcry led to the Partial Test-Ban Treaty.

Peak levels in Britain around 2 and 3 May 1986 were about 10 Becquerels (Bq) per cubic metre of grass. In areas of high rainfall, this translated to ground-level contamination of up to 30,000 Bq per square metre: equivalent, in terms of short-term whole-body dose rates, to about six times the natural radioactive background.

In the aftermath of Chernobyl, the Soviet authorities evacuated everyone from within a 30 km radius of the plant, and people from as far as 100 km away in specific downwind directions. In all, 135,000 people had to be evacuated. Topsoil was removed over a 1,000 square mile evacuation zone and buried as contaminated waste.

If the Chernobyl accident had happened in the UK – and the CEGB denies that it could – the consequences would have far exceeded the planned response of the authorities. This would also have been true for most other European countries and the US.

The previous worst accident to affect Britain was the 1957 fire in a military reactor at Windscale (now renamed Sellafield). The estimated release of iodine-131 was 20,000 Ci (Curies); some radioactive polonium was also released. Two million litres of milk collected from an area of 500 square kilometres were poured away.

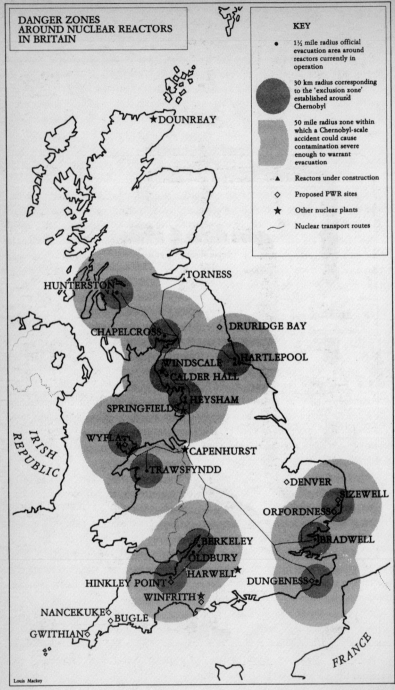

DANGER ZONES
AROUND NUCLEAR REACTORS
IN BRITAIN

KEY

• 1½ mile radius official
evacuation area around
reactors currently in
operation

30 km radius corresponding
to the 'exclusion zone'
established around
Chernobyl

50 mile radius zone within
which a Chernobyl-scale
accident could cause
contamination severe
enough to warrant
evacuation

▲ Reactors under construction

◇ Proposed PWR sites

★ Other nuclear plants

— Nuclear transport routes

★ DOUNREAY

HUNTERSTON

★ TORNESS

CHAPELCROSS

◇ DRURIDGE BAY

WINDSCALE ▲ HARTLEPOOL

CALDER HALL

HEYSHAM

SPRINGFIELDS

WYLFA

★ CAPENHURST

TRAWSFYNDD

IRISH
REPUBLIC

◇ DENVER

SIZEWELL

ORFORDNESS ◇

BERKELEY

OLDBURY

HARWELL ★

BRADWELL

HINKLEY POINT ◇

WINFRITH

DUNGENESS

NANCEKUKE ◇

◇ BUGLE

GWITHIAN ◇

FRANCE

Louis Mackay

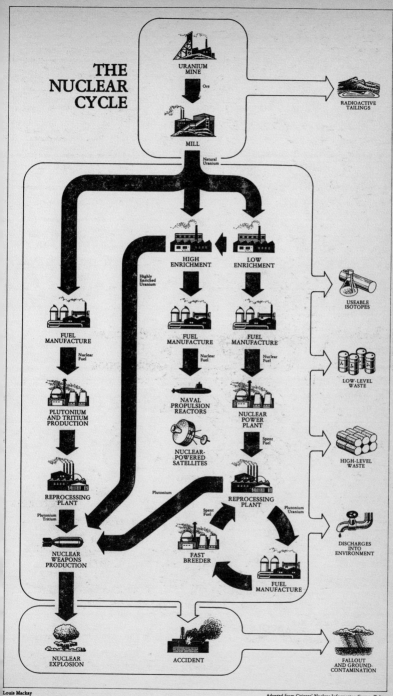

THE
NUCLEAR
CYCLE

URANIUM MINE

Ore

RADIOACTIVE TAILINGS

MILL

Natural Uranium

HIGH ENRICHMENT

LOW ENRICHMENT

Highly Enriched Uranium

USEABLE ISOTOPES

FUEL MANUFACTURE

FUEL MANUFACTURE

FUEL MANUFACTURE

Nuclear Fuel

Nuclear Fuel

Nuclear Fuel

LOW-LEVEL WASTE

PLUTONIUM AND TRITIUM PRODUCTION

NAVAL PROPULSION REACTORS

NUCLEAR POWER PLANT

Spent Fuel

HIGH-LEVEL WASTE

NUCLEAR-POWERED SATELLITES

REPROCESSING PLANT

Plutonium

REPROCESSING PLANT

Spent Fuel

Plutonium Uranium

Plutonium Tritium

FAST BREEDER

DISCHARGES INTO ENVIRONMENT

NUCLEAR WEAPONS PRODUCTION

FUEL MANUFACTURE

NUCLEAR EXPLOSION

ACCIDENT

FALLOUT AND GROUND-CONTAMINATION

Louis Mackay

Adapted from Citizens' Nuclear Information Centre, Tokyo.

49

Translating Chernobyl to the UK

The UK authorities have detailed plans for evacuation only from within a radius of 3 km. This encloses an area one-hundredth the size of the Chernobyl evacuation zone of 30 km. Outside the USSR, only Finland has evacuation plans extending anywhere near 30 km, with contingency plans for up to a further 20 km. In France the radius is 5 km, in the Federal German Republic 10 km, in the USA, 16 km. It is difficult to believe that the differences correspond to variations in nuclear power station safety in these countries. It seems much more likely that they represent different assessments of the worst accident *worth planning for*.

Table 2.1
Nuclear sites in UK and local populations

Site	Type[a]	Date of operation	Population[b] within 20 miles in thousands
Berkeley	Magnox	1962	859
Bradwell	Magnox	1962	704
Chapelcross	Magnox	1959	163
Dounreay	Prototype FBR	1977	5
Druridge Bay	Proposed PWR	?	674
Dungeness	Magnox	1966	242
Dungeness B	AGR	1984	
Hartlepool	AGR	1984	520
Heysham A, B	AGR	1984	482
Hinkley Point	Magnox	1965	459
Hinkley Point B	AGR	1976	
Hunterston	Magnox	1965	391
Hunterston B	AGR	1976	
Oldbury	Magnox	1967[c]	959
Sellafield	Reprocessing	1952	81
Sizewell	Magnox	1966	148
Sizewell B	Proposed PWR ?		
Torness A	AGR	1987	43
Trawsfynydd	Magnox	1965	62
Winfrith	Prototype SGHWR	1968	365
Wylfa	Magnox	1971	51

[a] FBR = Fast-Breeder Reactor, AGR = Advanced Gas-cooled Reactor, PWR = Pressurised Water Reactor, SGHWR = Steam-Generating Heavy Water Reactor.
[b] Source: Openshaw (1986). Note that the Chernobyl evacuation zone had a radius of about 20 miles.
[c] Since early (and continuing) use as weapons plutonium production facility.

If one draws a 30 km evacuation zone around all the UK nuclear stations, it is evident that most zones include large populations. The Hartlepool advanced gas-cooled reactor (AGR), for example, has over 300,000 people within such a zone, and only came to be sited in this largely suburban area because of relaxed siting regulations for AGRs in the late 1960s.

As for the older, Magnox-type reactors, which have been operating since the 1950s, Berkeley, Bradwell, Hinkley Point, Hunterston and Oldbury all have over 500,000 people living inside a 30 km evacuation zone – much larger populations than those the Soviet authorities had to evacuate.

The largest Soviet partial evacuation zone had a radius of 100 miles (160 km). Some idea of what such an evacuation zone would mean in the UK can be gained from the fact that only three regions in the whole of the UK are over 100 miles from a nuclear reactor – parts of Lincolnshire, the western tip of Cornwall and central-western Scotland. With unfavourable wind directions, a 100-mile evacuation zone would mean, for Bradwell (Magnox) or Dungeness (Magnox and AGR), the evacuation of London (over seven million people), and for Trawsfynydd (Magnox) or Heysham (AGR), the evacuation of Birmingham, Manchester or Sheffield. Glasgow and Edinburgh are already within the smaller 30 km radius of Hunterston (Magnox and AGR) and Torness (AGR) respectively. In the west, Bristol, Weston-super-Mare and Gloucester are all within 30 km of the Hinkley Point, Berkeley and Oldbury plants (three Magnox plus one AGR).

The UK authorities are not remotely prepared for an emergency on this scale and have no plans for evacuating such numbers of people or such large areas. In any case, where could these people actually be evacuated to?

In the case of Chernobyl, where the populations evacuated were much smaller, emergency telephone numbers took over a week to reach the district councils – rather slower than the arrival of the radiation cloud itself. The councils also found that their radiation monitors were not suitable for monitoring the contamination of foodstuffs, being intended for measuring the much higher doses expected after a nuclear attack.

The thinking behind planning for nuclear accidents in the UK and elsewhere in Western Europe is to prepare not for the worst accident possible, but rather for a class of accidents in which the planners in some way optimise the effect of the money that is spent on planning and preparation. They believe that the worst case is so unlikely that it is not cost-effective to prepare for it. So they prepare for what they believe to be the more likely accidents, which they think will have much smaller consequences. If the worst does happen, however, the plans will clearly be inadequate.

Finally, it is important to remember what Chernobyl proved – that the effects of nuclear reactor accidents are international. Nuclear plants are situated in most Western European countries; all of them are far nearer to the UK than Chernobyl is. The nearest nuclear reactor to parts of the English south coast is in France, as many French plants are sited along the northern French coast. Yet there are no plans in the UK for coping with accidents which might occur at these plants. It was Britain's good luck that it lay so far from Chernobyl, and that it took an entire week before the wind blew the cloud over the UK.

As far as other countries' nuclear activities are concerned, our safety depends not only on the abilities of our own administrations, over which we have some limited control, but also on foreign administrations over which we have none. This can have quite absurd consequences. Thus the Danes, who decided against nuclear power stations, have a nuclear reactor within a few kilometres of their capital city, across the Kattegat strait in Sweden. Many other nuclear reactors and facilities in Europe are sited very near to national boundaries. Often this is because of the need for access to cooling water from sea or river, but another consideration is that such a policy reduces the number of people in one's own country who might possibly object, while the population of the neighbouring country is usually not even consulted.

How Nuclear Reactor Accidents Happen: Windscale, Three Mile Island and Chernobyl

Until Chernobyl, the two most serious nuclear reactor accidents to have occurred were at Windscale in Cumbria on 10 October 1957, and at the Three Mile Island Unit 2 nuclear plant near Harrisburg, Pennsylvania on 28 March 1979.

Windscale

Pile No. 1 at Windscale was one of a number of primitive reactors whose purpose was to produce plutonium for nuclear weapons. These 'piles' did not generate electricity, so unlike Calder Hall there was little to disguise their true purpose. Natural uranium fuel (uranium-235 and -238, which is transformed into plutonium-239) was contained in aluminium cans, which in turn were housed in cavities manufactured inside a graphite 'moderator'. The piles were also used to produce polonium, which was used as a 'neutron initiator' in nuclear weapons.

An accident almost occured in 1952 when it was discovered that the graphite in the pile, when heated above a critical temperature, suddenly released energy. This energy is known as Wigner energy and arises from deformations in the graphite caused by radiation. By 1957 it had become a standard procedure to release Wigner energy and so avoid a dangerous build-up in the graphite. This involved raising then lowering the power in the pile. Surprisingly, the physicists who controlled the pile had no operating manual to guide them.

After the 1952 incident, a Wigner energy release had been performed after every 20,000 MW (megawatt) days of operation, but by September 1957 this had been increased to 40,000 MW days, probably because of military pressure to increase plutonium production. So when the pile was shut down on 7 October 1957 it had more Wigner energy stored in it than ever before. Thermocouples to measure the temperatures in the pile were not best placed to monitor the Wigner release and the pile overheated. The cans fractured, leading to oxidation of the uranium fuel, releasing more heat which triggered the graphite fire. This was finally put out by pumping in 5 million litres of water over a period of a day. It was a desperate measure, carrying the risk of creating a hydrogen–oxygen mixture which could have exploded. The Cabinet papers released in January 1988 add little to our understanding of the accident itself, but tell us a great deal about the political concerns of the day. Prime Minister Harold Macmillan opposed publication of Sir William Penney's report into the accident because he feared prejudicing Britain's chances of sharing US nuclear secrets, obstructed at that time by the US McMahon Act.

Three Mile Island

On 28 March 1979, TMI Unit No. 2 was having difficulty starting up; the maintenance force was overworked and understaffed owing to an economy drive. The accident started, as it did at Chernobyl, in the cooling system, which sprang a small leak. Moisture then got into the pneumatic system which drove some of the instruments. This was wrongly interpreted as a fault in the turbine, causing its automatic shutdown. As this stopped the cooling water, the emergency feedwater pumps came on. The controls told the operators that the pumps were working satisfactorily, but unknown to them, both the emergency feed pipes had been mistakenly left closed after maintenance two days earlier. The operators might have seen that the valves were shut, had not one been obscured by a repair tag hanging on a switch above it. With no coolant in the system, the steam generator boiled dry and the reactor 'scrammed' (shut down). Graphite control rods were dropped into the core to absorb neutrons and thus to stop the nuclear reaction. But the core, in the absence of cooling, was still dangerously hot and the water pressure in the core was rising. A further safety device – a relief valve – opened to relieve pressure, but then stuck open. The indicator light warning the operators of this failed. They waited in vain for the pressure to rise again as the valve closed.

At this point the accident was still only 13 seconds old, which gives some idea of the speed at which the crisis overtook the system and its operators.

Two additional reactor coolant systems were now switched on and radioactive water continued to pour out of the jammed open valve (into a tank not intended for this, which then overflowed into an auxiliary building). Next, a high-pressure injection system forced water at a much higher rate into the core. This ran at full pressure for two minutes before being turned down manually. The core was steadily uncovered. The operators were now presented with conflicting readings on two dials, one showing pressure rising, one showing it dropping. They did not know which was correct. In the control room three audible alarms were sounding and many of the 1,600 lights on the control panel were blinking. After eight minutes, the operators realised that a tag was obscuring the emergency feed pipe indicator, but by then most of the damage had been done.

After 2 hours and 20 minutes a relief shift worker spotted the jammed relief valve and it was shut, preventing further melting of the core. In another 30 minutes there would probably have been a complete meltdown of the core, threatening the containment of the building. Some 22 hours after the start of the emergency, a soft but distinct bang was heard in the control room resulting from a hydrogen gas explosion which fortunately was not repeated.

The President's Commission blamed everyone, but primarily the operators, for the accident. Given that the experts could not even agree upon the precautions which should have been taken at various stages by the operators, this was probably a fair judgement.

Chernobyl

Controversy over the exact cause of the Chernobyl accident will continue. As the editors note in their introduction to this volume, the story which emerges from the official Soviet report to the IAEA in Vienna put the blame squarely upon the operators of the plant. But the report also acknowledges – albeit indirectly, in listing a series of design adjustments – that the reactor's design made it particularly vulnerable to certain operating errors.

Ironically, it seems that the Chernobyl accident resulted from tests intended to investigate and improve the safety of the reactor. The experiment was designed to see how long residual energy in the electricity-generating, spinning, steam turbines would last and continue to power emergency back-up systems, after their powering steam supply was cut off.

One other important fact emerged from the report. The RBMK-1000 design has what is known as a 'positive temperature coefficient' (not to be confused with the 'void coefficient'). This is jargon for a reactor system which produces more energy as it gets hotter. Uncontrolled, any temperature rise spirals upwards (as happened in the Chernobyl accident) until damage is caused. The Soviets intend to undertake expensive design modifications, including the provision of better controls and larger numbers of control rods. They intend to try to get rid of the positive temperature coefficient by using more highly enriched uranium fuel. For comparison, the proposed PWR reactor at Sizewell is designed to have a negative temperature coefficient at normal power (although it can go positive during power raising or lowering).

Existing Reactor Designs and Accident Scenarios

The design of all engineering systems – such as large software packages, major civil construction and aerospace vehicles – invariably involves many trade-offs between competing requirements and constraints. Nuclear reactors are not immune from this basic feature of engineering. The requirements one might stipulate for a nuclear power reactor design, could include the electricity power output, the operating life and various safety features. The list of constraints involves factors such as the behaviour of water under temperature and pressure, and the budget for design and construction.

The most basic requirement is to be able to control the fission process in a given mass of fissile material, and to extract the heat generated so as to produce steam to drive turbines and thereby produce electricity.

Reactor designs may differ in respect of fuel, core geometry, moderator and coolant, and in the relationship between these variables. Each choice will involve its own special problems and trade-offs.

According to Freeman Dyson, writing about commercial power reactors, 'We are left with a very small number of reactor types in operation, each of them frozen into a huge bureaucratic organisation that makes any substantial change impossible, each of them in various ways technically unsatisfactory, each of them less safe than many possible alternative designs which have now been discarded.'[1]

Reactor accidents are not new and serious accidents – leading to partial meltdown – have occured in all the generic forms of reactor, with the exception of the pressurised heavy water reactor (PHWR), so far as we know.

In the case of the gas-cooled reactor (GCR), there was the Windscale reactor fire of 1957, described above. The 'advanced' gas-cooled reactor (AGR) design's main difference from the Magnox is in its use of much safer stainless steel cladding in place of 'Magnox', which is the trade name for a magnesium alloy with a relatively low melting point which will ignite at 645°C even in an inert carbon dioxide atmosphere. The main reason for changing to the AGR design was to achieve a smaller core size and higher thermal efficiency. The AGR must still contend, however, with the apparently slight possibility of a 'loss-of-coolant accident' (LOCA) coupled with a breach of primary containment leading to a graphite fire. Walter Patterson has pointed out that there is no safer reactor than one which doesn't work, and the endless teething problems with AGRs – causing a 17-year delay in the start-up of Dungeness B – have rather undermined confidence in the design.

In the RBMK, Chernobyl-type design, unlike in the gas-cooled reactor types familiar in the West, the graphite is separately cooled using a flow of inert gas, but the graphite operating temperature is higher, with a correspondingly greater risk of a graphite fire. The main fuel elements are water-cooled; if the water comes into contact with the high-temperature graphite, dangerous steam pressures can quickly result (which is what happened at Chernobyl), leaving little time for corrective action in the event of a loss-of-coolant accident.

It is not clear that the RBMK's containment is inferior to Western designs. Only the light water reactors (LWR), which include the PWR type, have full secondary containment. 'Western experts now agree that a large structure of heavy steel and concrete did in fact enclose the Chernobyl reactor. Moreover, it appears to have been designed to withstand pressures that are comparable to those in many American reactors.'[2]

The LWRs have high power density, making them difficult to handle under faulty conditions, as Three Mile Island illustrated all too clearly. Although, for the LWR, there is the ameliorating factor that the coolant (water) also acts as the moderator (so a loss of coolant will cause the chain reaction to stop), heat is still produced by the radioactive fission in the core. Therefore, such a high power density design is inherently unsafe, and must be compensated for in practice by the addition of a whole battery of engineered emergency cooling mechanisms. Safety then comes down to a reliance on the detection of problems and the execution of corrective actions, assuming these have all been thought through.

As far as the liquid metal fast-breeder reactor (LMFBR) is concerned, an accident at the Enrico Fermi 1 reactor near Laguna Beach, Detroit, in October 1966 was due to a safety modification to the design (to prevent the core becoming critical again – i.e. recriticality – in the event of meltdown), which had been insisted upon by the US Advisory Committee on Reactor Safeguards. The 'improvement' resulted in a blockage of liquid sodium coolant, damage to the core, and part meltdown. A report by the AEC (completed before the accident and immediately classified) predicted that, given unfavourable wind conditions, 133,000 people would receive high doses of radiation, of whom half would die. Another 181,000 could receive serious doses of radiation (150 rads). In the event they were lucky and didn't have to evacuate Detroit; but it was a close call.

The high heat capacity of sodium compensates for the very high power density in an LMFBR, but if the control rods failed at the same time as the coolant pumps, the liquid sodium could boil, leading to 'voids' causing increased activity which could, in turn, lead to core disruption and possible recriticality. In the worst possible case a (very inefficient) nuclear explosion, equivalent only to a fraction of a ton of TNT, might be generated; but this might be enough to breach containment. A major concern with the FBR is the very large quantities of plutonium and fission products in the reactor at any time, larger even than in current thermal reactors.

Each reactor design has its strengths and weaknesses. It is interesting that in the cases of Enrico Fermi 1, Three Mile Island and Chernobyl, attempts to guard against the most feared accident scenario led to, or distracted attention from, other dangers which can now be seen as equally serious.

To be sure, the RBMK design has a number of undesirable features, but so do the other generic forms of reactor currently in use, not least the most widespread of all, the LWR (especially the PWR).

Releases from Reprocessing Facilities
The routine releases from the Sellafield reprocessing plant into the Irish Sea are, of course, no accident. In the 1970s, the permitted levels were 6,000 Ci of alpha emitters and 300,000 Ci of beta emitters per year. In 1978, for example, 31 per cent of the alpha quota and 64 per cent of the beta quota were released. For comparison, the equivalent French plant at Cap de la Hague has permitted levels of only 90 Ci for alpha and 45,000 Ci of beta. Although strenuous efforts have been made to reduce the emissions from Sellafield, they remain very much higher than levels released by other countries.

Other Potential Causes of Nuclear Reactor Accidents
Besides the possibility of accident or malfunction within nuclear plants themselves, there are various factors which add to the risks nuclear plants pose to life.

Earthquakes, corruption or cost-cutting, war or terrorism, may all lead to nuclear releases. Clearly an earthquake of sufficient magnitude could devastate a nuclear reactor. Countries in earthquake zones, such as Japan and Taiwan, are particularly at risk.

Corruption or cost-cutting may result in contractors not paying sufficient attention to quality control in the construction of the plant and its fuel elements. Such factors may be expected to be more prevalent in the Third World, where money is short, although one should not assume that plant-siting and construction in the First World are immune to becoming jeopardised in this way.

In war, nuclear plants may be hit deliberately or accidently by armour-piercing, high-explosive, or even nuclear weapons – with what possible results, we have already described.

Terrorists, whilst unlikely to have sufficient explosive power to breach

Table 2.2 Characteristics of principal reactor types in operation

Common name	CANDU	Magnox	AGR	PWR	BWR	RBMK	FBR
Name of Example	Pickering (Canada)	Dungeness A (UK)	Hinkley Point B (UK)	Zion (USA)	Browns Ferry 1 (USA)	Chernobyl 4 (USSR)	Phénix (France)
Generic class	PHWR	GCR	GCR	LWR	LWR	LWGR	LMFBR
Fuel (effective enrichment)	natural uranium oxide (none)	natural uranium (none)	uranium metal oxide (2%)	uranium oxide (3%)	uranium oxide (2.2%)	uranium oxide (1.8%)	plutonium and uranium (20-27%)
Fuel cladding	zirconium alloy	magnesium alloy	stainless steel	zirconium alloy	zirconium alloy	zirconium-niobium alloy	stainless steel
Moderator Vessel	heavy water pressure tubes	graphite welded steel	graphite pre-stressed concrete tubes	water welded steel	water welded steel	graphite pressure steel 'pot'	none stainless steel Secondary
Containment	No	No	No	Yes	Yes	No	No
Fuel coolant	heavy water	carbon dioxide	carbon dioxide	water	water	water	liquid sodium
Average power density	16.2 kW/l	1.1 kW/l	4.5 kW/l	102 kW/l	49 kW/l	5-10 kW/l	646 kW/l
Coolant pressure	85 atm	19 atm	40 atm	150 atm	68 atm	65 atm	1 atm
Coolant outlet temp.	293°C	245°C	634°C	318°C	285°C	284°C	562°C
Steam for turbines	using heat exchanger	using heat exchanger	using heat exchanger	using heat exchanger	direct from reactor	direct from reactor	using heat exchanger
Fault response time	hours	hours	hours	minutes	minutes	minutes	seconds/minutes

Table 2.2 (cont.)

Source: Adapted from W. Patterson, Nuclear Power, 1983.

Notes
1. The generic names are: PHWR=Pressurised Heavy Water Reactor, GCR=Gas-Cooled Reactor, LWR=Light Water Reactor, LWGR =Light Water Graphite-moderated Reactor, and LMFBR=Liquid Metal Fast-Breeder Reactor. The common name acronyms are: AGR=Advanced Gas-cooled Reactor, PWR=Pressurised Water Reactor, BWR=Boiling Water Reactor, FBR=Fast Breeder Reactor. RBMK translates as Russian Graphite Moderated Channel Tube.
2. Many zirconium alloy pressure tubes are used in the CANDU and RBMK reactors in place of one large vessel, although both have a concrete primary containment structure, comparable to Western reactors that do have secondary containment. The last two Magnox reactors have concrete pressure vessels.
3. Secondary containment refers to a reinforced (often hemispherical) concrete reactor building, containing the reactor vessel and primary coolant circuits, which has been specially designed to withstand possible steam or chemical explosions following breach of some of the coolant pipes or the reactor vessel.
4. In the case of the PWR and BWR, the coolant and moderator are one and the same; in the CANDU they are the same, but are separately contained.
5. The average power density (in kilowatts per litre) is proportional to the ratio of the thermal output with the effective volume of the core. The RBMK value is an estimate. Local variations, in time and space, from these values are called 'transients'.
6. Pressure is given in atmospheres (atm).
7. The outlet coolant temperatures should not be confused with the core temperatures, which will be higher (e.g. in the case of the RBMK, between 550 and 750°C).
8. The steam from the BWR or RBMK reactors is 'wet' and must go through a separator before reaching the turbines. The steam generating heat exchanger takes heat from the primary coolant circuit, except in the case of the FBR which includes an additional intermediate circuit (of liquid sodium).
9. The fault response time, in relation to a Loss of Coolant Accident (LOCA) or transient, is closely related to a ratio of power density to the thermal capacity per unit volume of the core.

the core directly, could sabotage steam pipes and water cooling systems or cause a sudden disconnection from the electricity grid, leading to problems in power dumping. Actions of this sort could most easily be taken by infiltrators actually working at the plant. Fear of terrorism is one factor which has led nuclear plant operators to become obsessive about secrecy. The true nature of the so-called 'plutonium economy' is another. Secrecy, in turn, leads to public mistrust of nuclear plant operators.

Is There a Safe Reactor?

It is possible to envisage nuclear reactors which are less inherently dangerous than those currently used for power generation. The following characteristics are desirable: low power density; high heat capacity; natural convective cooling in the event of pump failure; little reliance upon 'engineered' safety systems; modular designs with minimal radioactivity in the core at any time. Such features would vastly reduce both the likelihood of accidents and of worst-case consequences. The chances of a serious accident, however, could still not be totally discounted.

Despite years of academic interest in such reactor types, however, there is little sign of any trend in the nuclear industry towards building reactors with these features. This is for two reasons: an institutional tendency to lock in on one design after substantial sums have been invested in its development; and economic pressures working against the operating practices required in the safer reactor types. In the latter case, there is a clear trade-off between cost and perceived safety.

Assessing Risk

Risk assessment, particularly in relation to matters nuclear, is undertaken by very specialised groups of 'experts'. There are two important aspects to this assessment: first, the likelihood of various possible accidents, and secondly, the estimated cost of those accidents.

The total risk usually calculated is a complicated combination of these two factors. The CEGB, for example, multiplies the cost of an accident by the chances of its occurrence to arrive at a final risk factor.

Taking the likelihood first, nuclear experts calculate the chances of various degrees of meltdown leading to releases of nuclear materials. In the absence of years of operating experience and many varied instances of accidents upon which to base figures, predictions can only be based on hypothetical projections of all the possible combinations of events in a plant. For example, calculations have to be made concerning the probability of each valve sticking, of various types of design failure, and so on.

The next problem is that the history of accidents is the history of the unexpected, and that some of the most important possible failure routes may not even be included in the analysis. Certainly no planner had predicted the precise series of accidents and operator errors that occurred at Three Mile Island – the hydrogen problem, for instance, was not even considered.

W.D. Rowe has usefully defined several types of risk assessment. Two of them he dubs the 'tip of the iceberg school' – in which the potential hazard is always greater than the risk calculated – and the 'count the bodies school' – in which the risk calculated is always less than the potential hazard.[3] The latter school is typified by highly numerate forms of risk assessment, probabilistic and economic cost-benefit analyses, while the former is usually based upon a more sociological or historical framework. Generally speaking, the nuclear industry comes from the 'count the bodies' school, and the opposition from the 'tip of the iceberg' school.

In the US Nuclear Regulatory Commission's Reactor Safety Study, the likelihood of a risk and its likely consequences are combined in a chart plotting the probable number of accidents per year against the probable number of deaths caused.[4] The likelihood of various manmade accidents and natural disasters is set against the records of 100 nuclear power plants. Comparing accidents in which ten or more people died, the figures show that earthquakes, dam breaches and aeroplane crashes of this gravity will occur once every ten years, whereas nuclear plant accidents occur only once every 10,000 years. Accidents of the former type, in which 1,000 or more people die, occur every 20 years, while the comparable figures for reactors are once in a million years. The obvious conclusion is that nuclear reactors are much safer than any other form of activity on the planet – the risks are about the same as the chances of being hit by a large meteorite. Even when the hazards of the entire fuel-cycle, from mining to production, are taken into account, nuclear power is nearly risk-free, whereas coal power kills an estimated 10,000 people a year. So what is the fuss about? Is it pure irrationality, as the nuclear industry would claim?

First, we need to ask what evidence we have that the figures are correct, and what they are based on. Few people make assessments based upon such a narrow set of values as the nuclear establishment's risk assessors.

The Likelihood of Accidents

Starting with the figures issued by the nuclear industry, when one looks at the accident-'cost'-versus-likelihood curves which the nuclear industry present in their defence, one sees that the worst accidents are always the least likely. It is in fact vital to the nuclear industry's case that the worst-case accident is *very* unlikely. For Sizewell, for example, the CEGB presents figures of 10^{-6} core melts per year (i.e. one core melt every million years) and a worst-case melt leading to a release of radioactivity from the reactor core of 7×10^{-8} per year, or once every 15 million years.[5]

Gittus and Dunbar of the CEGB compared the risks as follows: risk of accidental death – 3 x 10⁻⁴ per year; deaths due to 'degraded core' accidents – 2 x 10⁻⁹ per year (for individuals living near the plant). The argument is somewhat academic, because whilst on average three people in 10,000 die in accidents every year, amounting to about 15,000 for the UK, 2 x 10⁻⁹ deaths for a population of even 1,000 individuals 'near' the plant amounts to 10⁻⁶ deaths per year. It is of course impossible to kill less than one person, so this at least could mean one death every million years.

It is not highlighted, however, that the worst case considered by the CEGB (called 'category UK-1', when containment is 'bypassed' and up to 90 per cent of the radioactive xenon and krypton, 70 per cent of the iodine, and 50 per cent of the caesium and rubidium in the core would be released) could cause 1,000 to 6,000 'early deaths' once every 10,000 million years, or even 10,000 to 100,000 fatal cancers, in circumstances requiring the evacuation of three million people (but only once every million million years!). Obviously these individuals would come from places not 'near' the reactor.[6] One (unpublished) study has calculated that the results of this worst case would mean that milk would have to be thrown away as far off as Rome.[7]

But where do these truly geological periods of a million years here, another million million years there, on which the nuclear industry bases its case, come from? Risk experts Slovic and Fischoff criticise the NRC's multimillion-dollar study as follows: 'in assessing the probability of a core melt in a nuclear reactor, [the Reactor Safety Study] used the very procedure for setting confidence bounds that has been found in experiments to produce the highest degree of overconfidence.' With regard to dam engineering – much simpler than building a nuclear power station – they state: 'The Committee on Government Operation (US Government 1976) has attributed the collapse of the Teton Dam to the unwarranted confidence of the engineers who were absolutely certain they had solved the many serious problems that arose during construction.'[8]

Subsequent authoritative US studies of the nuclear accident risk figures (by the Union of Concerned Scientists, for example, in 1977) conclude that the risks have been drastically underestimated due to errors and omissions. They estimate that the correct figures could be 100 to 1,000 times greater, which makes the risks of nuclear accidents as high or higher than those of many other man-created accidents. The UK Health and Safety Executive, however, say that 'The comments in the report are not relevant to the situation in Britain and Europe more generally.'[9] They give no reasons for this dismissal.

But predicted nuclear reactor accident figures would differ from 'normal' accident figures in another very important respect, even assuming they were not totally incorrect in the first place. A characteristic of calculated or presented nuclear accident figures is that as the consequences of an accident increase, the probability falls off much faster than for 'normal' accidents. This faster fall-off of the death rate was in fact suggested as far back as 1967 as likely to provoke less public anxiety.[10] To achieve such a result, the reactors would have to be engineered in such a way that in worst-case accidents, additional safeguards would reduce the death figures more than for normal accidents. The Flowers Report recommended this approach, but many reactors were built and designed well before this time, and there is no hard evidence that reactors have been, or indeed could be, designed in this way.[11] Reactor designers can calculate, quite accurately, the chances of the more likely sorts of accidents, but with probabilities of the order of one in 10,000 the chances of drastic errors are high – simply because all the theoretical combinations of station conditions cannot be known.

This is the first problem for the experts, because in a highly complex system such as a nuclear reactor with, say, 400 separate components, maybe 40 can interact with each other. This creates over one million million combinations of possible failure conditions (out of these 40 components alone, ignoring the other 360). Whilst all the possible combinations could be examined by computer, the analysis will only be as good as the program – which in turn will depend upon the imagination of the programmer. Unfortunately, the history of accidents is often the history of the unimagined and the unpredicted. In a simple system of, say, 400 components one would expect no more than 1 per cent, or four components, to interact in a highly complex way, leaving only 11 possible combinations of failures (ignoring the remaining 396 components). For less likely types of accidents, the experts simply have to extrapolate – or to put it more crudely, guess. This is all they can do because they have no hard evidence upon which to base their figures.

Even at the level of calculating the chances of an individual tap or valve failure, experts may not be using correct figures. After Three Mile Island, Babcock and Wilcox expressed surprise at the number of cases in which the pressure release valve on the reactor core stuck open, although this was well known to the operators. There is clearly no way in which any expert can estimate how often a back-up battery will be unfilled due to human neglect or error, or how often a repair worker will hang a tag over a vital dial or drop a vital bulb inside a control console.

More seriously, severe building flaws have been discovered in nuclear reactors. In a recent study, it was found that the steel reinforcing cables in the reinforced concrete around the reactor cores were inadequately stressed, leading to reduced safety margins in eight UK reactors.[12]

In the US nuclear 'Diablo' reactor, which was constructed as an exact mirror-image of an earlier reactor, several of the control systems were connected up as if it were the other reactor. When new earthquake protection criteria required the strengthening of part of the structure, the wrong parts were strengthened while the parts that needed strengthening were left untouched – until a chance check by an engineer found that the wrong mirror-image set of plans had been used.

Various apparently trivial incidents show the excessive sensitivity of nuclear plants to the unexpected. In 1980 a worker in the North Anna No. 1 plant of the Virginia Electric and Power Company caught his shirt on a 3-inch handle on a circuit breaker. Pulling it free, he caused the reactor to shut down automatically, for four days.

In another plant, plumbing complexities meant that at one stage radioactive water was mistakenly fed to the drinking fountains![13]

In 1978, in the Rancho Secco 1 reactor in Clay Station, California, a worker dropped a control-panel light bulb whilst changing it. The bulb short-circuited some controls and the reactor shut itself down automatically. But the damage to the sensors meant that the operators could not know the temperature of the core, which dropped rapidly, threatening the core itself due to differential shrinking.

The journal *Nuclear Safety* catalogued these and many other, much more complex accidents with the intention of showing how safe the nuclear industry is. Yet similar accidents keep happening and for many of the same reasons. Operators are confronted with situations which rapidly go out of control and about which they do not have enough information to make a decision – if, that is, they are aware that anything is wrong at all.

Whilst the majority of accidents – 60 to 80 per cent – are eventually blamed on 'operator' error,[14] this is not the whole story. If the operator is confronted with totally unexpected combinations of events, no one can say what should have been done until after the event. Operators are overwhelmed by multiple equipment failures, false signals and bewildering interactions between systems.

Charles Perrow, one of the consultants to the Presidential Commission investigating Three Mile Island, wrote in 1984, before Chernobyl:

> We have not had more serious accidents of the scope of Three Mile Island simply because we have not given them enough time to appear. But the ingredients for such accidents are there, and unless we are very lucky, one or more will appear in the next decade and breach containment. Large nuclear plants of 1,000 MW have not been operating very long – only about 35 to 40 years of operating experience exists, and that constitutes 'industrial infancy' for complicated, poorly understood transformation systems ... For all nuclear plants, the steam generator and the core embrittlement problems are awesome. Small failures can interact and render inoperative the safety systems designed to prevent a steam generator failure from being catastrophic. Trivial events can place stress on the embrittled core in ways unimagined by designers.[15]

By 1983, the US Nuclear Regulatory Commision had drawn up a list of unresolved safety issues. These included:

- *Water hammer* – pipe vibration causing damage.
- *Pressurised thermal shock* – damage due to sudden cooling.
- *Decay heat removal* – systems to remove core heat after shutdown.
- *Containment emergency sump* – possible blockage in system following a loss of coolant, leading to lack of reactor cooling.
- *Earthquake-resistant design.*
- *Hydrogen-control measures.*
- *Bolting degradation or failure* – cracking or shearing of bolts.
- *Safety supplies* – possible failure of battery supplies.
- *Radiation protection plans.*
- *Containment integrity checks.*

Given all these problems, how can any expert accurately calculate the chances of an event? Clearly they cannot; nobody knows enough about these systems and how they might go wrong.

There is another neglected factor. If the worst-case accident is caused not by the expected chain of random unconnected events which the assessors assume, but by some linked chain of non-random events, one could get into a situation where the worst accident was not the least likely. An analogy is provided by an aircraft crossing the Alps without radar or air traffic control. It will either crash into the mountains or it won't. Whilst there are whole series of more likely but less serious accidents, resulting in the deaths of a few people, in this (admittedly extreme) case a quite likely accident is the death of everyone in a major crash. In nuclear power terms, the equivalent is the possibility that a plant might be, say, sabotaged or subjected to terrorist attack (there have already been cases of sabotage in the US, with the loss of control systems as a result). In this case the probability of the worst-case accident must rise. The risks of a warhead convoy or waste train being hijacked are also not included in the published figures. This was a major concern of the Flowers Report on nuclear power, that nuclear power would require excessive security measures at plants and in the transportation of weapons and waste.

The Deficiencies of Probabilistic Risk Assessment

Probabilistic risk assessment (PRA) is the name given to the kind of analysis used by the nuclear industry to assess the chance of various classes of serious accident, including the consequent effects. In the preceding section we saw how flawed such an analysis is likely to be in practice. Could the analysis be improved to the point where public confidence in the figures can be sustained?

There are two basic analytical tools used in PRA – 'event tree' and 'fault tree' analysis. An event tree traces the possible outcomes from a given initiating event. At each branch point in the tree the analyst asks the question: will this safety feature 'x' work? And then assigns a probability Px to the 'no' branch and 1-Px to the 'yes' branch following that branch point. This process is repeated through as many branches as are required until final outcomes are arrived at. Some of these will have no ill-effects (because a sufficient number of safety features have worked), some will have small effects, while others will have large effects. The probability of each outcome is obtained by multiplying the probabilities leading from the initiating event through the branches leading to the outcome. The analysis must take account of many different event trees – for many different initiating events. Then the serious outcomes can be grouped together and their probabilities added, to give an overall probability.

The other sort of analysis, known as fault tree analysis, works in the reverse direction: from outcomes back to likely causes.

The US Nuclear Regulatory Commission's WASH-1400 (Rasmussen) Report, which used these methods, arrived at a chance of 5 in 100,000 of a core meltdown in one reactor year. They then multiplied this number by three other factors to arrive at their risk for what they term the 'maximum credible accident'. These factors were, first, the probability (1 in 10) of a *substantial* release of radioactivity following breach of containment; secondly, the probability (1 in 10) of unfavourable weather (such as a wind blowing towards the nearest population centre); and thirdly, the probability (1 in 100) of a large exposed population at the aforementioned centre. This all leads, according to the WASH-1400 analysis, to a 5 in 1,000 million chance per reactor year of the 'maximum credible accident'.[16]

These figures, which are used as a model by the nuclear industry, can be criticised on many grounds.

First, the starting figure of 5 in 100,000 can be questioned. The basic event/fault tree analysis has serious limitations. There is no way of ensuring that every failure sequence has been allowed for or that the data base of component reliabilities is complete and up to date. The analysis fails to model human performance or common mode failures, and treats failures as discrete events, independent of time. WASH-1400 considered only two 'representative' plants, whereas in practice even reactors based on a single design, such as the AGRs, have evolved with each new commissioning, solving some problems but no doubt introducing others.

The 'common mode failure' problem is serious. If a reactor has three control rod systems, each with a one in 10,000 chance of failing per reactor year, and if all three must fail in order for an accident to occur, then, assuming they are completely independent, that means a chance of one in a million million per reactor year – an infinitesimally small probability. However, suppose these three control rod systems fail due to some common external cause, such as an earthquake, a terrorist bomb or even bad design in the power supply. Then the chance of all three failing is just the same as the chance of one failing: a dramatic increase in the probability. How should these numbers – the independent and dependent probabilities – be combined to arrive at a realistic assessment of risk? WASH-1400 simply puts a finger in the air and takes the geometric mean (the square root of the product) of these two extremes, without any justification. This heavily weights the answer in the direction that understates the common mode failure.

Considering the factors which collectively make up another factor of 1 in 10,000, one may well ask where the first figure of 1 in 10 for a 'serious breach' of containment comes from.

In addition, when considering the likely consequences, WASH-1400 uses an averaging technique which unquestionably underestimates the maximum risk. For instance, considering wind directions, the normally prevailing wind may happen to blow directly towards a population centre (take Hinkley Point and Bristol). The averaging technique in WASH-1400 does not take proper account of such a case.

What all these considerations amount to is that the WASH-1400 figures may have underestimated risks by factors of as much as 10,000 or more. Hence the criticism of these figures by other authorities.

How the Nuclear Industry Presents the Figures

Even given identical calculations as to the chances and consequences of a nuclear reactor accident, there are radically different ways of presenting the results for public consumption. In the aftermath of Chernobyl, Lord Marshall frequently used an analogy with smoking to illustrate the effects of low levels of radiation: the cancer risk for someone receiving a dose of one rem would be equivalent to that for another individual smoking one twentieth of a cigarette every Sunday for 30 years starting ten years later.

This analogy was used by Marshall *et al.*, in describing the effects of 'big' nuclear accidents, involving one rem exposure to 10 million people (viz. Sizewell and London).[17] It is worth noting that 100,000 people die every year in the UK from smoking-induced causes, yet expressed as a risk factor per cigarette, the figures appear misleadingly small. People smoke more heavily than Lord Marshall's hypothetical individual, and in our assessment, nuclear reactor accidents can produce higher doses to large populations than the nominal one rem. In any case, the one rem could only ever be an average figure concealing the much higher doses received by populations nearer the site of an accident. The use of averaged figures will almost always underestimate the consequences.

The use of individual risk factors, like those based on smoking or driving, ignores the fact that a nuclear accident is a risk to areas and populations, not merely to individuals. The chance that, say, 90 per cent of the people in Heysham might die in car accidents is infinitesimally small; but the chance that this number die as a result of an accident in one of the four neighbouring nuclear reactors, whilst still arguably small, is a realistic possibility.

Lastly, it should be reiterated that the basic radiation-induced cancer rates assumed by Lord Marshall were those based on ICRP figures which many, including the US National Academy of Sciences, believe to be too small by at least a factor of ten. The radiation risk figures were revised in 1987–8, acknowledging that radiation was in fact more dangerous than had previously been thought.

Public Perception of Risk

Some risk analysts acknowledge the existence of what they call 'bounded rationality' or 'social rationality'. This sort of rationality asks such questions as: 'If such a catastrophic accident is possible, why take the risk?'

The simple economic, probabilistic analysis does not take account of such factors as dread, fear of the worst case, fear of being trapped in threatening circumstances beyond one's control, delayed effects, unfamiliar effects, and uncontrollable events. All these factors have been identified as highly important by some researchers. In surveys, nuclear power, along with nuclear warfare, terrorism, crime and military activities in general, came very high on people's 'most dreaded' lists. This public reaction, which cuts right across political boundaries, has been shown most starkly in the fiercely hostile local reactions to proposed nuclear waste dumping.

Nuclear power scores so highly because the effects would be largely unknown or 'invisible' – radiation cannot be sensed; its consequences take time to appear and then are not easily identified; also, some risk is transmitted to future generations. The average person can take no precautions or avoid the danger (nuclear plants are everywhere); there are no obvious benefits (in the US and the UK, nuclear energy provides, respectively, only about 9.4 and 11 per cent of electricity requirements). For many, nuclear power has significant deficits in the shape of creating waste or nuclear weapons. The nuclear industry does not and cannot measure or allow for these factors, or for the likely cost of any alternative energy systems. The CEGB as a whole is hostile to alternative forms of energy, as has been shown by their assessment of wave and tide power as having no future, an assessment published on the very day that the Norwegians decided to pump a large sum of money into just such a project (partly inspired, it so chanced, by British research).

The CEGB's own costing systems involve some highly 'creative' accounting. Much of the research costs are offset by government, while in construction costings the expected energy benefit to be enjoyed in the future is allowed against the cost.

In sum, there is much common sense in the public's conception of risk. If the consequences of an accident are catastrophic, even if the chances of the accident are remote, why take the risk at all? Another point concerns the very small probabilities claimed by the nuclear industry for various disasters. A chance of one 'event' every 1,000 years is meaningless to most people. As we have seen, the figures are anyway highly questionable.

But even if they were correct, what would they mean? In any one year, the probability cannot tell you whether or not an accident will happen; either it happens or it doesn't. If it does, it is disastrous; if it doesn't, one does not worry any the less about the future. The possibility of a nuclear accident is not like the dangers of air travel or crossing the road. Everyone has some control and choice over such activities, which is patently not so in the case of nuclear power. Numerical risk analysis also rarely takes such factors as prolonged worry into account. The analyses by the GEGB certainly do not. These are all good reasons why the public's analysis differs from the CEGB's. The fundamental point at issue is whose perception of risk counts: the public's or the nuclear industry's experts? Certainly if the public perception of risk were given credence by government, nuclear power would be finished tomorrow.

The Consequences

The consequences of a reactor accident which most readily come to mind are the medical ones resulting from exposure to radiation. It is no easy calculation to translate the 'activity' of the radioactive emissions – the clicks on a Geiger counter – into doses absorbed in human tissue. This is because the 'received dose' is produced by both external sources of radiation as well as internal – i.e. incorporated – ones, where the latter will depend on the radionuclides' biological access to the body, whether by eating or breathing, or via open wounds.

The Effects of Exposure to High Levels of Radiation
Of the shorter-term effects from a nuclear weapon, acute whole-body doses received from radioactive fallout would be the most widespread, extending up to hundreds of miles downwind of the explosion. In a very serious nuclear reactor accident, such consequences would be unlikely to extend beyond 15 miles.

The medical consequences of acute exposure to radiation are complex, but fall into three broad categories, depending on the degree of exposure.

'Bone-marrow' radiation sickness results from a dose of between about 150 and 450 rads. There is a short period of lethargy, nausea and other more minor symptoms, followed by a symptom-free period of about ten days. Towards the end of the second week, a minimum is reached in the number of white blood cells, blood-clotting platelets and other blood constituents, resulting in both an increased susceptibility to infection and the development of spontaneous haemorrhages (seen as bleeding gums and facial spots on the victims of Hiroshima and Nagasaki). These effects may be fatal (depending on the age and general health of the victim, and also on other injuries that may have been sustained – like burns and blast injuries), or the victim may gradually recover from this 'acute radiation sickness'. However, blood disorders can continue for months if not years afterwards; later, as the Japanese experience has shown, cancers may develop, affecting also those who received sub-lethal doses (less than 150 rads).

'Gastro-intestinal' radiation sickness occurs at higher doses, damaging the cells lining the small intestine. This results in massive haemorrhaging and loss of body fluids, after which, if the victim survives, there follow the symptoms of the bone-marrow form, but sooner and with a low chance of survival. At even higher doses (in excess of 10,000 rads) the central nervous system is affected, leading to convulsions, coma and death within hours.

Until very recently, the widely accepted LD50 dose (the dose which, over a short period, would kill half of those exposed) was 450 rads (surface tissue dose). However, this figure is partly based on Hiroshima and Nagasaki data which have been re-evaluated. The WHO is now using an LD50 of 180 rads in calculating the effects of nuclear war.

Risks from Low Levels of Radiation

It used to be thought that there was some low threshold dose below which there would be no ill effects, however large the exposed population, but it is now generally accepted that there is no 'safe' dose. Of course, the risk increases with the dose, but the risk of an individual getting cancer as a result of exposure to radiation increases cumulatively. Thus, although a dose equivalent to a year's background dose (about 0.1 rad) may not be very much, it must be counted in addition to the background, and many such small additional doses can result in significantly increased risks, particularly for those who work in the nuclear industry or are repeatedly exposed to radiation from manmade sources (the most significant of which, for most people, is the medical X-ray).

Adding all the various risk factors together, it is estimated by the International Commission on Radiological Protection (ICRP) that if a population of 1 million were exposed to a dose of 1 rad (roughly ten times the average annual backround dose), then about 100 of these are likely to develop cancers *as a result of that radiation* over the next 10 to 50 years. Dr Rosalie Bertell, who has researched this area in depth, has presented findings which challenge this prediction. She estimates that a more correct figure would be in the range of 369–823 cancers, 11 to 30 years after exposure, and 549–1,648 within the lifetime of the exposed people.

These are still very low risks compared to the other risks we face.

Indeed, in Britain there is, on average, a one in five chance of an individual developing cancer at some stage in life. However, this comparison, although valid, is rather misleading. The risk of getting cancer increases with age, because cancer is principally a disease of old age. Obviously, there are environmentally linked cancers, the most striking of which is lung cancer (only 2.3 per cent of those who get lung cancer have not smoked). It is flippant to say that everyone has a 100 per cent chance of dying, but to some extent, the 20 per cent of us who die of cancer do so precisely because the 'ageing process' has taken its toll. Premature deaths that could be avoided – such as those due to smoking – are quite another matter.

It is clear that none of us want the risks of a premature death increased by some preventable cause, and in the case of low-level radiation, where there is controversy as to its long-term effects, this uncertainty is bound to cause anxiety. It could be argued that in Britain the psychological consequences of the Chernobyl accident, in terms of anxiety and stress, far outweighed the radiobiological hazard. However, it would be both arrogant and insensitive to suggest, as the nuclear industry has done, that this fear was based on 'over-reaction' and 'ignorance', when it is clear that the 'experts' are themselves ignorant in many important respects. The recently completed review of the Hiroshima and Nagasaki bombings and the late deaths due to cancer provides belated support for Bertell's higher estimates, suggesting that the ICRP figures underestimated risks by a factor of 15.[18] Estimates of genetic damage are also almost certain to be revised. If cancer risk factors can change overnight by a factor of 15, then people may legitimately wonder whether they will change again after further painstaking research. In the face of the fragile consensus that appears to exist in this area, it may be prudent, if not entirely rational, for people to assume the worst when contemplating the nuclear facilities on their own doorsteps.

Environmental, Economic and Social Consequences

An atom of caesium-137 differs from caesium-133, the common isotope, only because of its radioactive nucleus. Chemically they are identical. So when radioactive fission products are released into the environment they carry on as normal, so to speak, until, having been incorporated into the leaf of a plant or the flesh of an animal, they undergo radioactive decay, thereby causing damage to the delicate biochemical structures into which they are integrated. Caesium, like every element, has its special chemistry, and the actual 'mix' of radionuclides emitted from a reactor accident can vary greatly according to the reactor design and the seriousness of the accident. It is therefore difficult to generalise about which food chains are most critical. It was discovered that the global fallout from atmospheric weapon tests prior to 1963 had led to higher levels of caesium-137 in individual Laplanders and Inuit (Eskimos) than in other populations because these people depended on reindeer (or caribou) meat and these animals fed on lichen which was very efficient at retaining certain radionuclides, including caesium-137. The effective biological 'half-life' – that is, the time it takes for a radioactive isotope in the food chain to decay by half – depends on numerous complex factors.

In the case of reindeer and lichen, concentrated doses result from the fact that the lichen draws its moisture directly from the air, and the soil is therefore unable to act as a filter. Another factor is that the caesium is incorporated into the growing shoots which are eaten first by the reindeer. The reindeer then excrete some of the radioactive isotope back to be reabsorbed by the lichen. Similar but much more limited problems have confronted some British hill farmers whose sheep have been judged unfit for consumption. Initially, radioactivity levels in sheep carcasses fell off fairly rapidly, but as soon as the sheep began eating the new shoots, the levels rose again.

The economic costs of clearing up after a reactor accident are potentially huge. The US AEC Report WASH-740 of 1957 considered a 'maximum credible accident' involving a 200 MW plant 30 miles from a city. Some 3,400 deaths and 45,000 injuries were predicted, with clear-up costs amounting to 7,000 million US dollars, at 1956 prices. The likelihood of such an accident occurring was calculated at between one in 100,000 and one in 1,000 million per year per reactor. Even these miniscule probabilities are uninviting to insurance companies when set beside such staggering costs, and indeed they were only prepared to offer cover up to $60 million, with the Federal Government offering a further $500 million. This still left a shortfall of $6,440 million of uninsurable risk. The situation is essentially the same today: nuclear power is an uninsurable risk.[19]

Following Chernobyl, the economic consequences were felt most keenly by isolated communities dependent on crop farming or animal husbandry, particularly by the Laplanders in northern Norway and Sweden. We can only speculate over the final costs to agriculture in the Ukraine, often referred to as the bread basket of the USSR, but they will be immense and their consequences will be felt for many years to come.

The social costs incurred by a serious accident are even harder to quantify but no less real. Displaced populations may have to be monitored for years, and live with an inexact probability of eventually contracting cancer as a result of the radiation received. People cannot easily attach a meaning to these probabilities, and the result will be widespread anxiety. Numerous communities which previously existed in the Chernobyl region and which are now dispersed may never be able to return to their previous lifestyles. This is a social cost equivalent to displacement by war or invasion. The Lapp culture, dependent as it is upon the reindeer, may not survive the effects of being unable to sell reindeer meat for what may be many years. As we contemplate consequences such as these, it is well to consider the costs which have already been exacted, for example, in the injured health of uranium miners in Namibia and Mexico working in terrible conditions; the probably irreversible damage done to our environment by nuclear accidents and plants such as Sellafield; and the fact that nuclear power, instead of providing 'atoms for peace' has, for so many countries, been seen as the route to greater strategic power through the covert acquisition of nuclear weapons.

We were told that nuclear power would be cheaper than power from other sources, but in the run-up to a potential privatisation of electricity generation in Britain, the government has said it will require privatised utilities to generate 25 per cent of their electricity using nuclear plant. This compulsory 25 per cent arises because otherwise no private company would accept the risks involved in nuclear power. They could get no insurance underwriter to cover the full cost. Now, finally, the chairman of the Central Electricity Generating Board, Lord Marshall, has admitted that nuclear power has never been cheaper than other forms of generation.[20]

Government knows the true costs, including interest repayments on capital for construction and the future burden of decommissioning nuclear power stations: no businessman would willingly pursue this option. The original US nuclear business only got going when reactors were virtually given away, and now, after Three Mile Island, nuclear business in the US has ground to a halt.

The costs of nuclear power are therefore already with us, but they would be as nothing beside the consequences of a serious accident, such as Chernobyl, with the wind blowing *towards* a nearby city.

Civil–Military Links: Siamese Twins

The original impetus behind the first atomic installations was the production of weapons-grade material to make nuclear weapons. The production of nuclear weapons depends upon facilities to process and enrich uranium and plutonium; without these facilities there could be no nuclear weapons. The energy generated was a by-product which enabled the first power station in the UK, Calder Hall at Windscale, to be presented to the public with the slogan 'Atoms for Peace' in the early 1950s.

In the UK, the CEGB formally separated the weapons production and civil energy production programmes, but the programmes are still inextricably intertwined by Sellafield, which takes in radioactive materials and processes them to enrich the quality of the uranium or plutonium for use in reactors or in weapons. Once material enters it is not separately labelled 'civil' or 'military'. There is only one processing line into which all material goes; it is only the degree of enrichment that indicates in which category the material is classified. Thus 'civil' material may enter and come out as 'military'. The civil books could, however, be balanced by the retrieval of an equivalent weight of suitable civil-grade material, possibly originating from a nuclear warhead.

The spread of nuclear power stations around the world is opening a door through which countries without nuclear weapons may obtain high-grade nuclear material with which to build them. A country may desire nuclear power stations not for electricity generation but to obtain weapons-grade material. To obtain it, however, a plant's operating cycle must be changed from the most energy-efficient one, in order to obtain the best plutonium. As more and more countries acquire nuclear power stations and, more importantly, reprocessing plants, the amounts of nuclear material in the world are increasing along with the number of potential sources of supply. According to French arms dealers, there has been a thriving nuclear black market operating from, amongst other places, the Sudan, with Israel, South Africa, Iran and Iraq all known to be in the market for materials. The Israelis performed a pre-emptive strike on Iraq's Osirak nuclear reactor, believing it to be preparing for nuclear weapons material production. Thus one must assume that the Iraqis (and presumably the Iranians) are now seeking weapons-grade material by easier means than by operating a nuclear reactor.

Of particular concern is the failure of international agencies – such as Euratom, the European Community's nuclear safeguards commission – successfully to monitor and control the spread of nuclear materials. Whitehall refuses to allow the European Commission to release documents regarding safeguards at the Sellafield reprocessing plant to the European Parliamentary Committee of Energy investigation. In 1979, an official of Euratom admitted that it had 'agreed to cover up the loss' of 560 barrels of uranium from the ship *Scheerburg*.[21] Some 200 tons from this shipment was diverted to Israel for its secret bomb-making programme. The UKAEA has itself exported at least 200 kg of plutonium to Nukem in West Germany, one of the companies under investigation for illegal plutonium disposal and sales to Libya and Pakistan.

Several kilogrammes of enriched nuclear material are known to have been exchanged for millions of dollars on the black market. Israel and South Africa have collaborated for many years on the production of battlefield nuclear weapons. Mordechai Vanunu, a former nuclear technician who publicly confirmed some of this information, was recently sentenced to 18 years' imprisonment after secret trial in Israel, following his illegal abduction from Rome airport. South Africa has the uranium, Israel has the technology. In January 1988, astonishing evidence emerged that a West German company had allegedly been exporting enriched nuclear material suitable for bomb-making to Libya, Pakistan and the Soviet Union. Some £7 million in bribes had been paid out, and two people committed suicide during the official investigation.

As long as nuclear technology spreads and the existing nuclear powers show no signs of significantly reducing their nuclear arsenals, the number of countries seeking and obtaining weapons-grade material seems likely to increase. This is one further significant danger connected with nuclear power, as more and more reactors are profitably exported to Third World countries.

Direct export of weapons-grade nuclear material is banned under the provision of the 1968 nuclear Non-Proliferation Treaty (NPT). This treaty is highly important: not only was it intended to limit the spread of nuclear weapons, but it also contains the only commitment by the superpowers and Britain to general nuclear disarmament, a commitment which, with the exception of the 1987 INF treaty, has so far has been flagrantly dishonoured. Until the nuclear powers begin to honour their obligations in this respect, the NPT will be seen as a hypocritical agreement by the original nuclear 'club' to exclude other countries. The example set by the nuclear powers is also that possession of nuclear weapons equals world influence and power, and this further encourages the proliferation of nuclear energy and the acquisition of nuclear weapons.

SANA (Scientists Against Nuclear Arms) has evidence that the UK has, in direct contravention of the spirit of the NPT and possibly of its letter, exported 200–300 kg of highly enriched plutonium to the US, suitable for making some 40 nuclear warheads.

The Global Spread of Nuclear Power

Nuclear power is now seeing its largest growth in the developing and Comecon countries, while it appears to be on the decline in the US and to some extent in Western Europe. Poland, China, Romania and Cuba are building their first reactors. India and South Korea have notably ambitious programmes.

Among existing producers, France, Belgium and Taiwan have the largest programmes as a share of their total electricity output, while Japan and the German Democratic Republic have sizeable expansion programmes.

During 1985 the total installed nuclear power capacity in the world increased by 14 per cent, with 32 new units. At the end of 1986 there were 394 reactors on stream, with a further 137 under construction. During 1987, 21 reactors came on stream and total world capacity increased by some 9 per cent. By the end of the year, 416 reactors were connected to electricity grids world-wide, and nuclear power generation accounted for 16 per cent of world electricity output. Nuclear power plants now produce as much energy as the global electricity output in 1954.[22]

Conclusions

The risk analyses presented by the nuclear industry underestimate the risks of nuclear accidents. Even using the criteria of the nuclear industry, nuclear power may in fact be *more* risky than many other large-scale industrial activities.

Accidents have happened and will continue to happen. In systems as complex as nuclear power stations, designers are caught between two fundamentally conflicting requirements: first, to design an inflexible system in which the operators go by the rules, and thus *cause* no failures themselves; and then, to make provision for operator flexibility to allow for the unexpected and permit the operators to take remedial action when faced with the unexpected.

Both Chernobyl and Three Mile Island showed the vulnerability of complex systems to profound misunderstanding by operators (who are supposed to understand them best) under pressure or as a result of unusual conditions (such as an experiment). The worst dangers seem to arise from operators having too much faith in the safety of their plant – perhaps as at Chernobyl; which is often compounded by mechanical failures – as at Three Mile Island. It is difficult to see how this 'human factor' can be designed out, without introducing new risks from computer control systems.

Thus there is not much that can be done to decrease the likelihood of future nuclear accidents. Along with nuclear weapon systems, nuclear reactors will continue to pose the risk of a much graver potential catastrophe than other forms of power generation or other industrial activities. As reactors proliferate world-wide, the possibility of a nuclear accident is multiplied, particularly in countries which are unable to finance the expensive maintenance of sophisticated nuclear plants. Sometimes, exported nuclear plants are of a type which could not obtain a licence in the exporting country (the US, for instance). This – the most cynical opportunism – is exporting potential nuclear disaster for profit.

The world is threatened by over 50,000 nuclear weapons, each of which could create death and destruction far in excess of even the most serious nuclear meltdown. Accidents will happen unless we take measures to reduce and eventually eradicate the risks. Chernobyl is 'here and now', but so are the nuclear weapons and the potential flashpoints – such as the US attack on Libya in 1986, or the Lebanon – which might catalyse their use. This should be remembered when considering the serious risks already posed by nuclear reactors.

Nuclear power and nuclear weapons are inextricably linked. Nuclear weapons rely for their continued existence and development upon nuclear reprocessing facilities, such as at Sellafield. Reprocessing of spent fuel is not needed for nuclear power generation; projections show that suitable uranium fuel will be readily and economically available for over 100 years to come. The true motive for reprocessing is to ensure a supply of highly-enriched plutonium for nuclear warheads. As a by-product of this activity, Sellafield not only pours out thousands of times more radioactivity than *any other* nuclear plant, but also increases another huge risk – that of nuclear war.

All activities incur some risk. In the normal course of events, people balance the benefits of an action against the risk. We all do this when we cross the road, drive a car or fly in an aeroplane. But nuclear power generation is not comparable to these everyday activities.

First, the public is excluded from the ability to choose whether or not to have its electricity generated by nuclear means. People are naturally suspicious of choices made in their 'best interests' by experts. Secondly, the only benefit to the public from nuclear power, namely electricity, can be produced more cheaply by other means such as coal-fired stations. Even electricity imported from Iceland, generated by volcanically-heated water, would be cheaper. Thirdly, the worst accident possible would make any air crash pale into relative insignificance. Such accidents could also occur as a consequence of terrorism or non-nuclear war. Fourthly, no one knows how to decommission a nuclear power station when its operating life is finished, but certainly it would be a complex, dangerous and costly process. Fifthly, once created, many of the radioactive elements in waste decay only very slowly, some taking centuries. They cannot be destroyed. Over the years, Windscale – now the Sellafield reprocessing plant – has dumped more low-grade radioactivity into the Irish Sea than was released by Chernobyl.

The nuclear industry classifies radioactive waste into three grades: high, intermediate and low. 'High' means used fuel elements; 'intermediate' refers to the reactor core and components; and 'low' means ancillary material (clothing, etc.). There have long been plans to cope with high-grade waste by solidifying it into glassy blocks, through the process of 'vitrification'. These would then be buried deep underground. For this to be safe, both the glass and the locality must be stable for thousands of years. Transport of the highly radioactive used-fuel elements to the vitrification facility itself poses another and more immediate risk of leakage, by accident or conceivably by terrorist activity. Intermediate-grade waste will apparently be buried in concrete coffins in shallow graves. The sites will need to be secure for up to 100 years. Low-grade solid waste is buried in clay trenches; liquid and gaseous waste is diluted and discharged straight into the environment. A very basic problem for the nuclear industry and the environment in the future is that nobody can be quite sure that these radionuclides can be safely disposed of. This problem is particularly acute with high- and intermediate-grade waste.

There is also the danger created by the possibility of illegal dumping of high-grade wastage labelled as low-grade – as has already happened in the Nukem affair. Problems of decommissioning and waste disposal are likely to be thorns in the flesh of the nuclear establishment for the foreseeable future, imposing a substantial economic and logistical burden as well as potential hazards for generations to come.

To put this in its true historical perspective: if the Romans had had nuclear power, we would still be guarding their waste sites and reactors today – assuming of course that they had not wiped out the possibility of future generations with the nuclear weapons that they would also have possessed. Some of the plans for disposal of nuclear waste today postulate the building of massive pyramids or stone circles to mark the dangerous remains for milleniums to come. Surely it would be the depth of irresponsibility to hand on such a burden to succeeding generations.

Notes

1. F. Dyson, *Disturbing the Universe*, Harper & Row, 1979.
2. 'Chernobyl, USA?', in *Scientific American*, July 1986.
3. W.D. Rowe, *An Anatomy of Risk*, Wiley, 1977.
4. Nuclear Regulatory Commission, *Reactor Safety Study – An Assessment of Accident Risks in US Commercial Power Plant*, WASH 1400, NUREG 75-014, NRC, Washington DC, 1975.
5. J.H. Gittus and I.H. Dunbar, Workshop on methods for assessing the off-site radiological consequences of nuclear accidents, 15–19 April 1985, Report EUR 10397, Luxembourg. See also CEGB proof of evidence, P16 and Addenda, Sizewell Public Inquiry.
6. Gittus and Dunbar, ibid.
7. P. Stott, Imperial College of Science and Technology, London; private communication with the authors, 1986.
8. P. Slovic, B. Fischoff and S. Lichtenstein, 'Perceived risk: psychological factors and implications', in *Proceedings of the Royal Society*, A 376, London, 1981.
9. UK Health and Safety Executive, 1981.
10. F.R. Farmer, 'Siting criteria – a new approach', in *Containment and Siting of Nuclear Power Plants*, IAEA, Vienna, 1967.
11. Royal Commission on Environmental Pollution: Sixth Report, *Nuclear Power and the Environment*, Cmnd. 6618, HMSO, London, 1976. Commonly known as the 'Flowers Report' after the Commission's Chairman, Sir Brian (now Lord) Flowers.
12. *Guardian*, 9 August 1986.
13. C. Perrow, *Normal Accidents*, Basic Books, New York, 1984.
14. Perrow, ibid.
15. Perrow, ibid.
16. Nuclear Regulatory Commission, *Reactor Safety Study*.
17. W. Marshall et al, 'Big nuclear accidents', *AERE Report* 10532, HMSO, London, 1983.

18. J. Rotblat, 'A tale of two cities', in the *New Scientist*, 7 January 1988.
19. US Atomic Energy Commission, *Theoretical Possibilities and Consequences of Major Accidents in Large Nuclear Power Plant*, WASH 740, AEC, Washington DC, 1957.
20. Lord Marshall on *Brass Tacks*, BBC 2 Television, 16 October 1987.
21. David Lowry in the *Guardian*, 23 February 1988.
22. *Nuclear Power: Status and Trends*, 1986 edition, IAEA, Vienna; UK Atomic Energy Authority.

Further Reading

H. M. ApSimon and J. J. N. Wilson, 'Tracking the cloud from Chernobyl', in *New Scientist*, 17 July 1986.

Hilary Bacon and John Valentine, *Power Corrupts – The Arguments Against Nuclear Power*, Pluto Press, London, 1981.

Rosalie Bertell, *No Immediate Danger*, Women's Press, London, 1985.

S. A. Fetter and K. Tsipis, 'Catastrophic releases of radioactivity', in *Scientific American*, April 1981.

Margaret Gowing, *Britain and Atomic Energy, 1939-45*, Macmillan, London, 1964.

Margaret Gowing, *Independence and Deterrence* (2 vols), Macmillan, London, 1974.

Tony Hall, *Nuclear Politics – The History of Nuclear Power in Britain*, Pelican Books, Harmondsworth, 1986.

S. M. Keeny, *Nuclear Power Issues and Choices*, Report of the Nuclear Energy Policy Study Group under the auspices of the (Ford) Mitre Foundation, Ballinger, USA, 1977.

G. H. Kinchin, 'Risk Assessment', in W. Marshall (ed.), *Nuclear Power Technology*, vol. 3, Clarendon Press, Oxford, 1983.

R. Klueh, 'Future nuclear reactors – safety first?', in *New Scientist*, April 1986.

H. W. Lewis, 'Probabilistic risk assessment merits and limitations', in *Proceedings of the Fifth International Meeting on Thermal Nuclear Reactor Safety*, vol. 1, Karlsrühe Nuclear Reactor Centre, Rinisland, December 1984.

S. Openshaw, P. Steadman and O. Greene, *Doomsday: Britain after Nuclear Attack*, Basil Blackwell, Oxford, 1983.

S. Openshaw, *Nuclear Power – Siting and Safety*, RKP, London, 1986.

Walter C. Patterson, *Nuclear Power*, second edition, Pelican Books, Harmondsworth, London, 1983.

Walter C. Patterson, *Going Critical*, Paladin Books, London, 1985.

R. J. Pentreath, *Nuclear Power, Man and the Environment*, Taylor & Francis, London, 1980.

3

Secrecy, Policy-making and the Nuclear State

MARTIN INCE

The Chernobyl disaster of 1986 marks a distinct break in the history of nuclear power, not merely in the Soviet Union but throughout the world. But it does not and will not mean the end of nuclear power, which will continue to be considered in many developed and Third World countries as an option for generating electricity. In this chapter, I shall consider just why nuclear power is certain to survive Chernobyl. Most of my argument relates to Britain, but I shall also draw contrasts with other countries and so try to illuminate just what scope Chernobyl and the nuclear industry's other problems offer for people who regard nuclear power as a bad idea.

To do this properly it is necessary to describe the different interest groups which support nuclear power and explain just what they think is in it for them. The most basic pro-nuclear position is the view held by electricity supply utilities in many countries of the world, at one time or another, that a nuclear reactor is simply 'a cheaper way to boil water', as David Freeman put it when he was managing director of the Tennessee Valley Authority, the biggest power utility in the United States. In this view, nuclear power is a technical option, to be preferred over the use of coal or oil (alternative fuels which can be used to 'boil water' and so produce electricity in power station turbine generators) when it looks more reliable, less expensive or in some other way superior. We shall come back to this school of thought soon. Suffice it for the moment to say that pure market forces have never been the sole justification for nuclear power in any country.

More important is the power of the state. No country has ever implemented a nuclear power programme against the wishes of the national state. Instead, most national bureaucracies – especially energy and finance or economics ministries – contain a sizeable lobby in favour of nuclear power, generally consisting of people who regard it as economically desirable, people to whom it embodies an idea about 'progress' and 'the future', and of course people who have been cultivated by the nuclear industry at every level from outright bribery (not that there is any evidence of this in the UK) to good lunches. In addition, nuclear power is supported by extensive industrial power in all the countries in which it exists. Power station builders hope that it will bring them big business. On the world stage, major manufacturing firms like Westinghouse and General Electric of the US, Mitsubishi, Toshiba and Fujitsu of Japan, Siemens of West Germany, CGE of France and GEC of the UK are all beneficiaries of nuclear construction contracts. Over the last decade – since before the Three Mile Island accident – the commercial prospects for nuclear power have been drastically reduced, but few firms have left the field altogether, so there is an increased hunger for nuclear orders.

In addition, most countries have their own specialist nuclear companies and agencies which interlock with the public and private sectors. Britain, for example, has the UK Atomic Energy Authority (UKAEA), a state agency under the political wing of the Department of Energy. It also has the National Nuclear Corporation (NNC), a limited company set up to build nuclear power stations and owned by the state (via the UKAEA) and the engineering firms involved in nuclear projects, notably GEC. And it has British Nuclear Fuels Ltd (BNFL), a firm which is owned by the government, again via the Department of Energy, and which makes and reprocesses nuclear fuel for British and overseas customers. BNFL is a massive employer and a major source of big contracts for engineering firms, because of its large capital spending. It is especially important in the north-west of England, where its factories are concentrated, and especially in west Cumbria, where its Sellafield reprocessing works dominates the economy. This employment is a recurring theme in the support for nuclear power, partly because many nuclear activities are best carried out in areas away from major cities and population centres. Nuclear projects whose overall economic worth is questionable can become all-important to local economies, as with Sellafield or the UKAEA's fast reactor centre at Dounreay, in northern Scotland, while the project's vastly more numerous opponents are spread too thinly to be effective.

Nuclear power is also supported by groups which hope it will bring them some more general economic advantage. In the UK, nuclear power is supported by the Confederation of British Industry (CBI), in the hope that it will provide cheap power and therefore help British firms become more competitive internationally by reducing their costs. This particularly applies to electricity-intensive industries like papermaking or aluminium refining. There is also a strong trade union lobby in favour of nuclear power. In the UK this is dominated by the Electrical Power Engineers' Association, the Manufacturing, Science and Finance Union (formed in 1988 by the merger of two white-collar unions, TASS and ASTMS), and the Amalgamated Engineering Union. These unions' members work in, or build, power stations.

Nor should one neglect the role of political parties and their policies on nuclear power. Most right-wing parties in Europe support nuclear power on economic grounds; most left-wing ones are ambivalent, since they contain factions sceptical about nuclear power for economic and environmental reasons alongside others which support it for employment reasons. Green parties, where these exist, naturally oppose it root and branch.

Lastly, one sector of the national state with its own particular enthusiasm for nuclear power deserves a special mention – the military. The existing nuclear power systems now regarded by their supporters as 'commercial' were all developed for military uses. The British Magnox system, the Canadian CANDU system and the Soviet RBMK reactor – as at Chernobyl – were all designed to produce plutonium for bombs. The pressurised water and boiling water reactors were developed in the US for submarine propulsion. A constant supply of bomb material is one reason for nuclear weapons states' continuing investment in nuclear power, and the countries which are now acquiring nuclear weapons in the Third World, or are close to doing so, all use 'peaceful' nuclear projects as a cover for this activity. This link, which is about as transparent as it could be, is, of course, hotly denied by all involved.

Nuclear Power in Britain: Influences and Decisions

This list of nuclear power supporters is not comprehensive. There are academics, newspaper-editors, and ordinary voters who support nuclear power for a variety of reasons, ranging from the conviction that the world needs nuclear power to avoid running out of resources, to the general impression that it is desirable to have an alternative to coal as a country's main means of generating electricity. But the real story of British nuclear power is one in which the big interest groups cited above have been able to assure a high level of investment in nuclear power stations and related projects. The nuclear lobby – the sum of all the parts mentioned above – has not got all it wanted. But its defeats have been few, considering that they have been operating in what is allegedly a pluralist society which survives by balancing influences against each other. And the defeats which nuclear power has suffered have been due more to external forces – like slow growth in electricity demand during the 1970s and 1980s – than to successful political opposition to nuclear power.

Nuclear power in Britain was at its most unfettered between the Second World War and the mid-1970s. This is not the place for a complete history of British nuclear power, but the contrast between that era and this is important in showing just what political support nuclear power has in Britain, and how the world has changed for the supporters.

The United Kingdom ended the Second World War as a victorious power whose victory was due in part to the use of nuclear weapons against Japan. This circumstance left nuclear weapons politically well-placed in British public life and led to the UK beginning its own nuclear weapons development after the war, when the US put an end to tripartite cooperation on nuclear weapons with the UK and Canada. This decision to develop nuclear weapons was never debated in Parliament and was referred to only scantily in public announcements. The shape of the present British nuclear industry depends crucially upon decisions taken in the 1940s and 1950s. It was then that the Magnox reactors were developed, first in the form of 'piles' to produce plutonium for bombs and later as power stations used by the Central Electricity Generating Board (CEGB – for England and Wales) and the South of Scotland Electricity Board (SSEB). Later development of the Magnox reactor was to produce an enhanced and more efficient version, the advanced gas-cooled reactor (AGR).

During this period, nuclear developments were rarely controversial – planning inquiries into nuclear stations took mere days and were always successful for the industry. Even obvious losers from nuclear power, like the coal industry, had enough faith in the wonders of compound economic growth not to fear that nuclear power would harm them economically. And a sizeable industry grew up to supply nuclear stations, even hoping (with little success) to win export orders for them. The easy assumption that nuclear power was economically justifiable was never tested in detail; in recent years even the CEGB has admitted that Magnox power costs more than electricity from coal. In addition, the nuclear industry worried far less than it does now about the possible health effects of nuclear power, about the nuclear waste being piled up at Sellafield and elsewhere, and about the long-term future and disposal of the nuclear reactors and other plant being built without serious opposition around the country.

More serious for the long-term future of nuclear power in Britain than any of these issues was the vexed issue of 'reactor choice', the jargon phrase for a generation of key problems in British energy policy. The UKAEA had developed Magnox and the AGR, and the existence of these reactor systems in the British power system meant that they had their own supporters within pro-nuclear interest groups. But in the outside world, ordering of the US-developed pressurised water reactor (PWR) was proceeding apace, and its developer, the US electrical giant, Westinghouse, was selling it aggressively into developed and Third World nations alike. The Westinghouse PWR even crossed the Cold War divide to reappear in a close copy in the USSR, known in the industry as the 'Eastinghouse' machine.

The reactor choice debate was a political battle between the supporters of the AGR, the PWR, and two other machines – Canada's CANDU and the UKAEA's steam-generating heavy water reactor, neither of which had enough of a constituency to make much of a showing. The Westinghouse tactic was first to convince key people in the UKAEA that the PWR was to be preferred to their own AGR – a prime target being Lord

Marshall, now Chairman of the CEGB. Westinghouse also persuaded the country's biggest manufacturing firm, GEC, to take out a licence to build PWRs in Britain, although the licence has now been allocated to NNC and the reduced commercial prospects for the PWR in world power station markets has persuaded GEC to reduce its commitment to NNC. The CEGB itself was persuaded by the promise of lower power costs from the PWR, and after many years finally launched a bid to be allowed to build one at a place called Sizewell in Suffolk.

The epic Sizewell inquiry took years to graze across vast prairies of knowledge. It took in energy and economic policy, including the arcana of fossil fuel price predictions and exchange rates. It covered ecology and metallurgy, and it delved into cost predictions ranging beyond the twenty-first century into the twenty-second. But in the end, it was a trial of strength between several opposing armies. For the PWR: the CEGB, the NNC, BNFL, and – at one remove – the Department of Energy and the UKAEA. Against: environmental and anti-nuclear groups; unions, local authorities and others either threatened by future nuclear stations or by the damage which a British PWR programme would do to the UK coal industry; supporters of rival nuclear systems (mainly the SSEB, supporting the AGR), and a host of organisations with an interest in rival power systems from wave machines to district heating.

The Sizewell report of 1987, containing the inquiry's findings in hernia-inducing detail, is a comprehensive document. But its findings can be summarised in a few words. If the CEGB and the rest of the industry want the PWR, they can have it, unless the case for it is overwhelmingly defective on economic or safety grounds. Having found no such defect, despite many false starts by the industry before and during the inquiry, the senior judge running the inquiry, Sir Frank Layfield, recommended to the Department of Energy that the Sizewell PWR – and by implication a batch of several more to follow – should be allowed in the UK. Given a Conservative government keen on nuclear power, the debates in the Houses of Commons and Lords to approve Sizewell B were well-informed and interesting, but they were also a mere procedural formality.

The future for the British nuclear industry would be sweet indeed if it could continue to command enough of the political high ground to ensure this kind of favourable reception for its future plans. But an examination of the issues facing nuclear power in Britain indicates that this possible future will not come to be. First, let us think about the PWR itself. The CEGB wants a 'small family' of them, mainly in southern England, close to the centres of electricity consumption. Hinkley Point and Winfrith in the south-west and Dungeness and Sizewell (again) in the south-east are prime candidate sites, although others include Druridge Bay in Northumberland, and Wylfa and Trawsfynydd in north Wales.

But the idea of this small PWR family by no means unites the British power industry. The AGR supporters are still active in Scotland and elsewhere. So is the lobby for more coal-fired power stations. And as a commercial organisation, the electricity industry cannot be isolated from more general business considerations. If high growth in electricity demand continues into the 1990s, coal stations will come into their own – if only because they are quicker to build than nuclear ones. Two coal-fired stations are now in the process of being ordered. Recent history in the UK also shows, conversely, that low growth in power demand can wipe out whole nuclear programmes. In 1979 the Secretary of State for Energy, David Howell, announced that there would be a steady ordering programme of one nuclear station per year. Owing to insufficient electricity demand and the delays caused by the Sizewell inquiry, only two orders were ever placed.

Future political problems for the nuclear industry are all but inevitable. Although the CEGB has taken care to plan PWRs only at sites it already owns (except Winfrith, which is owned by the UKAEA), so reducing local opposition, various forces at high levels in government and industry are chipping away at support for nuclear power. One key aspect is the industrial one. There is simply a bigger and broader area of British industry standing to gain from coal-fired power station orders than from nuclear power, especially if the coal industry is counted into the equation.

At the same time, the nuclear industry is a branch of high technology and not immune to the general problems of high technology industry in the UK. The UKAEA's decades of being given billions of pounds by the government, against no collateral except a general promise of cheaper electricity at some point in the future, appear to be over. Indeed the government's new science and technology advisory group, ACOST, is examining the desirability of continuing to use thousands of skilled people to develop nuclear power systems, and it seems likely to conclude that a smaller programme designed to deliver specific and comparatively commercial developments would be a better bet, freeing highly qualified people for more urgent tasks in developing the UK's non-nuclear science and technology.

In addition, the UK's biggest nuclear research commitment – rather than the allegedly commercial projects of the CEGB and the SSEB – also seems to be running into the sand. At Dounreay, the UKAEA has spent 30 years trying to develop commercial fast reactors, dangerous and demanding machines capable of producing fresh nuclear fuel from uranium too poor for use in the present generation of thermal reactors. The cost of this research has now outrun the UK's national resources, after more than £2 billion has been spent at Dounreay. The UK has therefore joined a West European fast reactor consortium designed to develop the reactors themselves and the fuel to go with them. Dounreay's role is to house the fuel reprocessing plant for reactors which will be built, at least to start with, in France and

West Germany, using French technology. But it now seems certain that the reactors to produce the fuel for Dounreay to process will not be built for some time, making delay certain. The UK cannot develop new nuclear technology on its own. But international partnerships are subject to even more commercial and political problems than national programmes – and offer even more scope to opposition movements.

The theme of nuclear fuel reprocessing leads us to other areas of vulnerability for the nuclear power industry – its relentless manufacturing of waste products and its need for sites for producing and storing the waste. The UK's nuclear waste factory is Sellafield in Cumbria. It is important to realise that almost nothing of economic use happens here, even by the standards of the nuclear industry. Sellafield's main task so far has been to take 'spent' – i.e. used – fuel from the UK's Magnox power stations (plus the two in Italy and Japan) and to 'reprocess' it. The products of reprocessing can be listed simply. They are uranium (only a small percentage of the uranium put into a reactor is used up before the fuel starts to lose efficiency and has to be removed), plutonium, and wastes of various kinds, solid, liquid and gaseous. The uranium costs far more than fresh metal dug out of the ground in Australia, Canada or (like it or not) Namibia. The plutonium has no uses except as bomb material (of which more below). And the waste is hazardous material which has to be stored or disposed of.

The problems which the nuclear industry is creating for itself here are many. First, Sellafield is costing the nuclear industry a lot of money – billions of pounds in capital investment has to to be got back in fees paid by electricity utilities – and ultimately their customers.

Next, nuclear fuel reprocessing is inherently dirty. A solid metal or ceramic structure is deliberately broken open and chemically treated to allow access to the material within. (In the case of Magnox fuel, the industry is fond of claiming that reprocessing is essential because the fuel decomposes when stored in water. But the CEGB is turning away proposals from GEC, NNC and others to build dry stores in which the fuel keeps for long periods in a blanket of carbon dioxide gas.) BNFL is a massive economic power in Cumbria, and has taken charge of the local council and Member of Parliament. But the waste from Sellafield travels almost as widely as the Chernobyl cloud. Local and national governments from the Republic of Ireland, the Isle of Man, large areas of Scotland, the Faroes, Greenland, Iceland, Norway and elsewhere all oppose Sellafield, and opposition is bound to multiply in England as further Sellafield horror stories emerge.

In addition, the nuclear industry is constantly on the defensive in its search for sites to store the immense amounts of waste manufactured at Sellafield, especially where it is forced into areas where it does not dominate the local economy. At Billingham on Teesside, the chemical giant ICI told the industry to go away rather than risk unpopularity by allowing nuclear waste to be stored in its old salt mines, despite the dangers for one of the UK's largest manufacturing groups of seriously embarrassing the government. And at places like Elstow in Bedfordshire, Tory MPs have joined with local residents to stop plans for waste dumps getting even as far as the planning inquiry stage. (The nuclear industry calls such objectors 'nimbys', for the "not in my back yard" syndrome which it uses to explain away public antipathy to its plans.)

This being so, the political tactic for anti-nuclear objectors becomes obvious. Sellafield should cease being a reprocessing factory and should instead become the management centre for the fuel coming out of nuclear stations for as long as these keep running, as well as for the waste already created. This tactic would allow the objectors to cease seeming as if they are prepared to put thousands of people out of work, while presenting the environmental and economic points about nuclear power as clearly as possible. It would also allow Britain to clean its hands on the other issue concerning the British nuclear industry which is bound to draw increasing attention in coming years, namely its link with bombs – both British and US – and indeed with nuclear weapons proliferation into the Third World.

It is important to realise just how central this issue is to the British nuclear industry. The Magnox reactor was designed first and foremost for plutonium production. Two reactors – at Calder Hall on the Sellafield site and at Chapelcross in Scotland – are explicitly used for weapons plutonium manufacture; and a third, the Berkeley Magnox run by the CEGB, has actually been designed for enhanced plutonium output. In the near future Sellafield will probably get a separate production line for military plutonium manufacture, allowing the industry to claim that its hands are now clean, and in particular that no PWR plutonium is going into bombs.

But from the industry's point of view, this will not make the problem go away. The UK's Trident submarine programme involves a massive increase in the number of nuclear warheads on British submarines by comparison with the existing Polaris system. This means more plutonium. More importantly, the multinational fast reactor deal mentioned above is essentially a bargain to allow French fast reactor technology to become the standard throughout Western Europe. If the consortium's fuel reprocessing plant is built at Dounreay, the UK will be separating plutonium from spent fuel for a multinational grouping whose main partner, France, is not a signatory to the international treaty restricting nuclear weapons proliferation (the Non-Proliferation Treaty) and whose leading nuclear bureaucrats have made speeches and written papers showing commendable frankness about the links between their own fast reactor programmes and French nuclear weapons.

In addition, the nuclear weapons connection isolated by CND at the

Sizewell inquiry is one that is still active. The CND evidence concentrated on a deal whereby the US received plutonium from the UK in exchange for high-grade uranium for submarine fuel. The UK is still building nuclear submarines for its own navy (and trying to sell them to Canada), and has never taken up BNFL proposals to build a submarine-grade fuel works in the UK. At the same time, Trident, MX, cruise missiles, the B1 bomber and even SDI mean a massive US demand for weapons-grade plutonium, which has to come from somewhere, at a time when the US's own Magnox-type plutonium production reactors are nearing the end of their useful lives. The UK authorities may not get away with shipping bomb material to the US again but exchanges whereby plutonium goes there for civil purposes, allowing US supplies to be freed for bomb use, cannot be ruled out.

There is also scope for the UK to become embroiled in Third World nuclear proliferation scandals. This is not the place to discuss the hypocrisy of nuclear weapons states trying to tell other nations not to have nuclear weapons. But it is a fact that all the nations suspected of secret nuclear weapons programmes have carried out the suspect work under the guise of civil nuclear power, which also provides a core of knowledge about nuclear methods and materials of military as well as civil use. But major West European nuclear nations like France, the UK, West Germany and Italy all aim to be exporters, whether of equipment, entire power stations, or fuel services, leaving the door open to proliferation by accidental, fraudulent or even officially-sanctioned routes.

In addition, one should not ignore the scope for nuclear power's smooth progress to be interrupted by unpredictable events ranging from physical accidents to political misjudgements. Here the stage is global, since events occurring in the UK have effects on opinion and development elsewhere – and vice versa. A look at recent history provides copious examples, of which Chernobyl itself, the occasion and theme of this book, is obviously one. Another is the release at the start of 1988 of the state papers for 1957 under the 'Thirty Year Rule'. These documents made it clear that the government of the day had deliberately understated the likely health effects of radiation emitted during the 1957 fire in a plutonium production reactor at Sellafield, showing that the official report of the incident was largely nonsense.

The Sellafield fire is only one example of the way in which the troubling history of nuclear power will not lie down quietly. Another is the slow drip of stories about British behaviour – to British and Australian citizens – during the UK bomb tests of the 1950s, where it now turns out that many people were dangerously irradiated as a result of carelessness or callousness. While this has little to do with today's nuclear power stations, the effect on public opinion is still real.

But the worst publicity about nuclear power doubtless lies in the headlines of the future, not in those of the past. On the basis of accidents like Three Mile Island, Chernobyl or the Brown's Ferry fire of 1975, it seems certain that more disasters will occur to nuclear power stations. It is impossible to anticipate the number of ways in which a severe accident can happen. The nuclear industry is now under the spotlight more than ever before, and the public impact of its errors is now far more damaging. Three Mile Island, for example, had no severe effect on the British plan to adopt a very similar PWR technology for the UK – there was merely an official reassurance that the UK PWR would not be prone to precisely the same failure mode. But a repetition, especially in the US or France, would be far harder to shrug off.

Lastly, it is important to realise that nuclear power is a comparatively new technology. It is younger than microelectronics or satellite communications, for example, both of which have become fully commercial in far less time than nuclear power. And this new industry can only succeed if it prevails politically against a variety of opposing economic interests. Some of these are obvious: for example, as a means of generating electricity, nuclear power can only get anywhere by displacing other methods of electricity production and making inroads against other energy sources. Other opposing interests are less obvious. A recent example from the UK is the farming industry, which continues to suffer severe damage from the Chernobyl accident.

To begin with nuclear power's direct rivals, a key point is the modern climate of opinion about the future for energy production and in particular for electricity demand. During the 1960s, the CEGB and the SSEB had major expansion programmes which involved building coal, oil and nuclear power stations. In the case of coal-fired stations, major technological advances – especially increases in the size of generating units – were carried out alongside a shift towards ordering nuclear stations. Even the National Union of Mineworkers (although not all NUM members) was sympathetic to a nuclear power programme, seeing it as a necessary part of the future energy picture, not a deadly rival.

This climate has now changed, for two reasons. One is simply that the facts about nuclear power are better known than before and anti-nuclear movements better informed, more effective and more widely believed. The other is that a wider range of social groupings sees nuclear power as posing problems.

First in the list comes one estate of the realm whose own power is widely perceived as being on the wane but which is still a force to be reckoned with – the trade union movement. Many unions whose members have no direct involvement in nuclear power, from civil servants to agricultural workers, have anti-nuclear policies. So does the Trades Union Congress. Unions with a direct role in nuclear power have also started to take effective action against it. In the UK, the seafarers' union halted the dumping of radioactive waste in the Atlantic simply by refusing to do it – a decision against their narrow economic interest since the sea dump was work for British sailors. Now the only unions to hold out seriously in favour of nuclear power are those whose members work directly in nuclear power and the power industry in general. There is a larger task for the anti-nuclear movement here. But the nuclear lobby has only kept power station workers and builders on its side by a stupendous confidence trick, implying that nuclear power means jobs for workers which would be lost if nuclear power were abandoned. This is the opposite of the truth. Nuclear power in fact allows employee numbers to be cut, substituting capital for labour and reducing the number of power stations and power workers. This is a truth which the unions concerned are not likely to grasp spontaneously, since they are close to the industry's management and often take a management view on policy questions. Here, surely, is the raw material for a sustained campaign by anti-nuclear unionists.

The same argument – that nuclear power is central power, involving massive rural power stations – points to other interests trodden on by the nuclear industry. It is now possible for power to be produced in inner cities economically and cleanly, and local authorities, planning authorities, groups fighting fuel poverty and others are all in favour of reviving power generation as an inner-city industry. Events like the appearance of the Greater London Council at the Sizewell inquiry make the point that the link is already being made between massive nuclear programmes and the lack of resources for alternative means of power generation. The same goes for energy conservation – which in the UK has had to fight massive problems in gaining access to resources on the favoured terms available to nuclear power – and renewable energy, whose slow progress in the UK is linked by most of the practitioners affected to the political clout of the electricity and nuclear industries.

In addition, nuclear power's big British rival – coal – has to have a place in any list of the forces lined up against it. British Coal executives are often surprisingly indiscreet about the pleasure they take in the economic disasters which have beset nuclear power in the UK, the US and elsewhere. They are convinced that coal can be burned cleanly and can produce electricity more cheaply than nuclear power. More importantly, coal has some natural advantages over nuclear power. Coal-fired stations are cheap and quick to build, making them preferable to nuclear stations at a time when power demand is increasing apace. In addition, they are more potent generators of employment, since they create work for coal miners, the mining equipment industry, and others dependent on them, often in areas sorely in need of more investment and employment. The development of technology capable of cleaning up fossil-fuel power station emissions, including burners to suck nitrogen oxides out of the emissions, and new boilers or flue gas desulphurisation equipment to remove sulphur, means that coal-burning stations can be built with few environmental objections. This provides scope for full exploitation of its commercial attractions to power utilities.

At the same time, the UK has a substantial power station construction industry whose interests do not coincide completely with the electricity utilities' ideas on future investment. Because most power station investment around the world is in coal-burning plant, these firms have spent heavily on improved technology for building it. They are also alarmed at the low rate of ordering for new nuclear power stations, and chary of a heavy commitment to the PWR when it has gone heavily out of fashion, except in the UK, and when there are far more experienced manufacturers (in France, the US, West Germany, Japan and elsewhere) to compete for any available PWR business world-wide. Even GEC, whose predecessor English Electric signed the first British licence with Westinghouse to allow it to build PWRs in Britain, has offloaded the licence onto the NNC and reduced its NNC shareholding in line with the reduced commercial prospects of the PWR. The prospect of serious industrial opposition to nuclear power in Britain must sound somewhat unconvincing to the anti-nuclear movement. No doubt most senior industrialists have the same world-view as the nuclear magnates themselves; and after all, no company ever prospered by telling its customers that they didn't really want the goods they came into the shop to buy. But the clash of economic interests at work is evident and in principle ripe for exploitation. As well as large, rural power stations burning coal rather than using nuclear power, the British power industry would like to build city-scale combined heat and power plants using far more adventurous technology than British power utilities have so far chosen to buy, and for which there could be a worthwhile export market.

Finally in the UK, one should not forget that the dangers and problems of nuclear power can at any moment impress themselves forcibly on new and potentially influential groups. Thousands of British livestock farmers, for example, now regard nuclear power as a liability, because of the losses they have suffered on sheep meat after the Chernobyl accident. Not only have they lost money; they feel deceived by the nuclear industry and do not believe that there is an end in sight to the problems – genetic problems, for example, may affect future generations of sheep. Luckily for the nuclear industry, the damage has occurred mostly in Cumbria and north Wales, where the industry is politically and economically influential in the local community. But at other Chernobyl hotspots in Scotland and Yorkshire the same does not apply. It is unlikely that farmers will stop nuclear power in Britain. But nuclear power is a rural industry. We can expect bodies like the Country Landowners' Association and perhaps even the powerful National Farmers' Union to be a lot less sanguine than in the past when they consider new proposals for nuclear power stations and other nuclear plant.

Power, Protest, Decision: the Nuclear Establishment World-wide

The British nuclear industry is powerful, but not all-powerful. It gets away with a great deal, but by no means with everything it tries. It has an enormous number of friends in high places, but no monopoly on their attention. And as we have seen, there are significant economic interests opposed to nuclear power. How are nuclear decisions made in other countries? Taking a sample – I hope a representative one – it will be clear that some resemble the British case more closely than others. Some allow more scope for public opposition to official plans than others. But in many it would be quite wrong to over-emphasise the power of the nuclear industry in the context of the opposing interests with which it has to contend.

The first group of countries we come to are ones which it would be easy to neglect in an account of this nature. They are the nations – the vast majority – with no nuclear power at all. Developed nations such as the Republic of Ireland, Norway, Australia and New Zealand have all decided to stick with fossil fuels and renewable energy, despite, in many cases, determined attempts by overseas nuclear industries to sell them nuclear power stations on highly favourable terms. In some cases, an abundance of alternatives has ruled nuclear power out, along with the realisation that going in for nuclear power would involve massive investments of money and skill, and unforeseeable future problems, well beyond the scale of any benefits they might bring. The nuclear industry's present traumas must prompt many a sigh of relief in these countries' energy ministries. But the nuclear power station building industry has massive over-capacity and it has seen traditional markets dry up: it is likely to want to open up new markets for itself by influencing business and government leaders in countries that are presently non-nuclear.

The story changes when we consider the plethora of Third World countries with no nuclear power. Many of these are too small or too broke to interest even the nuclear industry. Third World debt problems are of particular importance here. They mean that the official credit sources, like the Export-Import Bank in the US, which provide the credit to make nuclear exports possible, are now not willing to deal with many Third World countries, especially for a single huge and risky investment like a nuclear power station. Also noteworthy here is the emergence of anti-nuclear, safe energy and environmental activity in the Third World (see Chapter 5) .

Next in any examination of nuclear power's friends and enemies today is the country where it all began, the United States. There is now a massive literature on the development of nuclear energy in the US, and the story is a fascinating one. To summarise as brutally as possible, nuclear power in the US was developed at government expense and continues to receive massive federal subsidies from civil and military budgets. But nuclear power stations in the US are bought mainly by private-sector utilities (although there are some federal ones like the Tennessee Valley Authority and the Bonneville Power Administration). They have bought nuclear power stations on the promise of cheap electricity and have in many cases been disappointed. Nuclear power projects have overrun on time and cost, and many have been cancelled or altered to coal-burning. At the same time, the US political system has made it possible for anti-nuclear objectors to cause even more massive delays to nuclear projects, since there is little difficulty making the case through the US public inquiry system that alternative investments offer cheaper power than nuclear energy, and do not pose unresolved safety problems. Fundamental to the problems of US nuclear power is the industry's inability to produce any evidence that it can dispose safely of the large amounts of spent nuclear fuel and waste it produces. Unresolved safety issues like this are far more effectively transformed into barriers to the granting of planning permission in the US planning system than in the UK.

Also important in the US energy picture is the existence of state regulatory bodies to keep an eye on the activities of power utilities. Many of these have refused to allow the increased power prices which massive nuclear investments involve. Others have taken to asking utilities to prove that nuclear investments are the best way of meeting the apparent demand for energy. In several states, power utilities now invest in energy conservation measures instead of in new power stations, in the knowledge that money so invested will yield a better and faster return, and bring praise from local inhabitants instead of writs.

The US nuclear industry remains a massive one, and is lobbying hard to get going again after over a decade of stagnation. But it is hard to see how it will surmount the enormous political and financial problems it faces at home – which serve only to encourage its enthusiasm for export business. It needs the money and it needs to be seen to be winning business abroad after the complete destruction of its domestic market.

The opposite extreme is illustrated in the case of France, whose nuclear experience differs from that of the US in all respects but two: France has built large numbers of PWRs; and it has now more or less stopped building them. But the reason why few PWRs are now being built in France is simply that the French electricity system cannot cope with any more of them. By 1990, over 70 per cent of French electricity may come from nuclear power – a figure at or beyond the maximum limit desirable for a stable electricity generating system.

This massive growth has been made possible by political and economic factors. In terms of economics, the French nuclear power stations have been bought at the cost, for the state power utility Electricité de France (EdF), of huge dollar borrowings which massively exceed its annual turnover. At the moment France has power prices close to those of other Western European nations, but EdF is lobbying for increases which will probably destroy the nuclear industry's claim that it has given France cheap power. The French are also dumping power cheaply in export markets, mainly the UK.

Politically, the French nuclear power programme has been through a complex history. France first developed a gas-cooled reactor system resembling the British Magnox one. This was destroyed by the arrival of PWR vendor Westinghouse, whose first step was to win over senior officials of the CEA, France's nuclear research authority, to the PWR – the same process gone through subsequently with the UKAEA in Britain. This led to a large PWR-based programme implemented by central direction, in which there was no role for public participation or local objection – although large sums were made available to communities agreeing to house nuclear power stations. No account was taken of the near-destruction of the French coal industry which resulted from this PWR programme, and there is no effective anti-nuclear lobby in France to argue against the programme on economic or safety grounds, despite the courage of some individuals and groups who have spoken out against it. Now the programme has reached its end in a world of falling fossil fuel prices, very different from the oil panics which helped it get launched. And the huge nuclear power plant industry which was developed to supply the stations has now run out of steam so decisively that a small domestic ordering programme is kept up at the behest of communist trades unions while the world is scoured for possible export markets. The lesson for overseas observers could hardly be clearer. A technocratic elite has been let loose, without democratic checks, in alliance with foreign big business, and the whole of France now has to suffer the economic consequences. So far no French PWR has suffered a severe accident. If one does, it is certain that the French would be unable to shut down their other PWRs until a massive programme of building alternative power stations had been completed.

Ask anyone interested in nuclear politics to name a country with the opposite of the French experience, and the answer will probably be Sweden. In a world of nations which are dropping out of nuclear power by default, Sweden is the one country which has taken a positive decision to do so. But this turn of events was by no means inevitable in Swedish history. Sweden is a major fuel importer, and therefore had an incentive to go for nuclear power and to avoid coal and oil imports. It also has a strong electrical engineering industry which has in the past seen nuclear power as a potential moneyspinner. On this basis, Sweden began a hefty programme of BWR and PWR construction. Only later did the Swedish environmental movement become powerful enough to force a national debate, a referendum, and a decision to build no new nuclear stations in Sweden and phase out the existing ones by 2010, replacing them with alternative generating capacity, or energy conservation.

A key element in this history is the Swedish approach to the problem, in which participatory democracy, including freedom of public information, was taken seriously by people and government. I would not – as an outsider with no direct experience of the country – advance the claim that Sweden is politically perfect. But the contrast with the secrecy and bureaucracy which have marked nuclear developments in France or the UK is informative. Also important is the way in which key actors in the Swedish economy found that they had little to gain from nuclear power. Power station builders can get more business from hydropower and combined heat and power stations, for example. But there are still groups in Sweden which favour readopting nuclear energy policies, mainly energy-intensive firms which are not persuaded that they will be able to get cheap energy once the nuclear power stations are gone. This means that conservation and alternative generation technologies, including renewable energy as well as fossil fuels, will have to be developed apace to persuade nuclear power supporters that they offer a real option.

The relationship between secrecy and openness, and between democracy and central decision-making, has an important bearing on nuclear power programmes throughout the developed world. Federal Germany tends towards the US model, because of the powers of the *Länder* and the existence of regional power utilities. There, partly because of the existence of a powerful green movement, nuclear power is in difficulty and coal seems likely to be the main winner. But the West German nuclear industry is clinging to its ambitions. For example, it has the truly horrific idea of building a national equivalent of Sellafield at a place called Wackersdorf, near the frontiers with Austria and Czechoslovakia. This scheme has been stalled for years because of countless legal, financial and environmental objections. Japan, on the other hand, tends towards the French model, with a hefty nuclear programme and its own version of PWR technology, which it is now developing with a second-generation PWR for home and export markets.

It would be easy to assume that the Soviet Union and the other Comecon countries have nuclear power policies of great simplicity, in which nuclear stations are built according to a central plan and with little regard for local sensibilities or environmental factors. This view seems to have much to support it. The massive nuclear waste disaster at Kyshtym in the Urals, which occurred in 1957, would have caused even the most centralist Western nation to think twice about embarking on a major nuclear power programme. There must have been repercussions behind closed doors in the USSR, but the nuclear programmes agreed by the energy ministry and the machine-building industry were apparently unimpaired. Will Chernobyl cause any major change in this outlook? One certain effect seems to be that RBMK reactors (modified, like Magnox, from a pile for plutonium manufacture) will no longer be built, although the existing ones will remain in service. In East Germany, the Soviet Union, Poland, Hungary and Czechoslovakia, the small environmental movements which have so far emerged have met with official disfavour, although the Hungarian movement against further damming of the Danube appears to be tolerated, and it seems that at least one Soviet nuclear station has been cancelled as a result of popular protest (see Chapter 4). Just how these movements will develop and what they will achieve are crucial questions, bound up with the general political future of the Comecon countries as well as with the nuclear issue itself. It must also be borne in mind that the same forces must be at work in Soviet energy policy-making as in the West. The USSR, for example, is by far the world's biggest coal producer, mining over 600 million tonnes a year. Most of this goes to power stations. It follows that there is a mining industry, a mining equipment industry, a coal-fired power station building industry and a cadre of coal-fired power station operators who have careers and pensions. On a lesser scale the same must be true for hydropower in the USSR – but not apparently for the whole field of energy conservation, in which the USSR has so far made very limited progress.

But there is one common factor in the Western nuclear nations' perspectives which is not a major consideration for the Soviet Union, and this is the hope that a domestic nuclear programme would give rise to a profitable export trade. The Soviet Union's only nuclear exports have been to other Comecon countries and to Finland, and even this limited trade now seems to have dried up.

The US, France, West Germany and other Western nations all retain hopes that the Third World will save them from the economic disaster of nuclear power's retreat at home. In my view, this is the most important factor affecting nuclear power policies in the Third World. Nuclear power is vigorously promoted by Western exporters and its appeal in developing countries is widespread among large industrial corporations, to state bureaucracies in energy ministries and to power companies. But when a Third World country is offered nuclear power by a Western company, it knows that the terms are harshly unequal. Most high technology companies in the West have more scientists and engineers, more economists and more financial muscle than the countries they deal with as potential export customers. The only advantage the recipients enjoy is that they have too little money to be able to pay for a nuclear power station, so they receive credit instead, and on a scale so massive that it stretches the language to describe them as 'buying' nuclear power stations at all.

That said, nuclear power's opponents in the Third World have a complex task in explaining just how little it has to offer there. The first and most obvious point is simply that nuclear power costs a lot of money, even if it is bought with soft credit which feels painless enough at the time. Other ways of generating or saving energy are normally less capital-intensive and create more employment. Since Third World nations have too little money and too much unemployment and underemployment, other technologies have more to offer. Moreover, the sums of money at stake increase the possibility of corruption in the placing of contracts, a problem which is also familiar from the arms trade.

In addition, the high level of technology in any nuclear power installation means that it consumes not only money but also other scarce resources in a Third World nation. It also demands the services of scientists and engineers in substantial numbers, both those educated locally and others who have been sent to the developed world for training. Some Third World nations, such as India, have huge numbers of skilled people – but they and the equipment and resources they use are still precious assets. Simply introducing an expensive alternative source of bulk electricity that does not benefit many people in most Third World nations (least of all those most in need) will not put these assets to best use.

Nuclear power poses even more severe technological problems in the Third World than elsewhere. Environmental protection is less highly developed; power station siting, to take account of considerations from earthquake hazards to local population centres, is likely to be less carefully appraised; the culture of industrial safety is likely to be less highly developed. And nuclear power is a peculiarly difficult technology to transfer to Third World countries, which rightly want to manufacture goods at home whenever they can rather than simply import them from abroad.

This last problem is thrown into relief by the 1975 nuclear deal between Brazil and West Germany, designed to make Brazil a major world power in the nuclear industry. The plan was to make Brazil independent as a nuclear power station builder and in nuclear fuel technology, and it was done without regard for the niceties of the international treaties on nuclear weapons proliferation. In fact money and technology problems have meant that Brazil has not yet emerged as a major force in world nuclear trade, nor has it established nuclear power successfully on its own soil.

This deal also illustrates the point that a Third World nation getting involved in nuclear power is necessarily entering a subordinate relationship with the developed world. The Philippines, for instance, handed over a large chunk of its nuclear policy-making to Westinghouse when the regime of Ferdinand Marcos decided to adopt the PWR. Argentina had the same experience until it decided to set up a contest by installing Canada's CANDU nuclear system alongside the PWR. The cost and chaos resulting from a switch of reactor type has meant years of confusion even for the UK; in a nation with limited resources, such as Argentina, the effect is multiplied.

The future of nuclear power in the Third World looks unpromising. Too few Third World nations can afford it; the examples above come from the richer nations like Brazil, but most of Africa and Asia are totally excluded from nuclear power because of the sums of money involved. There are strong intellectual arguments against the claim that nuclear power can solve any of the Third World's real problems. And most importantly, Third World leaders are strongly influenced by events in the developed world. They are now noticing that nuclear power is no longer in fashion; why should they buy something that the West has abandoned? The conscious mimicking of the West by Third World leaders may for once do some good.

But this is not to diminish the problems faced by the enemies of nuclear power in the Third World. Too few Third World countries are democracies, with real structures for expressing public discontent with nuclear power. Too few have environmental movements of real strength. It is interesting to note that nuclear projects in Third World countries have generally been slowed down or destroyed by the fall of Western-sponsored governments. The massive nuclear programme in Iran contracted by the Shah's government from the French did not survive the Shah himself – although it had become apparent even to him that it was a poor deal for Iran. The gradual democratisation of Brazil has coincided with the effective end of the West German deal there, although it occasionally shows signs of renewed life. The Philippines' programme, to Westinghouse's distress, looks unlikely to bring much new business to its Philadelphia factories after the revival of democracy under President Corazon Aquino. The same goes for nuclear power in Argentina now that the colonels have lost their former influence – or to be exact the admirals, since it was the Navy which primarily pushed nuclear power in Argentina during the years of military rule.

Conclusions

The picture painted above will be an inaccurate one if it has not conveyed an image of extreme complexity. Nuclear power is not an old technology, but already it has burrowed into the assumptions and plans of business executives, energy ministers, electricity utility managers and other people of power all over the world. It is a huge business employing large numbers of people. For that reason it is not going to go away. And remember that even if every nuclear nation in the world – 26 of the world's 169 nations at the end of 1987 – were to decide that nuclear power is unpalatable and to cease building and running nuclear stations, there would still be a radioactive legacy lasting tens of thousands of years from existing nuclear stations.

But it is vital to realise that nuclear power has competition, and not only in the normal business sense of the term. About 16 per cent of world electricity came from its 416 nuclear power stations at the end of 1987, but this means that 84 per cent comes from other sources, mainly coal and hydro-power. So non-nuclear electricity is bigger business than nuclear power, and is set to remain so. In many countries, like the UK, the common wisdom of governments and utilities is in favour of nuclear power, but there are bigger and more important industries, and in some cases careers, dependent upon other sources of electricity. And electricity is only part of the energy mix of particular countries; strengthening energy conservation and the use of rival fuels also weakens the proliferation of nuclear power.

However, if it were simply a question of rival considerations being weighed to find the most rational means of supplying electricity, nuclear power would never have got as far as it has. Some indication of just how bad an idea it has been can be gained from the figures quoted above, produced by the International Atomic Energy Agency (IAEA) in Vienna, the UN-funded marketing organisation for civil nuclear power. Any innovation which allegedly has a decisive economic advantage over its competitors, but which has just 16 per cent of the market after almost 40 years of lavish subsidies, cannot be all its promoters claim.

Still, nuclear power does seem to have a charmed life. It began its existence on the back of nuclear weapons, assuring it plentiful funding, and this is a connection which is still alive in the US, the UK, France, the Soviet Union, Israel, South Africa and elsewhere. As well as guaranteeing money, this connection means that the nuclear industry is always to some extent closed off by official secrecy from the rest of the economy, and becomes inherently a business for insiders and elites. Often it does not have to answer the hard questions about its economic viability – questions which would otherwise have brought nuclear programmes to a halt. In a television interview Lord Marshall, head of the CEGB, has described the Magnox power stations as the backbone of the electricity system – but when actual CEGB figures for electricity costs were produced in the run-up to the Sizewell inquiry, Magnox power turned out to be dearer than electricity from coal, in contrast to all the official pronouncements of many years.

Nuclear power is nourished by secrecy and centralised decision-making. So objectors to nuclear power tend also to object to state secrecy, in many fields. Secrecy has shrouded the true economic performance of nuclear power, which has still to prove itself against its main rival, coal, and against energy conservation. The same applies to safety information, as the case of the Windscale fire has shown. In general, the more information appears, the more alarming it is; continuing research on the health effects of radiation, for example, keeps finding that lower and lower levels of exposure are dangerous. In the same way, information on actual and possible pollution from nuclear power is rarely offered freely by the authorities and when it is, it tends to be alarming in two ways: the dangers revealed are worrying and so too are the questions *not* asked by nuclear power developers and the attitudes of mind they betray.

So the line-up opposing the massive forces behind nuclear power can be easily described: opposing economic interests, from home insulation to coal mining; anyone opposed to ecological hazards and arrogant gambling with the environment; and many of those opposed to the secrecy and lack of democracy which nuclear power inherently involves. These are disparate interests. The chief executives of coal-mining firms do not attend meetings to campaign against official secrecy, nor invite return visits from people who do. The nuclear industry, on the other hand, exists in a closed world of its own, where the key people in uranium mining firms, power utilities, power station contractors, energy ministries and the like know each other, share the same assumptions and are linked by common, strong, economic interests. On any rational basis of decision-making, these interests would have been set aside long ago in favour of more worthwhile directions for energy policy development. The task for the anti-nuclear movements of the future is to bring this about by combining and articulating the fragmentary power which they already possess.

Part II
The Movements

4
Lines of Latitude:
People's Détente, East and West

MARK THOMPSON

One certain effect of the Chernobyl accident has been to weaken public
confidence in nuclear power ... In the public mind, the nuclear industry is
back to square one – if not minus one.
Hans Blix, Director General, International Atomic Energy Agency[1]

Chernobyl has become the disaster that united East and West.
Moscow Trust Group statement, April 1987

As noted straightaway by a thousand pundits, politicians and anti-nuclear
activists, the radioactivity from Chernobyl paid no attention to national
or political frontiers – not even to the hallowed division between 'East'
and 'West'. This was the most terrible way in which the peoples of both
blocs were brought together by the moment of Chernobyl; but it was not the
only way. Another consequence of the disaster was a wave of protests
across West and East. Rallies and actions organised by anti-nuclear groups
took place throughout Europe, as well as Japan and North America, during
May and June 1986. On 10 May alone, a fortnight after the accident, 100,000
people took to the streets in Rome, and in the German Federal Republic
there were large demonstrations in Munich and Augsburg, and at
Breisach/Fessenheim on the Franco-German border. That same day there
were protests in Athens and in Yugoslavia, where 2,000 people marched
through the centre of Ljubljana. The day before, in Poland, activists of the
independent anti-militarist movement Wolnosc i Pokoj ('Freedom and
Peace') had drawn applause from sympathetic crowds when they carried
their banners – 'Our children are being killed', 'We demand full
information' – through Wroclaw. On 1 June, some 2,000 people marched in
protest at the construction of Soviet-model nuclear power stations in
Poland; and 3,000 people signed a petition calling for work on Poland's
first nuclear plant at Zarnowiec – being built with Soviet assistance – to be
suspended. In the Soviet Union, peace and civil liberties activists in
Moscow were twice prevented from circulating a petition. Students in
Czechoslovakia printed postcards calling for information about Chernobyl

and access to information on all aspects of nuclear power. In the German Democratic Republic, an Evangelical church group in East Berlin demanded that all nuclear power reactors be switched off, and the church in Potsdam called for a full debate on nuclear power.[2]

Chernobyl touched people who had never had cause to think about the nuclear issue before, and not only in the worst-irradiated areas in the USSR and Eastern Europe. Swiss fishermen on Lake Lugano who are still forbidden to work; the Saami peoples of northern Scandinavia, whose entire culture was irreparably damaged when their reindeer herds were contaminated by fallout; hill farmers in Britain who have now been told that their livestock may have to be monitored for the next 30 years: these peoples' lives were changed by Chernobyl, as directly as those of the Ukrainians in the Pripyat river basin.

Public opinion polls taken after Chernobyl all showed a significant rise in popular distrust of and hostility to nuclear power. They often showed, too, increasing scepticism about government information and advice on radiation and safety measures. This was hardly surprising, for as the peoples of East and West were united by radioactivity and dismay, so their governments were 'united' in their attempts to play down the danger, to absolve themselves and their nuclear plants of criticism, and to score political points. The CIA encouraged the notorious '2,100 dead' disinformation, so helping to justify Eastern counter-accusations that the Western media were slanderous and provocative. Western governments mocked shoddy Soviet technology and chorused that 'it couldn't happen here'. Mrs Thatcher took an early opportunity to declare that its secrecy over Chernobyl showed just how far the USSR could be trusted over disarmament verification procedures. European Community bans on food imports from Eastern Europe were called 'discriminatory'. In an access of pure Cold War paranoia, the Polish government tit-for-tatted the ('provocative'?) American gift of dried milk by donating 5,000 sleeping-bags for New York's homeless.

Meanwhile, Western radiologists and nuclear scientists were busily contradicting their own governments. It quietly emerged that there was not after all such a qualitative difference between Chernobyl and many Western reactors; and that the fallout was after all dangerous to Western health. Scientists also engaged in their own professional détente: one thinks of the US Environmental Protection Agency expert who arrived in Warsaw on 3 May and announced that he 'could not stress enough how small' the registered radiation was; and of the SSEB (South of Scotland Electricity Board) engineering director who said that 'We are not going to sit here and be critical after the event. We will learn everything we possibly can from the experience in Russia...'[3]

The Norwegian government commission's report on Chernobyl was studded with such remarks as: 'toxic limits have been exceeded, but this isn't dangerous,' and: 'one must be careful what one eats, but it doesn't matter if one isn't.'[4] The Polish commission set up by Premier Messner – at the insistence of scientific advisers – was equally illuminating: 'even if the source of contamination were still active – which it is not – the level of contamination would, over the next ten days, still on average be forty times lower than the level needed to cause concern.' But Poland was particularly rich in tragicomedy at this time. On the same day that Polish monitoring stations said their findings showed that there was no threat to health, Warsaw television announced that the intensity of radioactive iodine in north-east Poland 'may be harmful to infants, children and pregnant women'. The Zarnowiec nuclear plant under construction in northern Poland is, embarrassingly, a Soviet model; and everyone knew it because the government had been boasting of the fact. Government spokesman Jerzy Urban could not say whether Poland was told about Chernobyl by the USSR before they found out for themselves from the Swedes. Asked whether Poland would seek compensation from the USSR for lost exports, Urban replied that it would be difficult to ask the Soviet Union to compensate for damage done by the EEC. Then had the Soviet Union apologised? There was no need, because no damage had been done to Polish health or lives.

This broad equivalence of Eastern and Western governmental *and* popular responses is, I suggest, an essential fact about Chernobyl – and something that Western peace and environmental groups should have used and drawn attention to. Yet it passed largely unremarked, in Britain as elsewhere. The principal victims of the disaster – Ukrainians and other Soviet citizens, and Poles – were referred to in passing, if at all; and there was scarcely any show of solidarity with the environmental and peace groups of Eastern Europe. In the USA, where Chernobyl prompted 'the first wide-scale anti-nuclear protests in several years', with actions in 35 cities, apparently only one group invited a Soviet speaker to its rally.[5] (Honourable exceptions were the Austrian group which helped activists in Prague and Budapest in the most practical way – by going there and leafletting with them; and the US and British supporters of the Trust Group who distributed leaflets in Moscow's Gorky Park.) This was not of course callousness. Rather it was due, in part, to Western environmentalists' lack of experience in East–West networking and politics; but it was made inevitable by the vexed history of Western peace movements' relations with Eastern Europe. Before considering these relations, I shall look more closely at the East European and Soviet peace and ecology groups, starting with their responses to Chernobyl.

The Eastern protests were of course fewer and smaller than those in the West. Yet their significance cannot be gauged from their scale alone. The fact that they happened at all, in conditions so unpropitious to unofficial demonstrations, let alone demonstrations critical of the state, testifies to the strength of public fear and anger – emotions which were plain too in the manifestos and documents circulated by Soviet and East European independent peace and human rights groups in the weeks after the accident.

While Western anti-nuclear protesters were calling for nuclear stations to be closed down, these Eastern groups were much more concerned with their governments' readiness to risk people's health rather than give reliable information. The Czechoslovak civil liberties group Charta 77 – elder statesman among East European democratic-oppositional groups – released a statement on 6 May. In their habitually moderate, precise tone, the Charta spokespeople quoted the Czechoslovak government's public response ('continuous measurements are being taken on the territory of Czechoslovakia ... and for the entire period of these measurements no increase of radioactivity has been ascertained'), and went on to demand 'that you publish as soon as possible all available facts concerning if and on what level there was increased radioactivity during the individual days of the critical period on the territory of our country'.

While they insisted that Chernobyl made 'the safety of our nuclear power stations' all the more important, the Chartists did not express any anti-nuclear sentiments as such. The same is true of the statement put out by the underground leadership of Solidarnosc in Poland: 'The Chernobyl explosion', they said, 'has focused attention on environmental issues. Never before has it been so clearly demonstrated how strongly linked these are to issues of freedom of organisation and information.' The whole terrible business was taken as an instance of the Polish regime's 'reliance on the USSR', and its disregard for Poland's own ecological wellbeing.

The Krakow branch of Solidarnosc issued its own 'analysis of the situation ... prepared by scientists and specialists in nuclear physics', and necessitated by the 'inadequate information about the ... danger to the population as well as the lack of preventative health measures'. Wolnosc i Pokoj described Poland as 'a country on the brink of ecological catastrophe', pointed to the lack of social control over the nuclear power programme, and called for 'international security control of civil nuclear installations'.

In the German Democratic Republic, 'the independent peace and ecology movement and other concerned citizens' wrote a remarkable 'Open Letter to the Government and People of the GDR'. Entitled 'Chernobyl is Everywhere!', this eloquent document sets Chernobyl in the context of a history of disinformation and undemocratic decision-making by the nuclear-power industry and its lobby – a history which, the writers rightly insist, transcends the East–West bloc division. The letter locates nuclear power's home at the heart of technocratic industrialism, makes the all-important connection between civil and military nuclear technologies, and calls for 'a parallel process of balanced nuclear disarmament, on the one hand, and mutual decommissioning of nuclear power stations, on the other'. In June a petition calling for a referendum on nuclear power in the GDR was circulated. By summer 1987 it had gained more than 1,000 signatures; as one of the drafters has said, 'For GDR conditions, that is a considerable number, as the risks attached to signing are very high.'

In Yugoslavia, the Ljubljana peace movement sent a 'Declaration of Protest' to the Slovenian, Yugoslav and Soviet governments, condemning the lack of accurate information, demanding publication of the details of the Yugoslav nuclear power programme and a halt to any further development of that programme, pending a referendum. Only the Soviet independent peace and human rights group, the Trust Group, came out unequivocally against nuclear power. On 6 May the Group announced in a circular letter 'To all Friends and Colleagues in Independent Peace Movements of West and East' that 'from now on, our anti-nuclear programme includes the most negative attitude to nuclear power stations ... From now on, in our educational activities and our campaigning, we will be opposing both nuclear arsenals and nuclear power stations.' In Hungary the only demonstration was violently broken up by police. There was no word of civic unrest in Romania or Bulgaria.

The individuals who took their banners into the streets and put out these documents in May and June of 1986 are among those who are popularly and often misleadingly known in the West, when they are known at all, as 'dissidents', implying that they are self-segregated within their own societies, alienated and at odds with their fellow citizens – an interpretation that suits the establishments of both East and West, which portray these people as parasites or moral martyrs. Independent thought and activism in Eastern Europe is in fact very varied and complex, and groups such as Charta or Wolnosc i Pokoj are coalitions of individuals often with very different political and social outlooks. Reform communists rub shoulders with conscientious objectors, eco-anarchists with democratic oppositionists. What these individuals share is a will to change their societies from within, and a recognition that no measures of political reform 'from above' can in themselves achieve radical social change. Of course, groups like the ones I am discussing here do not have any monopoly on independence in their respective countries. Some 'oppositionists' are more interested in denunciation or 'bearing witness' than in social change; such people *can* fairly be termed 'dissidents'. Others again simply want to find room for their own 'alternative' lifestyles.

Now the evidence suggests that the groups which protested after Chernobyl do speak for large constituencies within their societies. (The complex exception here is the Trust Group, which seems since its inception in 1982 to have been marginal in Soviet society. This raises the crucial question of the legitimacy of East European regimes, which ultimately underlies all independent activity in the region, and to which I shall return.) It is certainly true of Charta 77, which remains the authentic voice of democratic socialism and reform communism in Czechoslovakia. And it is plainly true of Solidarnosc, the Polish labour movement (and much more besides) which still commands great popular support and authority more than six years after its defeat by martial law. The most affecting of the Polish responses to Chernobyl that I have seen is a letter addressed by a group of Polish women from a Warsaw factory to the Polish Bishops' Conference, and it echoes Solidarnosc's Krakow branch, though in humbler, 'unpolitical' terms:

> ... We do understand that a tragic accident may happen anywhere, even despite the strictest safety measures, and we sympathise with all the Ukrainian families who suffered most. However, we cannot understand why the authorities did not inform the population about the accident, about the danger of radiation and preventative measures, until four days after the disaster ... We think that in a critical situation like this, it is fully justifiable to expect the authorities at least to act in a sensible and responsible manner rather than to manipulate and use the information for short-term political gains.[6]

Also in May, a farmers' association linked to Solidarnosc appealed to scientists and doctors in Poland and abroad, including the World Health Organisation, to establish an international commission to monitor radioactivity in food, and to supervise Poland's nuclear plant construction.

In Yugoslavia, opinion polls taken after Chernobyl showed 80 per cent of the interviewees against the development of nuclear power. In Hungary and Poland, the underground press expressed the same anger with the national and Soviet regimes for their mendacity and delay in telling what they knew. A writer in *Beszelö*, Hungary's best-known underground newspaper, said that 'The Hungarian leadership has proved again that it does not have an active national interest which could induce an independent stance towards Big Brother.' An equivalent Polish paper, *Tygodnik Mazowsze*, declared that:

> The Chernobyl tragedy has once again shown Moscow's astounding arrogance towards its satellite countries. The Polish authorities found out about it from a Tass communiqué when the radioactive cloud was already over Poland. Soviet experts who arrived in Warsaw did not bring any concrete facts but only came to measure radiation levels in Poland.[7]

Evidence of this sort is bound to be piecemeal, as there are no reliable independent means of monitoring public opinion and the authorities prefer not to reveal information critical of themselves. (Warsaw Radio's 24 May report of an opinion poll which showed over half the respondents feeling that they were not told enough about the 'effects and handling of the accident' was an intriguing exception.) But all the signs are that very large numbers of people in Eastern Europe were not only frightened by the human and environmental implications of Chernobyl, but shocked by what the handling of the accident revealed or confirmed about their own governments. Hence the *Beszelö* writer's comment that 'It is not enough to describe Chernobyl as a technical catastrophe; what is being talked about is human and political catastrophe.'

As a last example, I can't resist quoting the writer Ludvík Vaculík, who distilled some very Czech humour out of state secrecy in one of his famous *feuilletons*, dated 'May 1986' and circulated in *samizdat* form:

> ... I tried to tune in to some foreign news broadcast to hear the latest about the cloud. But all I got was a nasty persistent whine.
>
> During supper, Mirek switched on Prague TV. There was the country's leading hygienist reassuring us that radiation levels were low. But she did recommend us to take showers and avoid stroking dogs. Mirek switched over to Vienna. Panic stations! They showed bulldozers clearing out children's sandpits, and sanitary inspectors going round the markets tipping boxes of lettuces off vegetable stalls onto the ground. It all looked a bit barmy. The Austrians were being told not to bathe in open-air pools or lie out on the grass, and to keep out of the rain. 'It must be dreadful over there,' said Mirek. 'I wouldn't want to live in Austria', I said, and Mirek thought it better to switch back to Prague.[8]

Subsequent developments among environmental activists suggest that Chernobyl marked the beginning of a sea-change in popular perceptions of nuclear power in Eastern Europe. It is important to realise that nuclear power is an issue on which there had been very little disagreement between the rulers and the ruled. The official policy has always been that exploitation of this resource is indispensable if the 'socialist' countries are to sustain economic growth, increase production and living standards, etc. And people assumed that nuclear plants could not be more dangerous to health and environment than the existing power stations. As John Harper wrote in the *Guardian* a year ago,

> Until Chernobyl, most of the Soviet bloc's environmentalists were actively in favour of nuclear energy. It offered an apparently cleaner way to generate electricity than fossil fuel-fired power stations. In Eastern Europe this is a particularly serious problem because most run on highly sulphurous lignite ('soft or 'brown' coal).[9]

The clearest instance of this change was furnished by the region's best-known environmental movement, which arose in Hungary in the early-to-mid 1980s, in protest at a joint Hungarian–Czechoslovak project, subsidised by Austria, to build a hydroelectric complex on the Danube. This single-issue movement contains several distinct though not separate groupings, of which the most prominent are the Danube Circle – recipients of the Alternative Nobel Prize – and the 'Blues'. The movement always favoured nuclear power over the ecological and agricultural havoc which the barrage project now seems certain, alas, to wreak. Two of the Danube Circle's leading lights told a foreign reporter, in the immediate aftermath of Chernobyl, that they would not fight nuclear energy.

Both accepted the official argument that the Hungarian nuclear plant at Paks is of a later, safer design than the Chernobyl reactor ... 'Compared with the dam or the coal-fired stations, nuclear power looks like a rational way of supplying our energy needs', Judit Vásárhelyi said. 'A nuclear plant doesn't destroy the landscape and we have installed more safety measures than the Soviet Union.'

The Blues, on the other hand, issued a post-Chernobyl statement criticising the Soviet authorities for not supplying prompt information, and calling on the Hungarian government to find other means of producing energy that would avoid both the perils of nuclear power and the damage of the barrage.[10]

But a recent (1987) account of Hungarian environmentalism says that the Paks nuclear plant 'has come to be regarded with suspicion by the population since the Soviet reactor accident.' Similarly, GDR ecology activist Wolfgang Rüddenklau recently admitted that 'the independent environmental movement' had 'held back on nuclear energy', but 'Then came 26 April 1986, the Chernobyl catastrophe, and we woke up.'[11] In November 1986 the GDR independent groups held their third annual ecology seminar; 100 people from 36 groups attended, and nuclear power was on the agenda. In Czechoslovakia, Charta 77's April 1987 document on pollution, called 'Let the People Breathe', discussed the dangers of nuclear power as well as the need for filters on coal-burning plants.

As early as 21 May 1986, the *Wall Street Journal* announced that 'Western speculation that the accident would trigger ecological groups in Eastern Europe to challenge their governments' ambitious nuclear energy plans hasn't come to pass.' It is worth pausing over this remark, which reveals such typically Western misunderstanding of the nature of autonomous activity, and the role of independent activism, in these societies. The reporter obviously missed the emergence of Czechoslovakia's first ever anti-nuclear power group, Antiatom, a mere fortnight after Chernobyl; but that apart, Rüddenklau provides an explanation which a moment's thought by the *Journal*'s staffer should have supplied:

> Nor were there spectacular campaigns and demonstrations by GDR environmentalists even after Chernobyl. We knew the issue was red-hot and we must accordingly act with caution. We have cured ourselves of running straight at an open knife ... If for example we were to demonstrate in front of the nuclear power station at Lubmin, the authorities would rejoice. It would be another chance for them to seize so justifiably.

Václav Havel, the Czechoslovak playwright and Chartist, once described the East European democratic opposition as working in the 'fifth column of social consciousness'. Such work may be invisible and has to be long term, an accumulative process, not something which can be 'triggered' into confrontation. Although they mobilise on specific issues, peace and ecological groups in Eastern Europe regard themselves as *social movements* rather than 'campaigns'. They want evolution, not revolution, and they see this as achievable by enlarging the sphere of *civil society* in their countries.[12] One of the best-informed British observers of the East European political scene, Timothy Garton Ash, was moved to write this, in the course of considering Chernobyl's effects on the region:

> If you look *from above*, at the formal, official structures of the system and the empire, you may well see 'no change' or, at best, very small change. But if you look *from below*, from the point of view of the individual man or woman living in one of these countries, then a great deal has changed, is changing and will continue to change – in practice, though not in theory.[13]

It cannot be stressed enough, however, that environmental concern in Eastern Europe and the Soviet Union is not limited to groups outside state institutions and structures; nor is environmental activism – in a broad sense – restricted to those whom Western media and politicians like to call 'dissidents', and their Eastern counterparts prefer to dub 'anti-social elements' or 'hooligans'. On the contrary; although these unofficial groups are now more numerous and more inclined to oppose nuclear power than at any time since they first appeared in the 1970s, the issues they address, and the *anxiety* they express, are echoed by state representatives and official bodies, as well as by sectors of the population which would rightly deny any connection, or even sympathy, with unofficial groups.

Czechoslovakia, Poland, the GDR and, to a lesser degree, Hungary have long been recognised as ecological disaster-areas. At one level, this means that nature has been devastated by growth-fixated, corner-cutting industrialism and quick-return agriculture. More than half the woodlands of Bohemia and Moravia are likely to be damaged irreparably by the end of the century. The GDR reportedly has the most advanced 'forest death' in the world, caused by acid rain, and its flora and fauna are being extinguished by large-scale chemical farming; Polish water pollution has made the country's major rivers unfit even for industrial use. The list of horrors could be extended for many pages.

But as one Polish activist put it to some visitors from Britain, 'This is not a matter of national parks – children are dying from air pollution and poisoned water, our natural resources are over-exploited, and much of this is past the stage where it can be reversed. Chernobyl was just an alarm signal.'[14] Environmental degradation endangers people's health on a scale and to an extent otherwise unknown outside the Third World. In 1980, for instance, in Czechoslovakia's northern Bohemia coal region, the still-birth and infant-mortality rate was 20 per cent (the highest regional rate in the UK was 5 per cent), and only 38 per cent of teenagers were free from respiratory, digestive, skin and bone diseases. In Poland, around Katowice, the annual fallout of 900–1,000 tonnes of dust per sq km results in 15 per cent more circulatory disease, 30 per cent more cancers, and 47 per cent more respiratory diseases than in the rest the country.[15] In Hungary,

> three-quarters of our drinking-water reservoirs are in danger and the drinking water of 1,500 communities is already unfit for human consumption. We are proportionately the fourth worst air polluters in Europe and the exploitative attitude to our forests continues ... More serious than the concrete facts, however, is that the rate of destruction is accelerating and that there are no mechanisms to stop this process within the present structures.[16]

Again, the litany could be extended almost indefinitely.

Threatening as it does the basic wellbeing of the people and ultimately the very 'foundations of industrial and agricultural production',[17] this situation has demanded the attention of the authorities. In the early 1980s the Polish and Czechoslovak Academies of Science produced long reports on the environmental crisis. The Czechoslovak report was not released, but Charta 77 publicised and endorsed its conclusions. The nine-volume Polish report warned of 'disaster throughout Poland' unless industrial policy were changed. Similar papers are submitted by other scientific associations, both official and unofficial. For instance, the Hungarian National Council for the Protection of the Environment and Nature – dismissed by a member of the Blues as 'nothing more than a piece of window-dressing' – recommended in a 1984 report that the Danube barrage scheme be scrapped or resited; and at least one member of the Hungarian Academy of Sciences is known to have supported the Danube

Circle. Concerned GDR scientists have contested the official dictum that economic growth must take priority over protection of the environment. In Czechoslovakia, Charta 77 is known as the channel for objective and expert criticism of environmental abuse.

In Poland, a report was issued after Chernobyl by the Social Committee for Learning and the Social Committee for Health – two technically illegal bodies comprising unnamed academics and medical experts, including members of the Academy of Sciences. The report declared that 'The behaviour of the Polish state authorities ... is indicative of incompetence and a desire to conceal the true situation and is no guarantee of safety in the future.' Also in Poland, five scientists who had been dismissed from the national nuclear research institute for objecting to the Soviet model of plant being built at Zarnowiec, sent an open letter on 16 May 1986 to the Minister of Energy, appealing for safety measures at the plant to be improved. Two weeks later, 18 senior academics wrote to to the Polish premier, asking that competent international authorities be given a voice in the construction of Zarnowiec. At the end of July the head of the Energy Problems Unit of the Polish Academy of Sciences, Dr Bojarski, published an article called 'Being More Modest about Nuclear Power', in the official Catholic weekly paper. He concluded with the thought that a country which still couldn't mass-produce the simplest sort of central-heating valve really must keep a sense of proportion in its nuclear plans ...

In the GDR, Poland and Yugoslavia the gravity of environmental degradation is now even acknowledged in the official media, if often obliquely and with scant mention of responsibility. And there is increasingly frank reference to environmental issues in specialist journals, though here too there is no open debate.[18]

There is an obvious tension here, indeed a potential contradiction, between the genuine if strictly limited scope for offically-sanctioned discussion of environmental questions, and the almost invariable repression of autonomous environmental initiatives. This tension is inevitable as long as official ideology promotes inexorable and limitless growth as a necessary condition of socialism, yet is unable to suppress all dissenting opinion on the human and natural cost of that ideology. (The constitutions of these states, it should be remembered, contain clauses about care and preservation of the natural environment.) The official Polish newspaper *Zycie Warszawy* bluntly summarised the purest ideological line in 1982: 'Environmental pollution is the price that has to be paid for industrial development and the development of civilisation.' Yet neither the Polish nor the other Warsaw Pact authorities can prevent ever more broadly-based criticism of this policy, from people within as well as outside official structures who find the price unacceptably high.

Thus, on the one hand, GDR state suppliers donate saplings for church-associated groups to carry out tree-planting sessions; while on the other, state police persecute the church environmental group at the Zionskirche in Berlin, seizing their library and rounding up their members, without 'provocation' (as happened in November 1987). The seriousness with which the GDR state takes environmental activism can be judged from the fact that an official forum, the Society for Nature and the Environment, was established in 1980, as an attempt to coopt unofficial groups. And the Ecology Club – the PKE – which set up under Solidarnosc in 1980, and collected 20,000 members within a few months, now serves a similar function in Poland. Likewise the Slovenian Association of Ecological Groups, in Yugoslavia – although the relative flexibility of political orthodoxy in Slovenia allows greater scope for unofficial attitudes within the Association. But the inherent ambiguity of such a body can rebound on the state; and the healthier the civil society, the more likely the body is to assert its independence. Thus in May 1986, the committee of the PKE issued an open letter to the Speaker of the Polish parliament, asking for a public debate – and recommending a referendum – on the future of the Polish nuclear industry. And on another recent occasion the PKE even offered to pay fines imposed on Wolnosc i Pokoj activists.

In 1987 there was a fascinating illustration of the anomalies of environmental debate in Eastern Europe when Christa Wolf – arguably the greatest writer in German today, and author of *Cassandra* (1983), an exploration through Greek myth of Cold War militarism – published her latest book, *Störfall*, in the GDR, her homeland. The book includes a record of the (autobiographical) narrator's reactions to Chernobyl. She explicitly rejects nuclear power: '... I informed somebody that the risk of nuclear technology cannot be compared with any other risk, and that even the least element of risk means that we must absolutely reject this technology ...' The narrator does not take the official Soviet line – that Chernobyl was a consequence of human error – but sees it rather as the entirely logical outcome of our technocratic society's misdirection. So the country's most famous writer voiced sentiments which had never been allowed official expression. What's more, the book was published in record time and to generally favourable reviews – even in *Neues Deutschland*, the party newspaper. To cap it all, the Deputy Minister for Culture has described *Störfall* as one of his favourite recent books, and Wolf was given a slot on television to read from her book.[19]

The Western peace movements which reacted (or didn't) to Chernobyl had of course existed before 1979, but the massive surge in their numbers and activity was catalysed by the NATO 'twin-track' decision, taken in December of that year, to deploy US intermediate nuclear force missiles in Western Europe – the famous cruise and Pershing – ostensibly to offset the build-up of Soviet SS-20s in the USSR.

In the five countries where the 'Euromissiles' were due to be deployed – Britain, the Netherlands, Belgium, Italy and the German Federal Republic – there were huge mobilisations against nuclear weapons. In the FRG alone, in the 'hot autumn' of 1983, between 2 and 3 million citizens were involved in a series of demonstrations. In the Hague, that same autumn, 350,000 marched against cruise; and in Rome, 600,000. The British Campaign for Nuclear Disarmament's national membership soared from under 5,000 in the late 1970s to 100,000 in 1984. Peace groups and organisations which had lain dormant through the 1970s were suddenly inundated with members, and not only in the deployment countries: peace activism was revitalised throughout the West. New groups sprang up, of almost every conceivable political loyalty and religious denomination. All at once nuclear weapons were a topic of everyday discussion and controversy. The scientistic blindfolds and euphemisms of nuclear weapons and defence jargon percolated into general usage. Women made an historic contribution to the 'new' peace movements, in the face of incredible aggression and mockery outside, and some uncertainty from within the movements themselves. Enthralled Leftist philosophers and sociologists propounded theories to account for this, the biggest and broadest social protest movement in recent European history.

It is dangerous to generalise about so multinational and heterodox a phenomenon, whose history still remains to be written and is still being made. But it seems safe to say that at its base lay two things: a fundamental fear and rejection of nuclear weapons, and a disgust with political justifications for their existence in ever-increasing numbers. This second element implied, in turn, a rejection of the undemocratic process by which decisions as momentous as those concerning nuclear weapons are taken.

The Western peace movements showed the (practical, immediate) strengths and the (analytical, longer-term) weaknesses which inevitably characterise such single-issue fundamentalist protest. They tended to resist tracing the nuclear conflict to its political sources, which were international. Hence their general indifference to bloc politics and to Eastern Europe (except, for obvious reasons, in the Federal Republic); and their sluggishness over Third World conflict – most glaringly, over Afghanistan. *Tygodnik Mazowsze* was, therefore, simply stating a truism when it remarked in 1987 that 'The greater part of the Western peace and ecology movements are still not interested in what is happening in Eastern Europe.'[20]

Not that this indifference was uniform or unanimous. Rather, it has provided the dominant context for internationalist initiatives within the Western movements. The most articulate such initiative has addressed itself above all to the question of relations with Eastern Europe and the USSR. It began with and grew out of a document called the European

Nuclear Disarmament Appeal, launched in London in 1980. The Appeal's originality lay not so much in its location of Cold War, and thus the arms race, in a divided Europe, as in its emphasis on the mutual interest of the superpowers in maintaining Cold War, and on the need for peace movements to be actively non-aligned in their work for a rapprochement between the two halves of Europe. The Appeal calls for unregulated, informal contact between people everywhere, who want to break down the blocs. 'The remedy lies in our own hands', it said:

> We must act together to free the entire territory of Europe, from Poland to Portugal, from nuclear weapons, air and submarine bases, and from all institutions engaged in research into or manufacture of nuclear weapons ... We envisage a Europe-wide campaign, in which every type of exchange takes place; in which representatives of different nations and opinions confer and co-ordinate their activities; and in which less formal exchanges, between universities, churches, women's organisations, trade unions, youth organisations, professional groups and individuals, take place with the object of promoting a common object: to free all Europe from nuclear weapons.
>
> We must commence to act as if a united, neutral and pacific Europe already exists. We must learn to be loyal, not to 'East' or 'West', but to each other, and we must disregard the prohibitions and limitations imposed by any national state.[21]

The Appeal quickly gained thousands of signatories from all over Europe, though very few from the Eastern half, and 'European Nuclear Disarmament' became a distinct and influential strand within the Western peace movements.

The signatory groups' main institutional activity has, since 1982, been the annual END Conventions, which bring together peace activists from all over the world. Their main practical activity – less visible but much more valuable – has been a dialogue between Western movements and independent Eastern intellectuals, and civil liberties and peace activists. The partners in this dialogue were united by a belief that the Appeal and its agenda provided a new basis for advancing out of the sterile reflex-reactions and antinomies of Cold War thinking. It got under way in 1981, and has continued with exchanges of letters and personal visits – what has come to be known as 'citizens' détente' or 'détente from below'. The difficulties have been immense. To start with, a backlog of prejudice and mistrust (why were the Western peace movements so pusillanimous over Solidarnosc in 1980–1? How could the Easterners tolerate US imperialism?) meant that, for progress even to be possible, both sides had to unpack and re-examine their basic political lexicons.

The crux of the dialogue has been the linkage of *peace* and *human rights* (but as the latter term is so enthusiastically commandeered by Western reactionaries who use it selectively, showing little concern for such rights in Third World countries whose repressive regimes are supported by the West, I shall continue to call them *civil liberties*). Participants in the dialogue from, for instance, Poland and the GDR differed in their analyses of this linkage and of Cold War itself; but on the whole, the East European partners tended to believe that the Westerners might be ready to settle for 'peace at any price' – even capitulation to Soviet dominance – rather than striving for 'peace with justice and dignity' (Charta 77). Conversely the Westerners tended to believe that their partners underestimated the nuclear threat and so did not grant mere disarmament its due importance. What the partners shared from the outset was a conviction that nuclear weapons are not the cause of the conflict which they symbolise so potently, and that peace protest must address itself to causes.

Nor was the dialogue taking place in a neutral environment. On the contrary: it became clear that non-alignment was indeed just what the Cold War antagonists could not tolerate.[22] The Westerners were accused of pro-Sovietism, or of being the Kremlin's 'useful idiots'; the Easterners were subject to all the persecution and abuse that their regimes reserve for independent thinkers and doers: they were constantly harassed and sometimes sacked, locked up, beaten up, hospitalised. At the same time they were being discouraged from a fruitless pursuit by members of other oppositional and unofficial groups, who for various reasons could not see the point of dialogue. And they were undermined from another direction by the Peace Councils: official bodies which never criticised Warsaw Pact policy and whose role was to coopt the Western movements' Eastward attentions.

It became clear, too, that certain vocal sections of the Western movements were not in favour of talking to unofficial groups in the East. One reason for this was that Western communist parties and some far-left groups involved with the peace movements would not endorse the criticism of Soviet policy which non-alignment obviously entails (END Appeal: We do not wish to apportion guilt between the political and military leaders of East and West. Guilt lies squarely upon both parties'). These groups, moreover, had often staunchly supported the peace groups during their barren years. Another factor, especially in ever-insular Britain, was the less conscious anti-Americanism among grassroots peace activists, who after all were busy opposing US weapons, and if they took a strategic political position at all, were 'against' Atlanticism. The grassroots and direct-action groups could hardly *practise* an internationalist analysis of the arms race in any regular way, even if they knew about and sympathised with it, as many undoubtedly did. To put it another way, they didn't have the chance to meet and talk with East Europeans.

Rather more important, though, was the reluctance to complicate or compromise (fateful word!) the 'single issue' of disarmament. (Women peace activists, too, were criticised within the movements because they insisted that the links between missiles and militarism, social violence, gender, etc. were no less urgent than disarmament itself.) This reluctance went with the vain hope – which stemmed from a fear of being dragged into party-political bickering and so losing ecumenical appeal – that it would be possible to avoid 'politicising' the issue.

On the level of policy, anti-nuclear fundamentalism favoured unilateral disarmament. As General Secretary Gorbachev has demonstrated, 'unilateralism' can be an open and flexible concept, embracing all sorts of initiatives; and although it has been abused – in Britain, perhaps irreparably – by anti-disarmers, the peace movements have done all too little to emphasise that openness and flexibility. By insisting on unilateral disarmament as a national act – a moral example to be set by a single country – which *might* have good international consequences by breaking the log-jam, the peace movements laid themselves open to highly effective propaganda accusations of shamelessly appeasing the insatiable Russian bear. (It is, incidentally, interesting to speculate how far this insistence, in Britain, is an inversion of our chronic post-imperial self-inflation – yet another case of granting ourselves more global weight than we can possibly possess.) This narrow interpretation of unilateralism was, in effect, nationalist. If you accept that each country's peace movement should work first and foremost to get rid of its own arsenal of weapons, whether they be NATO missiles or 'independent nuclear deterrents' (or, in Britain's unique case, both), then not only will non-alignment appear too 'theoretical' a position to be worth the effort of propounding and defending: it will actually be a damaging position, as it is very liable to obstruct the tactical political alliances which are indispensable if disarmament policies are ever to be implemented.

This, anyway, in the early 1980s, is how it looked to Western peace movements, which needed to strengthen their intrinsic alliances with social democratic and other opposition parties in the German Federal Republic, Britain, Italy, the Netherlands and Belgium (all the Euromissile deployment countries had pro-deployment, Right or Centre-Right governments). And social democratic parties, which have been a pillar of peace movement strength, often proved no keener than communist parties to cultivate dialogue with Eastern Europe's unofficial peace activists, although their reason is different: they won't risk disrupting East–West relations, and thus the détente of conventional *Ostpolitik*. This dialogue is bound to involve such risks, because, whether the issue is peace or ecology, what is at stake from both the authorities' and the unofficial groups' points of view is nothing less than the legitimacy of government, and political change, in Eastern Europe.

The East European groups which engage in this dialogue include the very ones whose statements after Chernobyl were discussed above: Charta 77 in Czechoslovakia, Solidarnosc and Wolnosc i Pokoj in Poland, church-related and other groups in the GDR, Hungarian environmentalists. While there are groups and individuals specifically concerned with the environment or peace, there is very little practical demarcation between one kind of activism and the other, for these are not 'single issues'. If a 'single issue' campaign exists for these groups, it is the campaign for democracy, social justice and civil liberties, which encompasses issues of peace or the environment.

Their understanding of 'peace' does not mirror the Western movements' standard stress on disarmament; peace, for them, means in the first place creating a society without institutionalised causes of conflict. Hence 'dignity and justice'. There can be no peace without the freedom of speech and travel, without the freedom to meet, organise, write and publish. As Jan Minkiewicz, now the Western representative of Wolnosc i Pokoj, wrote more than five years ago, in the first issue of *END Journal*: 'If the Western world wants a stabilised Europe, Left and Right must understand that Eastern European societies will continue to claim their rights and fight for them regardless of fluctuations in East–West relations and in disarmament talks.' Practically, for these groups peace campaigning means anti-militarist campaigning: raising questions about conscription, conscientious objection and militarism in education, rather than resisting particular weapon deployments.

We have seen how, after Chernobyl, East European protest was directed at state secrecy and undemocratic power. Something that strikes Western readers of Eastern unofficial texts on peace and environmentalism is the speed with which they become discussions of civil liberties and political change. To quote an example at random: the editor of the Hungarian magazine *Vizjel* ('Watermark'), the first independent environmental journal in Eastern Europe, said recently that, in the light of Hungary's environmental problems, 'the most pressing need' today

is for a unitary ministry of environmental protection with the necessary authority to carry out its tasks. In order to find a way out of this situation both discussions and social initiatives are necessary. For this reason work by environmentalist groups would have to be permitted and an effective legal procedure against environmental pollution should also be available to the individual citizen. In local communities, the conditions should be provided for genuine self-government.[23]

Here, as in the statements quoted earlier, the language of environmental activism merges naturally and inevitably with the language of political reform.

Exactly because the regimes of Eastern Europe are, in the eyes of so many of their citizens, not legitimate, these regimes perceive autonomous social initiatives as a threat to their power, even when these initiatives are as far from harbouring insurrectionary intentions as, say, a peace group's effort to ban war-toys. Outside parts of Yugoslavia, all the known attempts at independent peace activism in 'socialist' countries have been harshly treated, especially anything internationalist or to do with conscientious objection. The most notable early initiative was the Hungarian Peace Group for Dialogue in 1982, which was 'committed to the END idea' and, in a founder-member's words, was 'formed to heighten awareness of the nuclear threat and convince citizens that something could be done'.[24] The group collapsed under the weight of repression. Groups in the GDR which cultivated relations with END groups in the West were even more fiercely dealt with; and the Trust Group came to have almost as many members exiled in the West as inside the Soviet Union. As Václav Havel wrote in 1985:

> To speak out against the rockets here means, in effect, to become a 'dissident'. Concretely, it means the complete transformation of one's life ... It means becoming a member of that microscopic 'suicide pact' enclave surrounded, to be sure, by the unspoken good wishes of the public but at the same time by the unspoken amazement over the fact that anyone would choose to risk so much for something as hopeless as seeking to change what cannot be changed.[25]

While environmentalism is always viewed as potentially subversive, there is greater space for it than for independent peace activism (there could not easily be less). Even in the GDR, an environmental protest is more likely to be tolerated than a peace action which uses identical tactics. One reason is that, as we have seen, officially-sanctioned environmental organisations have some room for manoeuvre and effective action, and share some of the same ground as independent environmental groups. Another, related reason is that peace issues are seen as a challenge to the state in the incomparably sensitive area of national security, whereas the environment is a vaguer notion, less clearly bound to power. As in the West, peace is seen as directly 'political' whereas the environment is only indirectly so. Related again is the crucial fact that peace issues simply don't evoke anything like so much popular support as environmental ones: because official propaganda has appropriated and devalued the word 'peace'; because anti-Sovietism is widespread in Eastern as in Western Europe, and non-alignment is even more suspect; because any sort of peace activism is punished so harshly; because nuclear weapons there are hidden, invisible and undiscussible; because everybody experiences the horrors of environmental abuse every day, whether through their windows or in their poisoned bodies.

If independent peace politics have yet to touch a popular chord in Eastern Europe, in the Soviet Union itself they barely exist. Environmental questions, on the other hand, produced in the 1970s what one commentator has called 'the first mass movement of public opinion the country had seen'. The catalyst was the ecological plight of Lake Baikal. 'Scientists, lawyers, journalists and cultural celebrities' joined forces and eventually

> the state was persuaded to install purification equipment in the factories, and then to stop all discharges into the lake. The same coalition came together again to fight the proposals to reverse the flow of Siberian rivers so that their water could be used to irrigate the dry lands of the Muslim south. A gigantic scheme of great ecological risk, the river-reversal project was steadily criticised in what became a remarkable public debate in the Soviet media.[26]

The comparison with the beleaguered Trust Group is painfully obvious. The people who are brought together by environmental campaigns are not necessarily political radicals or potential converts to 'green' philosophy; here as everywhere, environmentalism tinges all parts of the political spectrum. Tolstoyan populism and a long tradition of Russian nature-romanticism lie behind many ecological utterances by 'respectable' Russian writers – some of whom were involved in the Baikal campaign – and accounts for the ecological content of so much Russian art.

The indifference or reticence of many Western movements towards Eastern Europe helps to explain their nationalistic reactions in 1986; 'Chernobyl can happen here' is a salutary response but hardly adequate by itself. Yet some Western movements did not protest at all after Chernobyl, for peace and environmental issues are still defined very differently in the West; the balance varies from country to country, but in general a division of labour brings nuclear disarmament under the peace movements' wing and puts civil nuclearism firmly on the environmental agenda.

So it was that in the Netherlands the Interchurch Peace Council, the country's most influential peace group – which has a fine record of 'citizens' détente' – did nothing about Chernobyl, leaving it to ecology groups. The same happened in Sweden, where the Swedish Peace and Arbitration Society, which is the biggest peace organisation in the country and has no political qualms about getting involved in East–West work, did not react.

In Britain, where the three biggest national peace and ecology organisations happened to hear the news of Chernobyl simultaneously, at a three-way meeting, CND and Friends of the Earth had problems after they decided on a joint response (the third, Greenpeace, did not get involved). The problems were those of organisations under high pressure, with different styles and no habit of collaboration. When they staged a silent demonstration outside the Department of Energy on 1 May, FoE turned up in black, while CND's contingent was kitted out in white radiation suits. Then the symbolic action turned into an impromptu march to the Soviet embassy, which aggrieved the environmentalists. These hitches were not reflected at local level: that autumn, CND and FoE groups demonstrated together at Sizewell and Sellafield nuclear power stations. But the two did not work together again at national level until they arranged the April 1987 anniversary rally in Hyde Park (in which Greenpeace too was invited but declined to participate).

At that local level, the same individuals are often the backbone of both peace and environmental groups, campaigning against nuclear weapons deployment one week and a new nuclear reactor the next. In this sense the organisations are lagging behind their memberships. This in itself is one excellent reason to question the division of labour. Are there others? Bruce Kent, the Chair of the organisation, wrote in 1986 that 'CND wisely remains a single-issue campaign';[27] yet how wise this is surely depends on what the single issue includes and what it excludes.

It seems to me that there are several reasons why the British movement – meaning that major part of it which is represented by CND – would benefit from redefining its 'single issue'. First, there is the fact, both scientific and political, of the link between civil and military nuclear technology, and the intimately related matter of undemocratic decision-making which shrouds nuclear affairs everywhere. CND regularly renews a commitment at its annual conferences to campaign against nuclear power; yet the campaigning in this area is never given the profile it deserves.

The mere fact of the power–weapons connection is quite well known by now; but it has just been given the most emphatic confirmation by Cabinet papers released under the 30 year rule. At the start of 1988 the public finally gained access to information about the Windscale reactor fire of 1957. The contamination, it emerges, was much worse than at Three Mile Island – known hitherto as the worst nuclear accident before Chernobyl. Although it presented no security risk, a Committee of Inquiry report prepared under the leadership of an official of the Atomic Weapons Research Establishment was suppressed by Prime Minister Macmillan, for fears that its revelations of incompetence would discourage the USA from cooperating with Britain in atomic weapons research (specifically, on the hydrogen bomb) and shake public confidence in atomic power. Secrecy, nationalism, civil–military interdependence, superpower might, all against a Cold War backdrop: it would be hard to *invent* a scenario which crammed so many nuclear weasels into one sack! The whole scandalous business is a timely reminder that military and civil nuclearism are two sides of a coin, and need to be treated as such by their opponents.

Secondly, the disarmament movements lost support (or more accurately, lost vitality) after the deployment of the Euromissiles in 1983–5, and seem set to lose still more with the signing of the INF treaty in Washington in December 1987. Not, of course, because there is no need for further disarmament – as if the loss of some 4 per cent of the global stockpile suddenly makes us safe! But because the missiles themselves, symbols of nuclear madness and of US dominance, will have gone (the Euromissiles' one virtue, after all, is their conspicuousness). The vital 'first step' of disarmament – which the INF deal is too easily taken to be – seems very likely to deflate movements which were so energised by governments' stark blindness to the plain sanity of their demands. There is a precedent here, in the demobilisation of the 'first-generation' peace movements after the Partial Test Ban Treaty of 1963.

Thirdly, it has become clear since Chernobyl that, as in the East, anti-nuclear power protest has much potential support where anti-weapons protest has little or none. In Britain, the memberships of FoE and Greenpeace, which both campaign vigorously against nuclear power, providing both expert information and local actions, have waxed as CND's has waned. In France, the country with the most developed nuclear power programme in the world as well as its own arsenal of nuclear weapons, ailing anti-nuclear groups have revived in the wake of public anger at the state's arrogant response to Chernobyl. For a full fortnight, the authorities denied that any radioactivity had so much as crossed French borders. An anti-nuclear coalition called the *Réseau pour un Avenir Sans Nucléaire* was resurrected; but the most practical and impressive response to state mendacity was the establishment of 'alternative' radiation information centres by concerned scientists. Called CRII-Rad (*Commission Régionale d'Indépendence sur la Radioactivité*), the project began in the south of France but has spread and grown. For almost a decade, both the military and civil programmes have been approved by all the major political parties and, overwhelmingly, by public opinion. Chernobyl may have cracked this consensus.[28]

Fourthly, with the INF treaty now signed, the peace movements are in a new international and strategic situation, very different to the frozen immobility of their formative moment at the end of the 1970s. It is already clear that NATO, having given an inch with the INF deal, will take back two inches if it can; the Alliance intends to make 'compensatory adjustments' for the doomed Euromissiles by deploying and developing new warheads, for use in the air and at sea. Yet there are gulfs of disagreement between the member states over the remaining nuclear weapons, and at the same time the US military commitment to Europe looks more fragile than at any time in NATO's history. Scarcely a week now goes by without the Federal Republic and France, or France and Britain, meeting to discuss defence integration and collaboration. A joint Franco-German army brigade, to be set up in October 1988, is described by Chancellor Helmut Kohl as 'the nucleus which will develop ... At the end of this road there must be a common European defence with a European army.' *Ostpolitik* diplomacy in central Europe is no less frenetic, with Western and Eastern political leaders expressing more interest in each other than for many a year, and West German leaders stating their impatience with US-imposed restrictions on technology exports to the Eastern bloc. (The Federal Republic, remember, has contracts to sell post-Chernobyl safety technology for Soviet nuclear reactors ...) The European Community and Comecon are moving closer together. The arch-conservative Bavarian leader Franz-Josef Strauss went to Moscow in January 1988, and pronounced 'the post-war period' to be 'over': 'We are in a new game, a new era has begun.'

In the Soviet Union, Mikhail Gorbachev has set in motion reforms which were unimaginable only five or six years ago, in the Brezhnevite stasis. People who spent the early 1980s as political prisoners are now establishing legal groups – 'clubs' – which debate and publish on controversial political issues. In Hungary the People's Patriotic Front, an official mass organisation, has raised the question of the eventual need for legal opposition parties. Ripples from the epicentre are beginning to affect even the most reactionary Warsaw Pact states. The Czechoslovak regime, comatose for 20 years, has a new leader who speaks of overhauling the economy (though he wants the *perestroika* – 'restructuring' – without the *glasnost* – 'openness'). Alexander Dubček, disgraced party leader of the Prague Spring, has surfaced after nearly two decades' silence, passionately defending reform communism in an interview with Italian journalists. At the end of 1987, GDR leader Erich Honecker paid his long-postponed first visit to the Federal Republic. Even in Romania there are twitches of official dissent and popular protest against President Ceausescu's despotism.

As these changes and new alliances are sketched, the Cold War appears more than ever an 'imaginary war'.[29] Yet there is no reason to think that the European 'new era' ushered in by Western and Eastern leaders will have much in common with the Europe adumbrated in the END Appeal, nuclear weapons-free and bloc-free. Imagine instead a continent combining the more technocratic and socially regressive features of both systems: libertarian economics and social values, meshing harmoniously with ever more centralised and less accountable political processes, as favoured by 'actually existing socialists' and Right authoritarians alike. Already the two superpowers are cooperating on joint nuclear bomb tests, to begin later this year. O brave new era!

Amidst this shifting landscape, peace and ecology groups need as never before to cultivate their own alliances, between and within East and West and North and South. The national disarmament campaigns by different movements should continue (I am thinking of British opposition to Trident submarines, or Swedish campaigns against arms sales and port-calls by nuclear-capable vessels), but they must not define the movements' political horizons. Internal reform and the loosening of superpower bonds yields increasing space for social movements to have real effects in West and East. Already this year, Hungarian officials have been calling for the legalisation of environmental groups. In the USSR, the official news agency Tass reported that a hydroelectric project in Lithuania has been dropped after more than 30,000 people wrote to the authorities in protest; and this year, in unprecedented admissions, the Soviet press has reported that construction of two nuclear plants is being abandoned after strong local resistance. The official Soviet line on ecology is shifting too: communism is no longer the indispensable precondition for resolving the crisis.[30] Western non-aligned groups, whose pressure on Eastern regimes has always been valued by independent groups for helping to ease their conditions, can help Eastern initiatives to use these new opportunities and enlarge the scope for autonomous activity.

Even in the headiest days of the early 1980s, disarmament movements were always minority movements; and one valuable result of the continuing experiment in non-aligned East–West dialogue is that we know now that neither the Western nor the Eastern conceptions of peace activism are sufficient to generate solidarity between social movements across the blocs. As we have seen, environmental issues enjoy far wider support in the East than questions of peace; in the West, it is increasingly clear that issues of nuclear disarmament are indeed, as Easterners have maintained all along, interdependent with environmental and civil liberties issues. For without full democracy, we know that the fragile achievement of the INF deal can easily be reversed or undone.

In the lean late 1980s – and, I suspect, in the 1990s – peace movements will either starve, more or less slowly, on their single-issue diets, or take the next step into environmental politics. In many countries green/peace coalitions are beginning to take shape under the auspices of green parties and movements. In Austria and Italy, the recent rise of green parties was intimately connected with campaigns against nuclear power. (It is significant that these campaigns, like other environmental issues East and West, very often foster transnationalism: think of the Franco-Belgian-German demonstrations at the French Cattenom plant; the Austrian–German protests at Wackersdorf reprocessing plant in Bavaria; the combined Danish–Swedish opposition to the Barsebaeck reactors; the Austrian greens' support for the Danube environmentalists.) The Italian *liste verdi* developed into a political force in the course of the campaign for a referendum on nuclear power – a campaign which was mobilised by

Chernobyl, and probably owed its eventual success to it. *Ecopacifismo* now has its own voice in the Italian senate. Can it be coincidence that Italian peace groups now appear finally to have overcome their differences in the interests of creating an umbrella organisation, the new *Associazione per la pace*?

Of course, the referendum was made possible in the first place by the Italian constitution, just as the constitutions of Austria and Sweden made it possible for anti-nuclear groups to campaign successfully against their national nuclear power programmes, and as the West German constitution makes *die Grünen* possible. In a country like Britain, without proportional representation in Parliament, social movements have no direct access to the legislature. (Nuclear issues – always at the razor's edge of state power – never fail to expose the limits of democracy.) Yet this makes 'alternative' alliances and the pooling of resources even more necessary than elsewhere. In Britain, the 'new' peace movements were born partly out of the anti-nuclear power campaigning of the 1970s. The shaky coalitions of that campaign disintegrated in the early 1980s; the time is ripe to rebuild and internationalise them.

Disarmament is intrinsic to green politics, whereas green politics are only latent in disarmament activism, and many Leftists resist any greening process. But increasing numbers of others are moving towards the 'red–green' interface so fruitfully explored by Rudolf Bahro and others. This exploration must continue if the Western environmental movements are to reach political maturity; for they, even more than the majority of Western peace activists, still fight shy of politics. Presciently, Bahro wrote in the early 1980s that 'The ecology crisis is insoluble without overcoming the confrontation between the Eastern and Western blocs, which drives on the arms race and economic growth on both sides, and is thus doubly suicidal.'[31] The foundations have been laid for an environmental dialogue across the blocs, and the first moves have been tentatively made by Western organisations such as Greenpeace and FoE. (International FoE's 1988 annual general meeting is going to be held in the East – Warsaw – for the first time.) These groups do not bear the burden of a heritage of Left politics: they may be able to avoid the sectarianism which has afflicted peace movements. But this is a weakness as well as a strength: there is no room for political naivety in any East–West contacts, whether official or unofficial or (preferably) both. There is no risk of these organisations being sidetracked into purely 'oppositional' contacts, but neither should they let the official bodies condition the terms of these contacts.

No strategic shifts have occurred to invalidate the END Appeal's basic analysis, and an environmental dialogue would be an enrichment of the process which it stimulated. In retrospect, the dialogue which I described above, initiated by the peace movement, has the appearance of a necessary space-clearing for a less constrained, more positive exchange yet to come. At times, what went on in the early-to-mid 1980s was not so much a dialogue as an attempt to create the *conditions* in which dialogue would be possible. The turning point may turn out to have been a seminar organised by Wolnosc i Pokoj in Warsaw, in May 1987. Although many people from the West were denied entry visas, and many Poles were prevented from attending, nevertheless an Eastern group succeeded for the first time in hosting a meeting of activists from both sides of the bloc divide. Participants were able to talk through, without fear of outside distortion or obstruction, their affinities and differences on civil liberties, disarmament, ecology, 'individual responsibility for peace', political issues and political values. This event, unprecedented in post-war, Cold War history, offers a model for the future.

Notes

1. Hans Blix, 'The Chernobyl reactor accident: the international significance and results', in *SIPRI Yearbook 1987*, Oxford University Press.
2. Much information in this chapter about Soviet and East European independent peace and environmental activity is gleaned from the following magazines: *Across Frontiers* (PO Box 2382, Berkeley, CA 94702, USA); *East European Reporter (EER)* (PO Box 222, London WC2H 9RP, UK); *END Journal* (11 Goodwin Street, London N4 3HQ, UK); and *Labour Focus on Eastern Europe (LFEE)* (c/o Crystal Management, 46 Theobalds Road, London WC1 8NW, UK). Also from the book *From Below: Independent Peace and Environmental Movements in Eastern Europe and the USSR*, published in 1987 by US Helsinki Watch (36 West 44th Street, New York, NY 10036, USA); and from 'The Chernobyl Challenge', a dossier compiled by the Rainbow Group in the European Parliament in summer 1986. Information on Poland also comes from *Uncensored Poland* bulletin, published by the UK Information Centre for Polish Affairs.
3. *Glasgow Herald*, 2 May 1986.
4. Quoted by Robert Paine, 'Accidents, ideologies and routines: "Chernobyl" over Norway', in *Anthropology Today*, August 1987.
5. Quotation from US *Groundswell* magazine (date unknown); with thanks to Bob McGlynn.
6. *Uncensored Poland*, 11/86.
7. *Tygodnik Mazowsze*, 15 May 1986.
8. Ludvík Vaculík, 'No worries', translated by A.G. Brain in *EER*, vol. 2, no. 2.
9. 'The lessons of Chernobyl', in the *Guardian*, 23 April 1987.
10. The *Economist* Foreign Report, 15 May 1986; 'Danube Blues', in *EER*, vol. 2, no. 2.

11. Hubertus Knabe,' "Unusual methods" – Hungarian ecology crisis', in *LFEE*, vol. 9, no. 2. And 'Nuclear power in the GDR: chipping away a cornerstone', in *EER*, vol. 2, no. 3.

12. The concept of 'civil society' needs to be defined differently for each political culture and system. In essence, as now used by East Europeans, it refers to a 'sphere different to and independent from the sphere of state activities and the political system' (Yugoslav sociologist Tomaz Mastnak, interviewed in *END Journal* 32). Independent self-organising activity takes place within civil society, and in a sense defines and constitutes civil society. The increasing currency of this term in the West is in large part due to the fruitful contact between intellectuals from both 'halves' of Europe.

13. T. Garton Ash, 'We should work like strontium', in *The Spectator*, 5 July 1986.

14. 'Conversations in Poland', in *END Journal* 26.

15. END Briefing Sheet: 'Ecology in Eastern Europe'. (Available from *END Journal*, address above.)

16. Ferenc Langmar interviewed in *LFEE*, vol. 9, no. 2.

17. Andrew Csepel's phrase, from his article in *EER* summer 1985.

18. See Michael Waller's paper, 'Autonomous movements for peace and the ecology in Eastern Europe', prepared for the 1987 annual conference of the National Association for Soviet and East European Studies.

19. Christa Wolf, *Störfall*, Luchterhand Verlag, 1987. (I owe this information to an END supporter who wishes not to be named.)

20. Quoted in *Across Frontiers*, summer-fall 1987.

21. END Appeal reprinted in E.P. Thompson and Dan Smith (eds), *Protest and Survive*, Penguin Books, Harmondsworth 1980.

22. See especially E.P. Thompson, *Double Exposure*, Merlin Press, London, 1985.

23. *LFEE*, vol. 9, no. 2.

24. Andrew White's article in *END Journal* 1.

25. Jan Vladislav, ed., *Vaclav Havel, or Living in Truth*, Faber & Faber, London, 1987, p. 170.

26. Martin Walker, *The Waking Giant: the Soviet Union under Gorbachev*, Sphere Books, London, 1987, p. xxiii.

27. Bruce Kent, 'The peace movements: hopes and achievements', in Dan Smith and E.P. Thompson (eds), *Prospectus for a Habitable Planet*, Penguin Books, London, 1987, p. 221.

28. With thanks to Bernard Dréano and Brendan Prendiville for information supplied.

29. 'The imaginary war' – title of Mary Kaldor's contribution to *Prospectus* (see note 27 above).

30. See Ze'ev Wilson, '*Perestroika* and *glasnost* in environmental

policy', in *Environmental Policy Review* (The Hebrew University, Jerusalem, Israel), 1987.

31. Rudolf Bahro, *Socialism and Survival*, Heretic Books, London, 1982, p. 55.

5

Lines of Longitude:
People's Détente, North and South

LOUIS MACKAY

The dense clouds of radionuclides carried into the sky above the Ukraine by the Chernobyl fire dispersed widely over Europe during the last days of April 1986. Radioactive isotopes of caesium and iodine contaminated the lichen eaten by Lapland's reindeer, the produce of Polish market gardens, the grass of Welsh sheepwalks and the wild thyme and rosemary growing on the *garrigues* of Provence. The indirect fallout travelled much further afield.

A month of confusion passed before the EEC managed to establish a maximum limit for contamination in foodstuffs. Even then, Britain and France went their own way with much less strict standards. In milk, for example, the permitted level of radioactivity according to the European Community rules was 370 Becquerels (Bq) per litre, while Britain allowed 2,000 and France 3,700 (the corresponding figures for the USA and Canada are, respectively, 56 and 10). In spite of the control measures applied to Eastern as well as Western Europe, dangerously irradiated food exports were soon being discovered in many parts of the Third World. Not for the first time, powdered milk, used to feed infants ten times more vulnerable to radiological injury than adults, was one of the principal commodities at the centre of a storm over double standards. A shipment from Poland with over 100 times the permitted level of radioactivity was discovered in Bangladesh in July. Over the course of the summer, similar shipments, involving a wide variety of produce from various European countries including Britain, were found in Malaysia, the Philippines, Singapore, Sri Lanka, Thailand, Egypt, Kuwait, Dubai, Iran, Ghana and Brazil. The governments of Thailand and the Philippines both complained that they had been threatened with the cancellation of big development grants unless they relaxed their radiation safety standards. As late as February 1987, a consignment of milk powder reading 6,000 Bq per kilo was intercepted by the Federal German authorities; it was bound for Africa after standing for months in a siding, loaded into 242 railway wagons.

Not surprisingly there was much public concern wherever such shipments turned up, and local consumer groups did what they could to alert people to the hazards. It was clear that major food companies were deliberately dumping tainted produce in countries where controls and safety checks were known to be inadequate – often relying on random sampling and on nuclear research facilities that were conveniently veiled in secrecy. For every contaminated load detected, it was likely that many would get through.[1]

To the extent that the dumping of irradiated foodstuffs has entailed the circumvention of European controls, it has been illegal. At the same time, a number of European countries, notably Britain, France and Spain, have aligned themselves with the commercial lobby seeking to raise safety thresholds by a factor of five or more – in spite of a new recognition by radiological protection agencies that radiological risks have been seriously underestimated. Here, Mrs Thatcher and her colleagues have been consistent with their attitude towards other environmental issues such as the contamination of water supplies by agricultural chemical residues, the pollution of the Irish and North Seas, the 1985 London Dumping Convention moratorium on radioactive waste disposal at sea and the destruction of the ozone layer by chlorofluorocarbons. On all these questions, Westminster has distinguished itself by its efforts to override the concerns not only of environmentalist groups, but also of other European governments wanting stricter controls. It is worth remarking in passing that what is revealed here is the strength of an inherent tendency towards deregulation in the face of threatened profit rates, which betrays the thinness of the pretence that there would be any possibility of assuring the responsible management of nuclear waste for the thousands of years it will remain dangerous.

Just as the radiological effects of Chernobyl were carried into the Third World, the political fallout also travelled far beyond Europe.

Before Chernobyl, anxiety over the Chinese government's plan to build an 1,800 MW nuclear plant at Daya Bay, near Hong Kong, was confined largely to small environmentalist organisations in the colony. The news shocked people into a realisation of what was being built some 35 miles away, and of the consequences for Hong Kong of a similar accident there. There was no possibility of evacuating the colony. Serious contingency plans did not exist. In the space of two months, a new coalition formed to oppose the project collected over a million signatures at subway stations and ferry terminals for a petition to Beijing. Heated debates erupted in the mass media and opinion polls conducted by the *South China Morning Post* put the level of opposition to the project at 72 per cent.

None of this was enough to persuade the Chinese government to change its plans. The deal with the British and French contractors, GEC and Framatome, was signed in Beijing in September 1986. But the level of concern in Hong Kong has remained high, amid a sense of resignation to the unlikelihood of seeing the project shelved. This has added to the intensity of the new political debates in Hong Kong, which has only nine years of British rule to run, and to a sense that the views of Hong Kong citizens have been unrepresented because the colonial administration, in the absence of any system of direct, democratic accountability, has been firmly under the thumb of the Thatcher government. Britain's main interest has evidently been in getting a contract for a British firm in return for withdrawing from Chinese territory. The UK Atomic Energy Authority has even provided advice to the Hong Kong administration on public relations techniques designed to play down disquieting facts. Thus, in Hong Kong, the Chernobyl accident has focused attention not only on the dangers of nuclear power, but also on the relationship of issues involving nuclear policy-making, democracy and freedom of information.

Across the South China Sea, criticism of Taiwan's nuclear programme has a longer history, with a considerable literature on nuclear hazards published by independent groups campaigning on environmental and civil liberties questions. Anti-nuclear feeling has been rising for many years, particularly since 1983, when plans were announced for a fourth nuclear power station. Taiwan's plans for waste disposal provoked particular concern. In May 1986, shortly after the Chernobyl accident, the decision to proceed with the new project was postponed indefinitely in the face of mounting popular disquiet.[2]

In India, too, reports of the Chernobyl accident served to boost anti-nuclear sentiment. In spite of India's relatively early acquisition of nuclear power, organised challenges to the well-entrenched nuclear establishment have only quite recently begun to gather strength. In academic circles, groups such as the Committee for a Sane Nuclear Policy (COSNUP) have become known for their efforts to stop the Indian government's slide towards realising the nuclear weapons capability it has possessed since 1974, and to promote a South Asian Nuclear Free Zone. But there are now also numerous grassroots campaigns opposing nuclear power. At Krakrapur, for example, in South Gujarat, the construction of two new nuclear plants in an area of seismic activity began to run into organised local opposition in 1985, much of it focused on the planned recycling of waste into plutonium and the links between the civil and military nuclear programmes. Leading opponents of the scheme now include a former Chief Minister in the Gujarat who had previously endorsed it. During the summer of 1986, the protestors prepared for a major demonstration on Hiroshima Day by visiting nearly 300 local villages with performances of a dance drama on Gandhian themes. The demonstration itself drew thousands of people, despite a prohibition by local authorities, and lasted several days. According to one of the organisers, Narayan Desai, the peaceful crowd was subjected to indiscriminate violence by the police, who shot dead a boy in one village and wounded another.[3] Similar vigorous protests have been gathering momentum against the project to build India's sixth nuclear plant in a tropical evergreen rainforest near Kaiga in Karnataka.

One source of inspiration to these campaigns was the defeat by local opposition of the Indian Department of Atomic Energy's plans, announced in 1982, for a nuclear plant at Kothamangalam in Kerala State – the first major instance of open resistance to nuclear power in India. Confronted with determined resistance from people in the area, with the support of an impressive array of public figures (including eight local professors, an archbishop, a former Supreme Court Justice and an ex-Governor of the state), the Site-Selection Committee backed off.

In Brazil, anti-nuclear organisations such as the Movimento Pacifista Brasileiro (MPB), formed in 1984 after the eclipse of the military dictatorship, and with the primary object of opposing any development of nuclear weapons, have been spurred by Chernobyl towards a much broader criticism of the Brazilian nuclear programme in general. The MPB has gained the support of many prominent figures in Brazil's political, cultural, scientific and ecclesiastical circles, including the physicist and rector of the University of São Paolo, Jose Goldemberg, and even the late President-Elect, Tancredo Neves. But until recently, the concerns it has voiced have been more the preoccupation of Brazil's intellectuals than of the general public. What alerted a much wider section of the Brazilian people to the dangers of nuclear mismanagement was the tragedy at Goiânia in the autumn of 1987 – described by an official of the World Health Organisation as 'the worst nuclear accident after Chernobyl'.

In Goiânia, a city of a million or so inhabitants in central Brazil, a gang of scrap-metal dealers broke open a lead cylinder they had stolen from a derelict clinic and discovered a glowing blue powder. They let some children rub it on their bodies to make themselves luminous. The powder turned out to be caesium-137 from the core of a capsule used in the radiotherapeutic treatment of cancer, which had been abandoned when the clinic had closed down.

By the end of the year, four of the irradiated victims were dead and buried in concrete. Many more were in hospital, severely ill with burns and radiation sickness. The official figures acknowledge 244 cases of contamination, but the true toll is believed to run to many thousands. Seven residential districts near the centre of the city had to be evacuated and former residents of the street containing the scrapyard are reported to have become 'untouchables' in the eyes of their relatives and neighbours.[4]

What the disaster revealed, apart from the deadly consequences of exposure to radiation, was the incompetence of Brazil's National Nuclear Energy Commission (CNEN), which is responsible for all aspects of nuclear safety and under military control. The Commission was caught wholly unprepared. The first teams sent to Goiânia lacked both the protective clothing and the equipment they needed, and it took them two weeks to map out the affected area. CNEN's president, Rex Nazareth, blamed a lack of resources for the fact that inspections of the country's 236 radiotherapy clinics had ceased three years earlier, and estimated that there were at least another 50 pieces of similar medical equipment lying abandoned around Brazil. Some Brazilian scientists have suggested that a series of similar accidents have occurred but remained unpublicised owing to CNEN's secretiveness.[5]

In Brazil, as in many other countries, economic pressures, technical difficulties, the overestimation of future energy demand and the availability of cheaper alternatives have prompted a drastic curtailment of what was originally an ambitious nuclear programme. Six plants have been cancelled and others have been bedevilled with one problem after another. According to Professor Goldemberg, 7 per cent of Brazil's massive external debt is tied up in non-functioning nuclear reactors.[6] The Brazilian civil nuclear programme, however, is seen to rest largely on the aspirations of the military sector which controls it. In the military field, Brazil admits only to working on a reactor for submarine propulsion (the silence with which HMS *Conqueror* shadowed Argentina's *General Belgrano* during the South Atlantic War left a deep impression in Latin America). But the existence of deep excavations on a military reservation in Pará state has long fuelled speculation that preparations for a weapons test were at an advanced stage – notwithstanding the Mutual Inspection Accord Brazil has agreed with Argentina. Meanwhile, Brazil, with some foreign help, has achieved a high degree of autonomy in the production of nuclear fuel and equipment – including the mastery of fuel enrichment. Brazil has itself become a nuclear exporter.

Goiânia, in demonstrating that the Brazilian authorities are wholly unprepared to deal with a nuclear reactor accident, has added force to the questioning of Brazil's entire nuclear programme.

The Goiânia accident, of course, involved not nuclear power generation but medical equipment – though it involved the same administrative structures. Similarly, other incidents not directly concerning nuclear power projects have contributed to a growing awareness of radiological dangers in Third World countries. On the Thai island of Phuket, 100,000 local people destroyed a tantalum plant posing a radioactive hazard in 1986. Since 1982, a controversy has been simmering in Malaysia's Perak state over the dumping of radioactive thorium hydroxide waste by the company, Asian Rare Earths (ARE). Each year ARE produces thousands of tons of this dangerous material as a by-product of minerals used in the electronics industry. In 1984, protests from residents near the original dumpsite, at Parit, forced the company to move it to Papan, a few miles away, where vigorous local protests and legal action again forced ARE to abandon its plan. As Gurmit Singh, President of the Environmental Protection Society of Malaysia, pointed out at the time, the Papan campaign, besides giving people a better understanding of nuclear issues, had a wider value: 'In a very important sense, the Papan residents have demonstrated that a local initiative at the grassroots level on a major environmental issue – while extremely rare in Malaysia – is possible.'[7]

Lacking an approved disposal site, ARE meanwhile stored its waste on a temporary dump beside the factory in the village of Bukit Merah, from where it leached into ponds. A contractor working for the company (but unaware of the hazards) even sold some of the waste to vegetable farmers to be used as fertilizer. A temporary injunction which stopped operations for over a year was lifted in early 1987 and the fight continues. In April, 2,000 people attended a demonstration against the company, which is 35 per cent owned by the Japanese giant, Mitsubishi Chemical (the rest by Malaysian interests). The Bukit Merah residents went back to court in October, shortly before the general clampdown under Malaysia's Internal Security Act, which put many of the campaign's leaders in custody, or under restriction orders.

As well as calling into question the motivation of foreign companies involved in joint ventures (Mitsubishi Chemicals would be bound by somewhat more restrictive legislation in Japan), the ARE case has shown that the authorities responsible for monitoring and controlling nuclear hazards in Malaysia are no more trustworthy than their counterparts in Brazil – or in Britain.

There are now some 400 functioning nuclear power plants in the world. Third World countries with plants operating or under construction include Argentina, Brazil, China, Cuba, India, Iran, Mexico, Pakistan, South Korea and Taiwan (as well as South Africa and Israel). Many more have research reactors. But just as the nuclear industries in the industrialised countries have found themselves facing increasingly bleak prospects at home, with a moratorium on further construction in many countries, and outright anti-nuclear commitments in several, so, in the Third World too, once ambitious nuclear programmes have been cut back. This is largely the product of the various factors seen in the Brazilian case – rising capital costs and a shortage of foreign exchange in countries burdened with soaring debt-servicing commitments, lower than expected demand for electricity, cheaper alternative sources of power, technical problems and the absence of any satisfactory solution to the problem of nuclear waste. But another reason, as Juan Eibenschutz, the Mexican representative at the Sixth Pacific Basin Nuclear Conference, held in Beijing in September 1987, admitted gloomily, is 'the social fear of nuclear power' created by the Chernobyl and Three Mile Island accidents. 'For Mexico', he said, 'and for the rest of the world, or at least the rest of the Western world, the future of nuclear power and particularly of the existing nuclear industry looks uncertain.'[8]

None the less, the pressures in the contrary direction are still strong – the fear of dependence on oil, the desire to keep open a nuclear weapons option, the evidence that nuclear capacity brings national prestige and international influence, and the economic leverage exerted by nuclear exporting creditors. And behind these considerations remains the assumption, generally shared by the ruling elites of the South as well as by the dominant powers of the North (and the international financial institutions which serve them) that Third World countries will find solutions to their problems only by following the models of market-led, export-oriented, energy-and-resource-intensive industrial development prescribed by the North.

In some newly-industrialising countries, especially those where information and expression of opinion is most rigidly controlled, there is still little sign of much opposition to nuclear power. In South Korea, for instance, which still plans to expand its nuclear capacity far beyond its existing six plants, the opposition has so far had little to say about the issue – although there has been some controversy even within government circles over the desirability of building additional reactors when coal-fired electricity is cheaper.

In general, though, anti-nuclear feeling is growing in the Third World as it is in the industrial countries, encouraged not only by the attention Chernobyl has drawn to nuclear dangers, but also by the example of one victorious anti-nuclear campaign in a Third World country – the Philippines, where Corazon Aquino responded to overwhelming popular feeling by mothballing the half-built Morong nuclear reactor as soon as she came to power.

The Morong project encapsulated a number of the deadly follies afflicting many nuclear schemes in the Third World. The reactor was a Westinghouse PWR of the ill-proven Three Mile Island type. The site was on the shore of the Bataan peninsula, which is cut by seven major geological faults and has the highest incidence of earthquakes in a seismically hyperactive country, with tremors recorded every ten seconds or so. Towering over the site, moreover, was the volcano, Mount Natib, whose eruption even the International Atomic Energy Agency described, in a highly critical report, as 'a credible event'. Nowhere with adequate geological stability could be found for the disposal of the high-level radioactive waste which the plant would have produced at the rate of 20 tons each year. The price Westinghouse originally quoted, US $500 million for two reactors, rose over eleven years to $2.1 billion for the Morong plant alone. In 1985, when the Marcos regime was $25 billion in debt, with interest rates three times their level when the contract was signed, the mere interest repayments on the loan for Morong were costing the Philippines $350,000 a day.

How was such a project ever hatched? According to Simon Watt and Conrad Taylor, who described the circumstances in *Inside Asia* magazine, the responsibility falls on 'the unholy marriage between Marcos, who needed prestige projects to justify his regime (and US loans to pay for them) and the US State Department and Westinghouse, who wanted sales'.[9] The deal is reported to have been lubricated, moreover, by a $35 million kickback to a cousin of Imelda Marcos acting as the Westinghouse agent. As Watt and Taylor point out, Marcos's electrification of the Philippines brought little benefit to the Filipino people, being consumed largely by 'big and dirty Japanese metallurgical concerns' in accordance with a strategy of export-oriented industrialisation based on foreign capital.

In the Philippines, opposition to nuclear power was one element in a much wider opposition to the Marcos regime. In the Third World generally, more than in Europe or North America, anti-nuclear campaigns, whether combatting nuclear power projects or other radiological hazards, tend to occur in the context of a much broader grassroots politics confronting the interconnected issues of the environment, development, social justice and civil liberties. The immediate hazards from toxic chemicals are no less threatening than those from exposure to radiation, as the holocaust at Bhopal has demonstrated. Indeed there are reports that one witness to the horror in Bhopal, finding himself in a city of the dead and dying, believed there had actually been a nuclear explosion.[10]

A great number of grassroots organisations active on environmental and related issues have come into being during recent years in many parts of the Third World (where the number of political organisations calling themselves 'green' is also growing rapidly – though some of them are perhaps using the term with questionable motives; 'greenness', a mark of marginality in the 1970s, is becoming a saleable political colour in the 1980s). In the Asia–Pacific region alone, there are several hundred registered environmental Non-Governmental Organisations. Some of them have become well known: the women of the Chipko movement, hugging the trees in Indian forests to save them from the chainsaw; the people of Cubatão, near São Paolo, where a pipeline explosion in 1984 killed 500, now fighting the chemical companies whose toxic pollution has caused purulent cysts, skin lesions and liver and kidney damage in the local population, the birth of children without brains, and the destruction of vegetation resulting in landslides; the Pacific island campaigns against the dumping of radioactive waste at sea; the Penan tribespeople of Sarawak who have formed human barricades to defend forest homelands they have inhabited since time immemorial from destruction by logging concerns.

Among these groups are many defending the rights of tribal peoples and other ethnic minorities against extinction in the name of 'development' or cultural homogeneity. Many small and vulnerable communities have been uprooted, injured or threatened as a result of specifically nuclear development – the Marshall Islanders, French Polynesians, and aboriginal Australians evicted or irradiated in American, French and British weapons tests, as well as the aboriginal North Americans, such as the Western Shoshone, on whose land over 800 nuclear weapons tests have taken place, including recent tests of British warheads.

What has stimulated the growth of environmental politics in the Third World is a consciousness not only of Bhopal and Chernobyl, but of the innumerable latent Bhopals and Chernobyls waiting to happen – along with the other human and environmental disasters threatened by the loss of forests, fertile topsoil and other vital resources, the poisoning of the air, the earth and the waters, and the squandering of desperately needed economic and intellectual resources on military budgets and technocratic priorities bringing no benefit to the poor of the poor world, but only greater poverty.

'Development', said Dr Vandana Shiva, a founder of the Chipko movement, addressing the 1987 European Nuclear Disarmament Convention in Coventry, 'has become total war.'

Sooner or later, in any exchange of views between supporters of the European peace movement and political activists from the Third World, the question of 'Eurocentricity' is likely to arise – to be met on the European side either with guilty nods or with indignant denials, or else with bewilderment.

Some of the criticism, as E. P. Thompson has recently shown in a spirited reply to the charges,[11] simply ignores the extent to which European peace organisations already take 'Southern' issues seriously. And some of the surrounding rhetoric stems from a spurious assumption that there exists a single, approved, Third World view, when many major issues are hotly disputed among and within Third World countries. In any case, there is a sense in which a Eurocentric perspective applied to Europe is legitimate – no less so than, say, an Indocentric perspective applied to India. After all, the premiss of self-determination is that no one is better qualified to describe the problems of a particular place, and to determine their solution, than the people who live there.

But the sense that Eurocentricity has been a problem is expressed not only in the bitter rhetoric of 'facile leftism' (of which E. P. Thompson provides examples), by people who regard the concepts of European and imperialist as being virtually synonymous; it is also felt in some degree by people who are thoroughly well-disposed towards the European peace movement. Rajni Kothari, for example, president both of India's People's Union for Civil Liberties and of *Lokayan*, an umbrella organisation bringing together a multitude of grassroots campaigns concerning the environment, the rights of women and the plight of ethnic minorities, has said,

> The European peace movement has had quite an impact in the Third
> World by simply focusing global attention on the threat to the survival
> of the species. On the other hand, a lot of Third World intellectuals and
> activists feel that the peace movement, having achieved this, is too
> Eurocentric and narrow in its thinking. As you know, a lot of people
> think there is nothing like the peace movement in the Third World. One
> reason for this is that the way they conceive of the peace movement is
> somewhat narrow. How can the peace movement, having mobilised
> European opinion, expand to cover other issues?[12]

As well as seeking to overcome ignorance and bad communications, as E.P.
Thompson concedes, 'we should listen to our critics.' Besides the general
point made by Rajni Kothari, that European peace groups need to widen
their focus, there are, it seems to me, a number of respects in which the
criticisms of Eurocentricity have some validity.

Although it is reasonable – indeed important – for Europeans to
concentrate on genuinely European concerns, it is not reasonable to imagine,
as it is sometimes made to seem, that the 'Cold War' (by which I mean the
whole problem of the existence of two blocs of rival interests centred on the
superpowers) is distinctively a European or Atlantic phenomenon, nor that
all we have to do is 'end the Cold War in Europe' and somehow peace and
justice for the whole world will magically follow. True, Europe, the
original seat of the Cold War, has been singularly stuffed with nuclear
ironmongery. And Europe's record, as the chief author of two world wars
(allowing some credit to Japan) is due cause for Europeans to contemplate
themselves apprehensively in the mirror of history. But today the Cold
War is global. The smallest islands in the biggest oceans find that they
are in Washington's unbounded backyard, and Soviet strategic interests
are by no means confined to Europe. If Europe were to be neutralised and
demilitarised tomorrow, much of the problem would remain. The tensions
and conflicts most likely to lead to global war lie far more in the Third
World, where so many wars are already raging, than in Europe.

Since 1945, some 30 million people are estimated to have died in over 100
wars in the Third World – not counting 'minor' conflicts with fewer than
1,000 killed. These wars have been increasing in frequency, in
destructiveness and in the proportion of non-combatants among their
casualties. Not all of these conflicts can be blamed on the superpowers, or
the former colonial powers; many of the South's wars have their origins
largely in local dynamics, which may be economic, ethnic, religious or
factional. But in certain cases – Vietnam, the Horn of Africa, Central
America, Afghanistan – the superpowers and their allies in the North
have obviously been among the principal actors. In many other wars, the

involvement of the North, though perhaps less manifest, has still been important – through covert or political intervention rather than direct military operations, and through the arms trade which not only fuels wars directly but also serves to distort development, to militarise society and political culture, and thus to create the dynamics of further conflict.

Interventionism – the product of seeing the world only as a domain of interests to be dominated, won or protected – and the arms trade form the principal links between the Cold War in the North and the hot wars in the South. Interference in local wars by one superpower soon brings in the other, polarises the conflict in Cold War terms and creates an investment in perpetuating the war rather than permitting any resolution through the victory of one side. The peaceful resolution of conflicts in which the big powers are involved is subject to the same limitations as the resolution of the Cold War itself. As for the arms trade, Europe now accounts for about one quarter of the world arms trade – barely less than the United States – and as the Gulf War has shown, there are few European countries without a grubby finger in the pie.

With the INF agreement, it seems that things may have relaxed a little in Europe. But even as preparations are made to pack the Euromissiles back into their boxes, similar weaponry is appearing on warships cruising the world's oceans. And as the economic power of the Pacific rises, so too does its strategic significance to the superpowers. In reminding his audience at the US National Press Club that the volume of US trade with Asia is 75 per cent above that with the Atlantic nations, US Navy Secretary James Webb recently remarked that 'East Asia is an indispensable part of our country's future', and that 'it provides the only point in the world where the direct military interests of the Soviet Union, the People's Republic of China, the United States and Japan converge.' As many observers have noted, the INF agreement has not brought about any discernible change in interventionist foreign policy objectives.

The problem is not just that the confrontation between the superpowers occurs in the Third World. The question of peace cannot be addressed adequately without recognising the conflicts of interest which threaten it, and in these the North–South dimension is at least as significant as the East–West.

The terminology of the rich North versus poor South is of course a simplistic shorthand. The South has its pockets of wealth and power, its internal ethnic conflicts and denials of self-determination, its home-grown regional bullies, its Marcoses, its Amins, its Duvaliers. And the poor world exists partly in the North – in the dispossessed sections of our own societies. But the economic relations between what, for the sake of brevity, we can continue to call the North and the South, are central to the problems of peace. And here European countries have some responsibilities not only as superpower allies, but in their own right. They need more attention.

Finally, European debates on healing the divisions imposed by the Cold War sometimes seem to rest on an unreal and impoverished notion of the continent as a homogeneous and self-contained cultural entity, which obscures the non-European weft that has always been woven into the complex patterns of Europe's cultural fabric. It was with the labour and the commodities of Africa, Asia and the Americas that post-Renaissance Europe built its power. Greek thought survives thanks to the Islamic universities which preserved the texts through centuries of Christian obscurantism. Christianity itself came out of Asia, and Greek culture may owe more to Africa than is generally acknowledged. Even our languages, Indo-European or Finno-Ugrian, belong to families shared with Asia; and English, French, Spanish and Portuguese remain today as the currency of constant cultural exchange with South Asia, Africa, the Caribbean and Latin America. By comparison, only one language, German, spans the river Elbe.

This is not in any way to denigrate the immense importance of building our bridges across the Elbe and restoring our broken community with friends and relatives in Eastern and Central Europe. It is only to beware of alienating friends and relatives in other continents, and friends and relatives in our own countries who have roots elsewhere, by neglecting what Europe's multiculture owes to them.

Beside the charge of being Eurocentric, that of being 'nuko-centric' has also been laid against the European peace movement. The very intensity of the anxiety people in the Western industrial countries have voiced about nuclear weapons has been seen by some as a symptom of their ethnocentricity and middle-class identity – as though nothing short of the spectre of nuclear holocaust could penetrate their cosy padding of comfort and privilege to remind them of what everyone else knows from their daily experience: life is short and dangerous. In El Salvador or Tigray there are more immediate things to worry about than the nuclear winter. It is perhaps an appreciation of the bomb as an existential icon – the white man's *memento mori* – that fires Third World enthusiasts for nuclear proliferation such as the African political scientist, Ali Mazrui, or India's K. Subrahmanyam.

Now the nuclear nightmares of people in the industrial countries are mingled with ecological terrors – new visions of the death of the planet. Is this what keeps people awake in the shantytowns? Or is it once again the neurotic preoccupation of mollycoddled Northerners, projecting their own mortality as the end of the world?

A serious case, pointing, if not exactly to this conclusion, then at least in this direction, has been argued. It deserves consideration, not least because it throws some light on the difficulties of communication environmentalists have with the unconvinced – both the risk-happy technocrats who are declared adversaries, and the people in-between who find the status quo at least real, and anything else dubious. In an analysis of the perception of environmental dangers, two US cultural theorists, Mary Douglas and Aaron Wildavsky, use 'some blunt instruments from anthropology and political theory' to shake what they see as 'ethnocentric parochialism'. They ask,

> What are Americans afraid of? Nothing much, really, except the food they eat, the water they drink, the air they breathe, the land they live on and the energy they use. In the amazingly short space of fifteen to twenty years, confidence about the physical world has turned into doubt. Once the source of safety, science and technology have become the source of risk. What could have happened in so short a time to bring forth so severe a reaction?[13]

They start from the premiss that there is no objective, value-free means of calculating total risks or choosing between risky alternatives. Scientists disagree with one another and are biased, like everyone else, by the conscious or unconscious desire to promote a particular social and moral order. Normally, research shows, people pay little heed to remote risks of any sort. The choice whether to worry first about foreign enemies, economic collapse, law and order or pollution involves a political decision 'a bit like aesthetic judgement' with a message about who should rule and what should matter. Any or all of these dangers, though unquantifiable, may be real; but Americans, in deciding which to focus on, are no more or less objective than the Lele people of Zaire, who, according to the authors, ignore a plethora of tropical ills in their concern to locate the moral responsibility for lightning-strike and bronchitis.

The debate over environmental dangers is said to boil down to a conflict between three competing cultures, respectively associated by Douglas and Wildavsky (in the US context) with big business, big government and a millenary utopianism which regards the other two cultures (competing within the status quo) from the powerless margins of society. Environmentalism is naturally ascribed to this third category. Each culture has its own package of sacred axioms, values, self-contradictions and fears to be invoked in self-justification. The 'cornucopians' of the market and the technocracy assume that the benefits of technology will outweigh the costs, and that risks can be kept within acceptable limits as they are better understood in the light of experience. The political consequences of doubting this are too great to contemplate since they threaten the whole structure of the society to which they are committed. On the other side, the 'catastrophist' Jeremiahs of the environmental movement assume the reverse, and their assumption arises similarly not so much from evidence as from a prior commitment – though in this case to the very social upheaval the cornucopians fear. In reality, of course, most people find themselves somewhere between the extreme positions, but none the less with a bias one way or the other.

Even though, as the authors avow, their own bias ultimately leans towards the industrial establishment, they provide some useful insights concerning both the dangerous complacency of that establishment, and some of the pitfalls and paradoxes of ecotopianism: an underlying pessimism concerning human institutions which conflicts with a proclaimed conviction in human goodness, a latent intolerance with a tendency to invoke 'nature' as the word of God, the spurious affectation of innocence by those who evade the responsibilities and dilemmas of exercising power, and an inclination to underestimate the resilience of societies – their capacity to cope with crises and to benefit from positive feedback.

It is because the ecological movement is seen as characteristic of the United States, that it is found to be ethnocentric; it is in the US that affluence has bred distrust in the culture that created it.'

Certainly, environmental politics in their present form developed earlier in the more affluent parts of the world; to some extent, rising safety standards are a function of rising material living standards. And if an unclouded optimism concerning technology as the means to salvation is to be found anywhere, it is perhaps more likely to be in poorer countries. There, people cannot fail to be struck that the technologically advanced countries lack many of the desperate problems they confront. If technology cannot help to solve them, then what can, and what is technology for? And appeals for reduced consumption, which are all very well in profligate societies awash with money and throw-away gadgets, are less likely to find a resonance in places where a surfeit of material comforts is scarcely the problem.

But as we have seen, environmental concern is not by any means confined to the North, let alone to the US. Ecological politics is on the rise in the South.

Naturally, the attention of people in Cubatão or Bukit Merah is likely to be focused first on the immediate hazard in their communities rather than on the more abstract notion of a threat to the entire planet. But the discovery that people in other parts of the Third World are in a similar position soon gives rise to an awareness that some deep-rooted general problems are at issue. One circumstance that is likely to attract attention is that the hazardous plant is often owned, wholly or in part, by a big multinational company based in the North. Another is that the rate of industrial accidents in the Third World is several times higher than in the metropolitan countries; according to the International Labour Organisation, moreover, that rate was *increasing* in half the 24 developing countries studied in 1984.

The reasons are clear enough. Investment in health and safety precautions is low. This applies to locally owned industries as well as to the operations of transnationals, but in the latter case a double standard is often evident whereby the company profits from industrial operations involving hazardous processes or toxic substances no longer permitted in the metropolitan countries. The laxity of controls and the scarcity of information allows the transfer of hazards to Third World countries. All attempts to establish an international code of conduct binding multinational concerns, for example through the UN and the OECD, are constantly blocked by the industrial countries – though often with the complicity of Third World governments which see the acceptance of the double standard, and a willingness to downplay the seriousness of industrial risks, as the price of securing foreign investment.[14]

This devaluation of the lives of people in poor countries arises from the impeccable logic of the market, in a system where 'market values' predominate – a system which puts the maximisation of profit before all else, and ignores the social costs (and even the long-term economic costs) which need to be weighed against short-term private benefits in any socially responsible industrial planning. This double standard, which is in effect 'racist', is merely one facet of a much vaster double standard inherent to our economic system which serves to preserve the privileges of economic power once they have been established. But as some critics of toxic industry have been careful to stress,[15] there are no grounds for complacency about industrial safety in the North, where cases of disregard for safety in the interests of profit are legion. Moreover, as has been said, the tendency in the face of the economic pressures confronting Northern governments is towards cost-cutting and deregulation – and destroying such power as the labour force may have possessed to act in defence of its own interests.

What is so often conspicuously absent from our discussions (in the technologically advanced countries) concerning the relationship between the risks and benefits of a particular technology, is any acknowledgement that the costs and risks of the system from which people in the North benefit (some more than others) might partly be borne in places where the benefit is not seen – in the South.

The capital on which the system runs is largely multinational, of course, so the benefits as well as the costs are distributed unevenly to various parts of the world – but not in the same way. The fact is that in the name of interests and objectives defined largely in the United States (or Europe or Japan), risks of many sorts are imposed on people elsewhere – economic risks, risks of war and environmental risks. The *knowledge* and *consent* required before a risk can be said to have been accepted voluntarily is lacking as far as these extraterritorial risks are concerned – indeed they are often ruled out of court. Bhopal is a case in point. There, details of

Union Carbide's chemical and production processes were treated as an industrial secret under US arms export legislation and the local population did not know the risks they were living with, nor how to minimise the effects of the catastrophe once it had occurred. Secrecy is just one of the factors which limit environmental controls throughout the Third World, and stand as obstacles to self-determination. As the UN Centre on Transnational Corporations noted in a report shortly after the Bhopal accident,

> Few countries have a good handle on what is going on where and why. The lack of information adds an air of mystery to the environmental image of transnationals, but most importantly, makes it difficult for government, workers and consumers to exercise informed choice.[16]

As far as the activities of multinational pesticide manufacturers are concerned, the relationship of risks to benefits presents a very different picture in the South from that seen in the North, as David Weir points out in a study of the Bhopal tragedy:

> WHO [the World Health Organization] has estimated that at least half the world's acute pesticide poisonings take place in underdeveloped countries every year, even though they use only one-sixth of the world's pesticides. In other words, people are being poisoned at a rate three times that of their counterparts in the industrialized countries. Every 42 seconds, somebody is being poisoned somewhere, leading to at least 10,000 deaths annually in the Third World alone. Furthermore, at least half of all the pesticides used in underdeveloped countries are applied, not to food crops grown locally, but to luxury items (coffee, tea, etc.) and to non-food crops (cotton, rubber) grown for export to the US, Japan and Europe. Therefore the major argument advanced in favour of Third World pesticide use – helping feed the hungry – is a highly questionable one.[17]

If X pays the cost of Y's benefit, who does the cost accountancy? Any analysis of risk perception in the US, or anywhere else, which neglects this aspect of the problem might well be accused of ethnocentricity.

Just as serious and growing concern over environmental dangers is not confined to the metropolitan countries, it is by no means confined to extremist bands of latter-day Anabaptists wandering the margins of society in the grip of millenary visions, motivated solely by a private grudge against the whore of Babylon. On the contrary, it is shared in some measure right across the conventional political spectrum, by people whose views differ widely on most questions – including the causes and remedies for the dangers they agree exist. Even the governments fail to ignore the problem altogether (here the market is more successful). The Brundtland Report, recently published by the UN Commission on Environment and Development, may have some failings from the point of view of many environmentalists, but its general conclusions endorse much of the environmentalist perspective – as well as its sense of urgency:

> When the century began, neither human numbers nor technology had the power to radically alter planetary systems. As the century closes, not only do vastly increased human numbers and their activities have that power, but major unintended changes are occurring in the atmosphere, in soils, in waters, among plants and animals, and in the relationship among all these things ... To keep options open for future generations, the present generation must begin now, and begin together, nationally and internationally.[18]

Environmental destruction is nothing new. Overgrazing was already turning lush North African pasture into wasteland in the time of the Pharaohs and the canals that watered Babylon also dried the deserts which eventually buried it. But in the past people could move on. There were plenty of green places left. There was time for regeneration. What is new is the realisation that this is no longer so, the sense that we are approaching global limits we have not seen before. This tale is told by satellite photographs – by technology itself. It is not a matter which reputable scientists dispute according to their ideological prejudices – though they may debate the time available for procrastination. And while the environmental costs of exploiting the resources needed to meet the demands of production are rising as never before, no limit to that production can be admitted within the dominant structures of politics. On the contrary, production is required to expand constantly in order to meet the material demands of the world's expanding population, in order to 'create wealth', in order to 'create work'. The very conception of a ceiling on production knocks the floor from under the systems we live by, whether we live in Manchester, Magnetogorsk or Montevideo.

The argument that the environment must wait while we cure poverty through overall growth and 'trickle-down' development is no longer tenable. The destruction of life-giving qualities in the places in which we live is part of poverty, as is the damage to health caused by pollution. And poverty perpetuates the destruction of the environment. The fact that 25 billion tons of fertile topsoil is being lost each year is partly due to landless peasants and pastoralists who have little choice but to graze the last grass at the edge of the dust. Neither problem will wait on the other and poverty, far from being alleviated by the pursuit of limitless and indiscriminate economic growth, is being aggravated. The most recent UN studies show unprecedented 10–15 per cent drops in living standards in

Africa and Latin America and, in the words of Dr Richard Jolly, UNICEF's Deputy Executive Director, 'hard evidence from 32 countries that things are getting worse'. In 1986-7, Africa's export earnings dropped by US $19 billion on top of a loss of nearly $15 billion in debt repayments. According to Dr Jolly, even within the IMF and the World Bank, there is 'increasing recognition of these issues by the high priests of financial orthodoxy'.[19] If so, it is not before time.

If we are to come to terms with the existence of limits on growth, our social systems are faced with enormous upheavals as the cost of adjustment to reality. The burden of those upheavals must not fall on those least able to bear them, either internationally or within our own unevenly developed national economies. This is the point at which environmentalists in the rich countries really do have to beware of ethnocentric prescriptions, as Raymond Williams emphasised in his pamphlet on socialism and ecology:

It is too easy, in the rich industrial North, to say that we have had our industrial revolution, we have had our advanced industrial and urban development, and we have known some of its undesirable effects, and so we are in a position to warn the poor countries against going down that same road. We have indeed tried to share that experience of indiscriminate production. But we must do it in a kind of good faith which is in fact rare. It must not become an argument for keeping the poor countries in a radical state of underdevelopment, with their economies in fact shaped to keep supplying the existing rich countries. It must not become an argument against the kind of sensible industrialization which will enable them, in more balanced ways, to use and develop their own resources, and to overcome their often apalling problems of poverty.[20]

An extreme and uncompromising environmental fundamentalism which declared itself against *all* growth, industry and technology, would be missing the interrelationship of problems and helping no one. But this is not characteristic of environmental movements in general, which well appreciate the importance of trying to distinguish between benign and malignant growth and development, and between appropriate and inappropriate forms of technology – those which serve desired ends and those which enslave. This is not a simple matter, of course, but the first requirement is a rejection of the technological determinism which says, 'you can't stop progress', when what it means is, 'you can't *steer* technology; it is a storm-blown, rudderless wreck of a ship and all you can do is sit tight on the provisions and hope for the best.' This determinism is used to disguise the fact that technology is *not* rudderless. It is steered towards particular ports of destination, with research and development grants and investment, chosen in accordance with particular interests, and navigated by the stars of the market. The chosen ports are where the captains and owners prosper at the crew's expense. There are other harbours on the map.

Environmentalism in the South goes together with a high consciousness of development issues, of the need to determine the direction of development in accordance with local needs, rather than submitting to a model of development imposed from outside. It therefore represents a political challenge to the status quo in the most important sense. It is clear that this self-determination of development requires the political power to choose and to resist. It involves democracy and it involves sovereignty over resources.

Allowing that environmental concern is justified, that it is political, and that environmental problems are interwoven with those of poverty and development, how is this the business of a peace movement?

For some time, sections within the European peace movements have been making the point that it is not enough to talk about weapons systems. A high level of armament may increase tension and the probability of unintentionally setting off hostilities, but the weapons in themselves are a poor excuse for a war. War requires a conflict of interest. Attention has been paid to 'the Cold War' because it is meant to persuade us that there is a fundamental conflict of interest between East and West. It is intended not as an excuse for real war, but rather as a means of disciplining unruly citizens and distracting attention from inconvenient discrepancies between ideology and reality. The Cold War is dangerous because people might really come to believe its propositions, and then there would be an excuse for a real war (if it were not for the restraining, 'deterrent' effect of nuclear weapons – thus are nuclear weapons justified). But it has been an axiom shared among a good many European peace organisations that there is no real conflict of interest between Eastern and Western Europe, and that even the conflicts of interest between the two superpowers are largely fictitious – false to the extent that their respective claims to represent freedom or social justice for the world are false. Rather, they share a good measure of covert common interest, which has been revealed in their common hostility to non-aligned tendencies within their own camps – an alternative common interest – and also, incidentally, in the tacit agreement to play down the significance of the Chernobyl accident, because a loss of public confidence in nuclear energy threatens shared assumptions concerning production and energy needs and controls. The Cold War is a system of mutual reinforcement.

Obviously, there are differences of *strategic* interest, but these are superficial unless they can be shown to rest on a more fundamental conflict of interest. The most threatening conflicts concern the control of resources and markets. Without the raw materials, food and fuel the industrial countries need to maintain their levels of production and consumption, they face economic and social disintegration. Here there is some reality to the conflict of interest between the superpowers; each wishes to retain the power to deny the other what it would need in a crisis, to ensure its own supply. But there are also conflicts *within* the Western bloc (and thus 'the West' is the concept to be defended, lest the sense that US interests must also be Europe's and Japan's be lost).

Vastly more real than these are the conflicts of interest between poor countries and rich countries. Once again, this simple terminology belies the complexity of the matter; varying degrees of industrialisation and of actual or potential self-sufficiency need to be taken into account, but the simplified scheme in which the North consumes the South's raw materials and gives little of benefit in return has enough validity for the present purposes. Many Third World countries are rich in the resources that could be used to overcome their own problems, but these resources are largely controlled in the rich countries, where they feed a malignant system.

Unless something changes, this conflict will intensify. Already it is acknowledged as the excuse for military intervention – to protect 'our interests' in the Gulf, for example – and for political intervention on a far wider scale. Intervention is the denial of self-determination and there is nothing for which people are more likely to take up arms, sooner or later, than the right not to be dictated to.

Nothing calling itself a peace movement has any business putting these issues aside. Unless ways are found to move towards a resolution of such fundamental conflicts of interest, no sustainable peace is conceivable – only a *pax borealis*, dependent on the superior armament of the North and the internal divisions of the South, fuelled by 'military aid'.

At the same time, it is obviously impossible for European peace organisations systematically to take up the enormous multitude of individual issues affecting the Third World. Rather than each movement trying to confront the whole mess of interrelated issues at once (with the result that they all end up making the same sort of generalised statements against sin and in favour of virtue that peace activists spend enough time making already), is it not better for different movements, with different focuses of attention to complement one another? Certainly, but they each still need a broad view, and a broad exchange of information, if they are to help rather than hinder one another. Besides trying to retain a general overview, are there any particular sorts of focuses and channels which might help the peace movements of the North to address Southern issues more coherently?

Jonathan Steele has recently outlined a number of priorities which arise more or less naturally from a concern with military and foreign policy issues.[21] The first is to block attempts to extend NATO's sphere of operations; this dangerous tendency has been manifested in the complicity of European governments in the bombing of Tripoli, and in some of the responses to the Gulf crisis – as well as in more explicit efforts on the part of the United States to expand NATO naval operations to the east of Suez. The second is to pressure European governments into acting as more effective restraints on the United States, to prevent Washington from seeing every Third World crisis only in terms of threats to its own 'legitimate' interests (it cannot be denied, of course, that many struggles in the Third World do represent a threat to the *illegitimate* interests of maintaining US *dominance*; once again, this distinction between legitimate and illegitimate interests is something the Cold War, invoking the Soviet threat, serves to obscure). The third is to support non-alignment in the Third World and de-alignment in Europe by opposing military bases, by promoting Nuclear-Weapons-Free-Zones, Zones-of-Peace and 'Zones-of-Non-Intervention', by supporting moves towards the progressive dissolution of the blocs, and by canvassing greater political support for non-aligned countries. Up to a point, these items are already on the European peace movement agenda, along with the questions of nuclear proliferation and the arms trade. Beyond this, says Steele, the peace movement and the 'development movement' must join hands 'to create the political conditions within Western Europe for a non-exploitative relationship with the Third World'.

Here, it seems to me, there are at least three kinds of issue, involving Europe's relations with the South, which follow quite naturally from European peace and anti-nuclear organisations' existing areas of concern: nuclear issues, issues entailing a specifically European responsibility, and issues involving grassroots citizens' initiatives where an affinity of interest is felt on both sides. Many questions obviously overlap two or more of these categories.

Nuclear Issues

Nuclear weapons proliferation would obviously be one item under this heading; it threatens Third World populations before anyone else with the dangers of regional nuclear arms races, to say nothing of regional nuclear war. Pakistan and India are playing on the brink of their own nuclear arms race, for reasons which have more to do with boosting prestige and distracting attention from internal problems than with any real basis for mutual fear. Brazil and Argentina, both within reach of a nuclear weapons capability, are keeping their options open. Israel and South Africa must now be considered full members of the Nuclear Weapons Club – as a result of their collaboration in what one Israeli academic, Benjamin Beit-Hallahmi, recently described as 'an alliance cemented in plutonium and sealed in blood', which 'should be taken very seriously'.[22] It is certainly taken seriously by a good many Third World countries, who need no better excuse to pursue their own weapons programmes. Iran, Iraq, Syria, Egypt, Libya and Cuba, among others, are working on them. And South Korea and Taiwan, both parties to unresolved civil wars, could assemble warheads within a short time if they decided to.

Europe has had a lot to do with the spread of nuclear weapons. Britain in particular, by doing nothing to encourage superpower nuclear disarmament, and now by expanding its own nuclear arsenal massively with the Trident system, has helped to discredit the Non-Proliferation Treaty of 1968 – flawed though this slender restraint was from the start, in its favour towards the existing Nuclear Weapons States. But European countries have also been a source of plutonium and nuclear enrichment technology – especially after 1978, when President Carter's Nuclear Non-Proliferation Act somewhat restricted exports from the USA. Even before this, there was the well-known case of the German company, Kraftwerk Union, wasting no time to take advantage of US reluctance to supply complete fuel cycle technology to Brazil. More recently, the revelation of an extensive black market in plutonium, centred on Khartoum, has pointed to British and US 'material unaccounted for' as the origin of up to 50 kg of the bomb material entering this black market each year.[23] On top of this has come the news of the scandal in the Federal Republic of Germany over the alleged supply of weapons-grade material to Libya and Pakistan among other countries, and involving corruption on a massive scale, which has prompted even Chancellor Helmut Kohl to express doubts about the future of his country's nuclear industry.[24]

Britain and France, meanwhile (unlike the United States), are planning a massive increase in plutonium production through new reprocessing plants, and looking for customers interested in buying the world's most lethal metal.

This is one reason why 'civil' as well as military nuclear programmes must be opposed and why nuclear power issues in the wider world need the attention of the European peace movement. But it is not the only reason.

The mining of the uranium on which nuclear power programmes depend involves serious health hazards to mineworkers in many Third World countries – and in industrialized countries such as Australia, Canada and the United States, where uranium mining often relies disproportionately on workers from aboriginal population groups in areas where radioactive pollution from tailings presents a wider hazard to indigenous communities. Third World countries with uranium mining operations include Argentina, Brazil, Turkey, India, China, Gabon and Niger as well as South Africa and Namibia.

The contracts under which the British government imported Uranium from RTZ's Rossing mine, in contravention of UN Decree No.1 on Namibia, expired in 1984. BNFL's lucrative trade with apartheid is continuing, however, since large quantities of uranium, not only from Rossing, but also from South Africa, are still entering Britain to be reprocessed into uranium hexafluoride and exported to Japan, the FRG and the USA (through a loophole in the US Anti-Apartheid Act). In this way the British nuclear industry is maintaining its interest in denying Namibian independence, and in upholding the Pretoria regime itself.[25]

With declining public confidence in nuclear energy in North America and much of Europe, Western nuclear exporters, jostling one another in their anxious search for markets elsewhere, have been finding means to pressure export-oriented newly-industrialising countries into nuclear energy programmes that defy any economic justification. The threat of trade quotas, for example, has been used to persuade countries such as South Korea and Taiwan, with markets Western producers find difficult to penetrate, to import nuclear technology from the United States and Canada, despite the availability of adequate, safer and cheaper sources of energy. 'With our big trade surplus with the US', one official of Taiwan's Taipower company said recently, in a moment of candour, 'and the rising protectionism imposed on us, it looks like the only way out is to keep buying these expensive plants from them in order to please the Americans.'[26] Four of Taiwan's reactors stand in an area of high volcanic activity in an island which has experienced over 2,000 earthquakes this century. And in the People's Republic of China, although the government's decision to buy one wholly foreign-built plant never rested solely on short-term economic considerations, the British government's guarantee that Hong Kong will buy 70 per cent of the output from Daya Bay with hard currency (in return for a contract for GEC) was obviously a major element in the economic case as seen from Beijing.

Japan too is looking for markets abroad as the home market becomes saturated. In partnership with Italian and US companies, Mitsubishi Heavy Industries has been bidding for the contract to build Indonesia's first nuclear plant.

The economic pressures involved in this nuclear trade are, of course, only one of many ugly symptoms of the much broader crisis in the world economy, in which the North–South contradiction is becoming more and more acute under the burden of debt repayments and protectionism.

European Responsibilities

There are, as we have seen, specifically European aspects to the nuclear issues affecting the Third World. Besides these, there is a host of military issues with a European dimension, which European peace movements are generally giving some attention to already, but often not enough: French nuclear testing in the Pacific; the entanglement of small dependent territories (British or French colonies) in basing structures and in the communications networks of 'battle management', and the SDI scheme; the eviction of the people of Diego Garcia by Britain; measures controlling access to strategic minerals – and other related questions. Underlying these, though, is the more general effect of European interests on the shape of development in Third World countries.

To what extent are the aid policies of individual European governments, and of the European Community as a bloc, serving the interests of peace, demilitarisation and self-determined development in poor countries, and to what extent are they merely self-serving, being geared to returns on investment, the creation of dependence and subservient export markets, dumping agricultural surpluses in return for cash-crop imports, and maintaining strategic interests described as essential to the 'defence' of our present patterns of consumption and wealth distribution? There is a need for well-directed aid as a catalyst to self-determined development guided by the real interests of the poor in the poor countries, but this must be the yardstick by which aid is defined. In a world where the rich are rich because the poor are poor, as Julius Nyerere has put it, the transfer of wealth from rich to poor is a matter of right, not of charity.

This is not only a matter of the malignant effects of 'military aid' – though the role of European arms companies in the Third World should be high on any peace movement's agenda. European companies are also profiting from the destruction of the environment and the neglect of health and safety throughout the South. In Brazil, for example, European chemical concerns such as Bayer and Rhodia are profiting from the sickness, death and ecocide which is their contribution to local development in the industrial outskirts of Rio and São Paolo.

An Affinity of Movements

Western peace groups seeking not merely to oppose nuclear weapons but to tackle the underlying problems of the Cold War through a strategy of 'détente from below' have long recognised certain independent groups in the Comecon countries, such as Charta 77 in Czechoslovakia or WiP ('Freedom and Peace') in Poland, as natural allies. Are there not similar 'natural allies' beyond Europe, and outside the metropolitan countries, confronting questions no less central to peace?

Rajni Kothari, whose comment on the narrowness of the European peace movement was quoted earlier, sees a natural affinity between the groups making up that movement and grassroots campaigns seeking to promote civil liberties in the Third World – and by 'civil liberties', as he is quick to explain, he does not mean merely the rights of journalists and academics, but civil liberties in the broad sense, including 'social, economic and cultural rights as well as political and legal rights'. Groups of this sort have been burgeoning in many parts of the Third World. In India alone, there are some 15,000, focusing on various facets of exploitation and inequality – including discrimination against women and ethnic minorities. By and large, environmental concern is part and parcel of their perspective; running right through them is a profound awareness, based on direct experience, of the consequences of current industrialisation policies: 'a fundamental erosion of the resources base – deforestation, desertification, forced migration, building of dams which displace people. All of this leads to a highly exploitive pattern of urbanization.'[27]

One reason why grassroots environmental politics is on the rise in the South as it is in the North, Rajni Kothari suggests, lies in 'the conviction that the modern state was no longer an agent of liberation, the conviction that organized political parties, including left parties, were not really interested in the problems of the poor ...' In many ways, this really is a new politics, challenging not only the ownership of the means of production, but also the nature and purpose of production, and the direction of development.

But just as the 'green' movements of the West, and the environmental associations now appearing in Eastern Europe, are new shoots sprouting from a gnarled old taproot, which no industrial development has been able to prevent from shattering the concrete from time to time with a crop of saplings and thistles, the environmental consciousness of the South has not appeared from nowhere. In the South, pre-industrial and even pre-agricultural ways of understanding the world are often far less deeply buried than they are in the North. There are deep-seated philosophical traditions – in the Gandhian movement, or in certain forms of Buddhism, as well as in the everyday consciousness of peasant, herding, and hunting cultures – in which the dependence of human beings on the natural world they are part of, and not masters of, is taken for granted. The values which are thus counterposed against the fetishes of a reckless and unbridled technocracy, and the deification of the market, far from being the transplanted hallucinations of a few cossetted and ethnocentric Americans and Europeans, draw on deep wells of knowledge and feeling that have seen the human race through most of its history, and which have only comparatively recently been in danger of running dry.

The sense that the 'social movements' of the North and the South have a common cause is not merely a Northern notion. It is reciprocated from the South – though not always uncritically – by such people as Rajni Kothari. The Asia-Pacific People's Environmental Network (APPEN), established in 1983 and based in Malaysia at the hub of a vast and growing network of citizens' initiatives, incorporates the experience of the European peace and disarmament movements in its training manual for activists along with studies of the Chipko movement, the grassroots opposition to the extension of Japan's Narita airport and the Nuclear-Free Pacific campaigns.

Grassroots organisations focusing on military issues (besides those involving the superpowers) do occur in the Third World – for example against the Indian government's plan, declared in May 1986, to build a missile testing range at Baliapal in Orissa state – but these generally have to contend with much more difficult circumstances than parallel campaigns in the West where, press calumnies, telephone taps and a certain level of police heavy-handedness notwithstanding, opposition can be expressed relatively freely. It is in this respect that environmental politics in the South has another significance.

Under authoritarian Third World regimes, as in Democratic Centralist political systems, issues touching on national security (or 'ideological security') are extremely difficult to confront; the would-be critic of military or foreign policy is easily silenced by the knowledge that she or he will be represented as acting in the interests of an enemy power, a Great Satan or an Empire of Evil, if not actually as a willing agent of such an enemy, with all the consequences that entails.

Environmental concern, however, is not so easily controlled. For a start, the dangers which are addressed cross frontiers and do not put one nation in opposition to another. More significantly, the government in question has little interest in being seen openly to disregard threats to the life and health of its citizens – threats which Seveso, Bhopal, Chernobyl and other tragedies have undeniably given some reality to. Up to a point, an 'official' concern with the same issues has to be expressed – at least verbally. The government may try to depict the environmentalists as being alarmist or neurotic, but it cannot easily represent their concerns as those of an enemy. This is not to suggest that Third World environmentalists escape state repression and misrepresentation; far from it. The wave of arrests under Malaysia's Internal Security Act in October 1987 fell heavily on environmental activists who were innocent of any part in exacerbating intercommunal tensions. The fact that they were targetted is, however, indicative of their success in drawing attention to environmental issues such as radioactive dumping and the destruction of forests – as well as in mobilising some vociferous public demonstrations. It may be read as a measure of official anxiety at the emergence of a form of civil politics with an evident popular appeal, but profoundly troubling to some powerful chemical and logging interests, involving a large measure of foreign capital.

On the other hand, environmental politics may find a certain sympathy even within parts of a ruling political establishment, and governments may even seek cooperation with some sorts of citizens' initiatives. Rajni Kothari, for example, describes 'a kind of process of greater legitimation for non-party, non-state action', evident when the state governments of

Jamnu and Kashmir, and Andrapradesh, asked the independent People's Union for Civil Liberties for help in restoring the democratic process after Indira Gandhi had attacked the Chief Ministers of those governments.

The broad grassroots politics of the environment and civil liberties which is developing in many parts of the Third World might therefore be described as having a higher 'political osmotic pressure' than any campaigns confined narrowly to nuclear, military or foreign policy issues would have. It is better able to penetrate the semi-permeable membranes dividing nations from one another, and dividing 'civil' from 'official' concerns. This enlargement of the grey areas in which politics 'from below' is able to operate represents a significant victory for self-determination in political cultures where the possibilities are severely limited.

Clearly, European peace organisations cannot contemplate trying to develop contacts with each of India's 15,000 grassroots campaigns; but in various parts of the South there exist umbrella groups such as *Lokayan* in India and APPEN in Malaysia, which serve as information centres, coordinating points and channels of communication for a multitude of groups in the region.

A certain level of contact and cooperation already occurs between such organisations and peace and anti-nuclear groups in the industrial countries; contacts with European environmentalist networks and development-oriented campaigns are more extensive. APPEN for example, is coordinated by Malaysia's Friends of the Earth (SAM), and thus forms part of FoE's web of environmental activity spanning all continents. And when the money for air fares can be found, the groups from the South are sometimes able to meet their nearest counterparts in the North at international conferences. What they ask us for, in the North, is a recognition that the problems of peace and energy policy are inseparable from the problems of development, and a willingness to exchange information and to publicise and amplify their concerns.

'Détente from below' means the involvement of 'civil society' in relaxing tensions which could lead to war. Since the world's most severe conflicts of interest entail the economic and power relations between the North, with its consumption, and the South with its resources and its poverty – making due allowance for the complexities lost from view in this overly simple terminology – 'détente from below' must have a North–South dimension.

Notes

1. Teh Chin Chai, 'Chernobyl fallout reaches the Third World', in Peter Worsley and Kofi Buenor Hadjor (eds), *On the Brink*, Third World Communications, 1987.
2. Trini Leung, 'Anti-nuclear-power movements in East Asia', conference paper, Penang, 1987.

3. Narayan Desai, 'Atoms for weapons', in *Peace News*, 31 October 1986.
4. *Guardian*, 12 October 1987.
5. 'Brazil report', *Latin American Newsletter*, 26 November 1987.
6. BBC2, *Newsnight*, 18 December 1987.
7. Gurmit Singh, 'Papan – More than just a dump', in *Inside Asia*, June 1985.
8. *Beijing Review*, 21 September 1987.
9. Simon Watt and Conrad Taylor, 'Playing with fire', in *Inside Asia*, June 1985.
10. Claude Alvares, 'A walk through Bhopal', in David Weir (ed), *The Bhopal Syndrome*, IOCU, 1986, p. 93.
11. E.P. Thompson, 'Eurocentrism, indocentrism and internationalism', in *END Journal* 31, December 1987.
12. Interview with Mary Kaldor, *END Journal*, April 1985.
13. M. Douglas and A. Wildavsky, *Risk and Culture*, University of California Press, 1982, p. 10.
14. Maria Helena Hurtado, 'The lessons of Bhopal', in *South*, June 1985.
15. E.g. Tara Jones, 'Hazards for export', in Les Levidow (ed), *Science as Politics*, Free Association Books, 1986.
16. *Environmental Aspects of the Activity of Transnational Corporations: a Survey*, UN, 1985.
17. David Weir, *Bhopal*.
18. *Our Common Future*, World Commission on Environment and Development.
19. The *Guardian Third World Review*.
20. Raymond Williams, *Socialism and Ecology*, SERA, 1983.
21. Jonathan Steele, 'East–West and North–South', in Dan Smith and E.P. Thompson (eds), *Prospectus for a Habitable Planet*, Penguin, 1987.
22. *Guardian*, 14 January 1988.
23. Tim Cornwell, 'Plutonium for sale', in the *Listener*, 5 November 1987.
24. *Guardian*, 25 January 1988.
25. Martin Bond, 'South African uranium: Britain's hidden role', *Sanity*, December 1987.
26. Trini Leung, 'Anti-nuclear-power movements'.
27. *END Journal*, April 1985.

Part III
The Alternatives

6
Alternative Energy

GORDON MACKERRON

In this chapter the possible alternatives to nuclear power are examined in terms of technical viability, economic attractiveness and environmental acceptability. The starting point is nuclear power itself – how dependent are Europe and the world on nuclear power, how cheap is it, and how easy would it be to remove? Secondly, what sort of energy policy could be formulated in the absence of nuclear power – how environmentally acceptable is coal (and how cheap), and what roles could conservation and renewable energy play?

Nuclear Power: Dependence

The first thing to remember about nuclear power is that, in energy terms, it is only capable of producing electricity. Electricity is important enough, but in terms of world use of final energy (energy, that is, at the point of delivery to consumers), it is less than 20 per cent of all energy use.[1] The direct effects of any phasing out of nuclear power would therefore be felt only in a limited part of the world's energy economy, though for the same reason the effects would be more severe within the electricity sector.

The degree of dependence on nuclear power varies widely within the industrialised world. In the OECD (Organisation for Economic Cooperation and Development) countries 15 per cent of the electric power capacity is nuclear, though at one extreme nuclear plants make up 55 per cent of the total stock in France, while countries like Australia, Portugal, Norway and Turkey have no nuclear capacity at all. However, measuring capacity somewhat underestimates the degree of dependence that exists in terms of electricity produced. This is because nuclear plants generally have lower running costs than fossil-fuelled generators and are therefore run round the clock where possible. Thus France generates 75 per cent of all electricity from nuclear power, and the OECD average is 22 per cent.

In the centrally planned economies the degree of dependence is rather less. Total nuclear capacity in the Comecon countries, concentrated very heavily in the USSR, amounts to some 7 per cent of all electrical plant, and nuclear generation accounts for 10 per cent of all production. China has two plants under construction but non operating yet (apart from military and research reactors).

The position in developing countries is varied. Although many developing countries have devoted large sums of state expenditure to nuclear power, the degree of dependence is limited in all cases except South Korea and Taiwan. Developing countries' nuclear capacity is collectively less than one-third that of France, and the total dependence in generating terms is only 6 per cent.

Nuclear power is therefore established as a significant but by no means dominant source of electricity supply. There has been a lull in the ordering of nuclear plant throughout the world in recent years, especially in the industrialised world, but nuclear plant currently under construction would add a further 145 GW (equal to 61 per cent of existing nuclear capacity). If all nuclear electricity generation were to be replaced by coal, this would require an extra 500 million tonnes of coal at the existing level of nuclear power, and 800 million tonnes if all current construction were completed. These are large quantities of coal: 500 million tonnes is around 20 per cent of world production of hard coal. The question of how quickly such substitution could occur is dealt with later in this chapter.

Nuclear Power: Costs

The real costs of nuclear power are passionately disputed, and – mainly because of the passion involved – both supporters and opponents of nuclear power have at times made dubious or fraudulent claims. The basic problem is that nuclear power raises issues of such fundamental importance that no technocratic calculus can possibly capture them all. Yet the apparatus of cost-benefit analysis has been pressed into service in a doomed attempt to achieve such 'capture'. The kinds of issue which no technique can sensibly handle include the reduction in civil liberties that nuclear power may entail, the scale of the worst accidents that could occur, and the problems for countless future generations that nuclear waste management may involve. This much is hard to dispute, and some dimensions of nuclear power must inevitably be left outside the realm of technique. But it *is* still important to glean what we can about those costs which are reasonably measurable. The approach here, therefore, is first to consider the evidence concerning the economic experience of nuclear power in the way a utility-company or government decision-maker would see it, and then to see how far such an experience is modified by taking account of some of the wider considerations that are not amenable to technocratic analysis.

The first and vital, if controversial, point is that throughout the 1970s, and for some countries into the 1980s, nuclear power has seemed an inviting economic prospect to governments and utilities. True, utilities have needed various forms of state backing, but it is important to recognise the attractions of nuclear power, quite apart from any military purpose, or (as in Britain) its use as a political weapon to defeat miners or other unruly workers. Two major features of nuclear power made it appealing to electric utilities. The first is that in a nuclear project, some two-thirds of costs are capital-related – and therefore apparently under the direct control of the investor. By contrast, the main perceived alternative, fossil-fired generation, has an exactly reverse structure, with two-thirds of the cost made up by fuel – which is clearly outside the control of decision-makers. To this initial appeal was added, in the 1970s, the firm conviction that the limitation in world supplies of fossil fuel would inevitably lead to constantly rising prices, whether of oil, gas or coal. In the late 1980s, nuclear power is less economically appealing to utilities, but it is not off the investment agenda in many industrialised countries. It is important to understand that while political and military motives may have played supplementary roles in many countries, there has been a clear economic rationale, from a utility point of view, for investing in nuclear power.

All this does not mean that there has not been a great deal of self-delusion and patent unreality in utility and government expectations of the economic performance of nuclear power. The great bulk of 'evidence' in nuclear economics in fact refers not to concrete historical experience of actual costs, but to forecasts of what *ought* to happen if a new plant were started now. Such forecasts have characteristically suffered from the 'appraisal optimism' which has been observed in a wide range of projects, private and public, power and non-power. This tendency to overstate the likely net benefits has been exaggerated in the case of nuclear power by two notable factors: first, there has been an unusually large lobby interested in promoting nuclear power over its competitors, and this has led to a differential optimism in favour of nuclear power; secondly, because nuclear power has been both complex and increasingly politicised, the conventional, static techniques of engineering economics have been increasingly inadequate as forecasting tools.

This has meant that even without any in-built appraisal optimism, nuclear costs have tended to be severely under-forecast. Over-rapid development, inherent complexity, rising safety standards and (in some countries) a more generally hostile regulatory and political climate have combined to make conventional, quantity survey-based techniques hopelessly inadequate for forecasting nuclear costs accurately, though they are still widely used. Internationally the most influential of these forecasts have come from official US sources, and they date back to 1967. They have massively underestimated the actual costs, and though they have attempted to keep up with real cost escalations they have remained essentially backward-looking. In the UK, the forecasts of AGR costs, initiated in 1965 when construction of the still incomplete Dungeness B plant was started, have likewise been valueless as guides to real costs:

they have been huge underestimates.

Despite this largely doleful history it is worth looking at recent official forecasts, partly because they do now show – if at times only indirectly – that the apparently substantial economic superiority once claimed for nuclear power has now been largely eroded. The official OECD body responsible for nuclear power – the Nuclear Energy Agency (NEA) – periodically reviews its member governments' views of the economic status of nuclear power, compared to its main potential competitor, power from large coal-fired units. The 1986 review-body[2] is unlikely to have been biased against nuclear power, containing, as it did, many representatives of the nuclear industry but no one with an interest in coal-firing. Its conclusions are interesting, because it is no longer argued that nuclear power is cheaper throughout the OECD; in some regions of the USA and Canada, nuclear power is officially acknowledged to be more expensive. The specific assumptions that were fed into the 1986 assessment were also biased in favour of nuclear power in two important respects – the value of the US dollar chosen (all costs of coal are denominated in US dollars), and the rate at which costs and benefits are 'discounted' (i.e. made progressively less valuable in today's terms, the further into the future they are expected to arise).

A re-working of the NEA figures by experienced Cambridge researchers who have not the slightest taint of anti-nuclear bias, and who merely changed the US dollar and discount assumptions in directions that any private businessman would be certain to approve, radically undermines the official wisdom.[3] Nuclear power now turns out to be cheaper than coal-fired power in fewer than half of the 20 regions covered. Thus the official presumption that nuclear power is automatically cheaper for future investments is no longer sustained even by an objective interpretation of official international figures.

A similar process of attrition has occurred in the case of the Sizewell PWR in the UK. Originally the Central Electricity Generating Board (CEGB) argued that a PWR at Sizewell would be so cheap that its total costs would be less than the running costs of the fossil-fired stations that it would replace at the bottom of the system. It would also, so they argued, provide power at much lower cost than coal-firing. As the public inquiry wore on, the CEGB's assumptions about construction cost were seriously questioned, and the world price of coal kept falling. By the time the Inspector, Sir Frank Layfield, produced his report, he expected total PWR costs to fall only just short of the less efficient stations' running costs; and by the time the government responded, coal prices had fallen so far that it was no longer clear whether Sizewell could even achieve the official minimum rate of return of 5 per cent. And all this was on the assumption that Sizewell's construction costs could be kept to the CEGB's original estimate, even when the CEGB *itself* was forecasting a cost overrun of over £100 million.[4] In these circumstances neither nuclear nor conventional coal-fired investment looked very profitable, and there was certainly no presumption that nuclear would be any cheaper than coal-firing. Once again the promise of jam tomorrow was beginning to wear thin.

Turning to the actual, historical experience of nuclear power, the record is much more patchy: most countries produce some figures showing the past costs of nuclear and alternative sources of power, but it is often difficult to make unambiguous interpretations of them.

In the UK, the figures for actual costs are probably more accurate than those of any other country. This is ironic, because until the early 1980s, the British data were particularly misleading. The old convention was to mix current with historic costs – for the capital-related costs, original-year prices were used, while current-year prices were used for fuel costs. This would not have led to any bias in favour of nuclear power if the profile of nuclear costs was similar to that for coal-firing (though it would underestimate the costs of *all* forms of power generation). But, as explained earlier, nuclear costs are predominantly capital-related while coal-fired electricity costs are mostly fuel-related. A technique which puts the prices of 10 to 15 years ago on capital, but current prices on fuel will systematically favour nuclear technology. Thus the only figures produced by the CEGB up to 1983 appeared to show that the early Magnox stations were susbstantially cheaper than all alternatives. It is true that the CEGB did provide a 'health warning' in the small print on its original tables, pointing out that the figures could not give a full economic appraisal, but as the Board did not provide any such appraisal, and used these highly flawed figures in a general public relations context in support of future nuclear power plans, the barrage of criticism which it met was hardly surprising.

By 1983 the CEGB had yielded to these criticisms and produced, for the first time, some methodologically better figures comparing nuclear costs with costs for power stations which were built at roughly the same time.[5] These showed a very different picture.

Using the offical interest rate of 5 per cent, the costs of Magnox stations up to 1983–4 were some 10 per cent higher than those of coal-fired stations of the same vintage, while the only AGR ever completed by the CEGB anywhere near its estimated time was still running 7 per cent dearer than its contemporary coal-fired plants. The other first-generation AGRs, at Heysham, Hartlepool and Dungeness, would clearly carry a much higher cost penalty. The CEGB also carried out a further calculation, covering whole lifetimes (i.e. including future operations) and these appeared to show nuclear in a more favourable light. Yet again, however, this was jam tomorrow: the future coal price figures used by the CEGB have already been shown to be much too high. As Lord Marshall, chairman of the CEGB, candidly admitted late in 1987, the economic benefits of nuclear power remain in the future.

The economic experience of nuclear power has not always proved so disappointing, on conventional, utility-based criteria. In France, for instance, Electricité de France (EdF) regularly reports that nuclear power generates electricity 30 to 50 per cent more cheaply than any alternatives. It can reasonably be objected that EdF has received large state subsidies, and also that the French authorities reveal such limited cost data that objective evaluation is difficult. Nevertheless the costs of nuclear construction have been low in France, and operating performance reasonably good. It is hard to argue, looking at costs through a government or utility lens, that nuclear power has not been cheaper than available alternatives. This is not the same thing as saying that the heavy French concentration on nuclear power has been wise, even from a technocratic point of view, but the French example is a good illustration of the strong economic attraction of nuclear power.

The experience of other countries has not all been so smooth as that of France. Nuclear costs in West Germany have been substantially higher than in France, and the fact that nuclear is still seen as an attractive option by utilities is mainly a consequence of the very high level of protection that the German government gives to the domestic coal industry – German power producers have to pay well over double the world market price of coal. And, as is very well known, nuclear power is now completely out of favour in the USA. What is perhaps less well known about the USA is that the essential problems of nuclear power have been almost totally economic, and had very little to do with safety or public opposition. The important thing about the Three Mile Island accident in 1979, from the viewpoint of the investment community, was not the public health risk but the financial risk. Any investment worth US $1 billion which can be written off in a few hours of poor decision-making, and which subsequently leads to an open-ended clean-up bill several times in excess of the construction cost, does not commend itself to private investors.

The question of financial risk is of course important in other countries. The current fashion for turning publicly-owned utilities into wholly or partly privately-owned companies sits uncomfortably with nuclear power. The financial risks, even in conditions where accidents are not considered seriously, are legion. One risk of taking on old nuclear stations is that they can quickly lead to uncertain and potentially uncontrollable decommissioning costs; while new projects involve risks of delays in licensing and construction, and thus much deferred profit. Such problems are at the heart of the debate over privatising the electricity supply in Britain at the moment. They mean that there is no serious likelihood of any purely private financial responsibility for nuclear power. In all cases state guarantees are needed to protect investors from the 'worst case' outcomes – only a few of which necessarily have anything to do with nuclear accidents.

Nuclear Power: Wider Costs

What conclusions can be drawn if an attempt is made to take account of some of the more diffuse costs to which nuclear power gives rise – the risks of serious accidents, the potential threat to civil liberties or the problem of costs handed down to future generations? There is not space here to weigh all these issues, and if I choose the single issue of future generations, it is partly because of its importance and partly because it gives insight into the misuse of technocratic analysis.

Perhaps surprisingly, conventional cost benefit analysis does attempt to take account of costs to future generations. It does this through the mechanical device of a discount rate, which has the effect of reducing the apparent present-day value of costs or benefits expected in the future. Thus a 5 per cent discount rate means that a sum of £105 expected in exactly one year's time has a 'present value' of only £100. The same sum expected in two years' time is reduced by a further 5 per cent to £95.24, and so on into the future. This technique of discounted cash flow analysis is used widely in all kinds of investment decision-making over short time horizons. In its own terms it can be a legitimate technique, and its purpose is to ensure that the investment under consideration will not earn less than alternative investments – £105 in a year's time is only worth £100 today because the alternative may be to put £100 into a building society today and it will turn into £105 next year through the agreed interest rate.

However, a technique which helps to ration investment decisions in the short term takes on altogether different meanings if extended generations into the future. For decisions with very long-term implications, it is necessary to take account of the philosophical and political meaning of applying discounting into an indefinite future. The power of discounting to diminish the apparent importance of future generations is remarkable: at 5 per cent a year, a value of £1,000 expected in 100 years' time turns out to have a present value of only £7.50. Most people have a clear sense that this is a fix, but there is nothing wrong with the logic: if you invested £7.50 now and could get a rate of return (interest) at 5 per cent every year for 100 years, you would have £1,000 in 100 years' time. The flaw is in the extraordinary assumption that anyone has the slightest idea of what interest rates or rates of return will be in 30, let alone in 100 years' time. This did not deter the CEGB in its Sizewell evidence from applying a 5 per cent discount rate 120 years into the future.[6] One imagines that they stopped at the year 2108 not because discounting becomes unimportant at that particular date, but rather because by that time any cost below infinity becomes so minute as to disappear from view, if seen through a discounting lens. To give an example, suppose the CEGB could foresee a waste management cost of £10 billion in the year 2109: using its 5 per cent discount procedure it would have valued it at only £22 million in present value terms, an apparent diminution by a multiple of 445.

In these circumstances, it is not hard to see how utilities are now able to take full and even generous account of long-term costs like decommissioning and waste management. What is the odd billion pounds or so in the middle of the next century if we only have to count it as around £10 million now? The CEGB, for one, does take reasonable account of such costs, and even if they were to prove underestimates by a factor of ten, this would hardly disturb the apparent economic balance as seen from today's vantage. But if we cannot know what the real productivity of the economy will be in the future, nor can we apply discounting in this blind way. The importance of this argument is that it does *not* depend on substituting some alternative line of philosophical argument about the importance of future generations and our moral or political duty to them. Rather it is a serious problem in the application of straight technocratic logic; it is simply not good business practice to discount indefinitely.

Once this is accepted, it becomes impossible to defend long-term discounting, and this has profound implications for the real economics of nuclear power. For at very low or zero discount rates, nuclear power shows up as inferior to alternatives, because the long tail of indefinite waste management costs eventually overwhelms all others. Strangely enough, the economics of nuclear power also show up poorly at *high* discount rates. This is because nuclear power has very high capital costs which occur in the early years. A high discount rate means that by the time the benefits in fuel savings emerge, they have become discounted heavily, and the high early costs of nuclear power come to predominate. In comparison with coal-firing, nuclear power therefore needs just those intermediate values of the discount rate (around 5 per cent) which governments or utilities normally use. At higher private-sector discount rates, nuclear power falls foul of its high early year costs; at low 'environmental' rates it falls foul of its indefinite waste management costs. It should be recognised that most renewable forms of energy are penalised even more heavily by high discount rates because they characteristically have an even higher early-year concentration of costs than nuclear power. But in terms of current choices between nuclear and coal-firing, nuclear economics are poised uneasily on an intermediate range of discount rates – much higher, or much lower, and nuclear power would appear very unattractive.

This discussion makes it clear that whether or not nuclear power looks economically attractive is not a matter of some iron law of business or engineering reality. Its appeal is rather a function of decisions about such characteristics of appraisal techniques as discount rates, where there is much room for legitimate disagreement.

The Costs of Non-nuclear Futures

It was a commonplace of pro-nuclear public relations in the 1970s to threaten humanity with catastrophic loss of civilised life if nuclear power were not vigorously promoted. Fred Hoyle's book title *Energy or Extinction?* was only slightly more extreme than the average run of this material. At the opposite extreme, there is an environmental view that nuclear power is such an expensive mistake that costs – seen in broad as well as narrowly financial terms – are bound to be lower if nuclear power ceases to operate. Neither of these extremes has much to be said for it.

What *would* happen if, for whatever reason, the world stopped using nuclear power as an electricity-producing technology? The answer to this is far from certain, and it depends very much on the period over which nuclear power was phased out, but the first point is that the 'lights will go out' view is alarmist and needs to be firmly rejected. If nuclear power were to be switched off overnight, there would be a short-term loss of power, but in any other circumstances this would be extremely unlikely. On the other hand, even if, as suggested earlier, nuclear has not in general been cheaper than fossil-fired alternatives, this is not the same as claiming that a transition to a non-nuclear future would be costless.

There are two reasons for expecting real costs to result from a nuclear shutdown, though the scale of costs will vary according to the speed and comprehensiveness of the phasing out, longer and geographically more limited shutdowns having lower costs. The first reason is that if a nuclear power plant is closed before the end of its working life, the costs of replacing it will in the short term be higher than those of keeping it running. This has nothing to do with whether or not nuclear costs *in total* are cheaper than alternative power sources. It is a consequence of the fact that nuclear *operating* costs are almost always lower than fossil-fired alternatives. Given that the expensive capital costs of the closed nuclear stations will already have been incurred, electric power systems lose the short-term benefits of low nuclear fuelling costs as they replace nuclear output with electricity with much higher operating costs. This leads into the second reason why costs would rise. A loss of nuclear output would lead to a big rise in the demand for fossil fuels. Elementary economic theory suggests that a rapid growth in demand will, other things being equal, tend to raise prices. This effect would be amplified in the case of fossil fuels by the fact that depletion (the best resources tend to get used up first) makes successive tranches of fossil fuel output more expensive, irrespective of immediate demand conditions.

It is difficult to attempt any calculation of these effects because they would be historically unprecedented. The impact of an extra 500 million tonnes of demand for fossil fuel, even if spread over two decades, could be very substantial. Estimates of the transitional costs of a nuclear shutdown in Britain alone, and phased over 15 or 20 years – both factors which will tend to keep costs relatively low – suggest that they would peak at about £1 billion a year some ten years after the start of a shutdown programme. These are substantial costs, though in fact they would increase electricity prices by no more than 10 per cent. By comparison, the new financial targets for the CEGB announced in late 1987 imply a price increase of around 15 per cent.

However, any more rapid transition would be even costlier, and countries like France – over three times as dependent on nuclear as the UK – would either have to contemplate very long transitional periods, or face very high costs. It would be wrong to underestimate the profound shock to the world's energy markets of a general or rapid shutdown of nuclear power: costs could be very high. On the other hand if, for whatever reason, nuclear power were to be completely shut down, the costs would not be likely to be of the 'end of civilised life as we know it' kind.

Long-term Alternatives to Nuclear Power: Demand and Conservation

Imagine a world in which nuclear power is coming to an end. How might energy develop? In particular, how could policy shape such a world ? This means looking ahead not just 20 years, but into prospects for the middle of the next century and beyond.

The most important contextual issue is the evolution of demand for energy, both in aggregate and for particular uses. The conventional 1970s vision of the long-term energy future was for energy demand to grow indefinitely, with nuclear power increasingly filling the gap that more and more serious depletion of fossil fuels would open up. This was the 'hard' path, and it was the one which dominated the decisions of governments, both Western and centrally planned. There was also a 'soft' path, promoted by Amory Lovins and others, emphasising renewable energy plus conservation as an alternative to nuclear, but it had little impact on policy.

The positions of both sides in the debate have become a little less stark, but the underlying visions have not changed much. In particular, despite rather more conservation than expected (not all of it the product of policy), the conventional view is still sceptical about the security and economy of a non-nuclear path. The differences between the current visions of the energy future are perhaps best illustrated by contrasting some 1980s versions of the two sides. The International Institute of Applied Systems Analysis (IIASA) in Vienna (a meeting-ground throughout the Cold War for scientists from both sides of the divide) is well known both for the complexity of its modelling and for its enthusiastic pro-nuclear advocacy. A long-term world energy study from IIASA in the early 1980s foresaw rapid and continuing growth in energy demand through the first half of the twenty-first century.[7] A very different British study of roughly the same vintage from Earth Resources Research (ERR) concluded that economic prosperity could be combined with substantial *falls* in energy use.[8] Generalised internationally, this difference suggests that IIASA expects world energy demand to be up to six to ten times as large as ERR. These figures are not wholly comparable, but such an enormous gap is highly significant. If IIASA were broadly right, and energy demand were to grow inexorably, then the future would be difficult without a technology to take the place of fossil fuels as they became increasingly scarce and expensive, and nuclear power is currently much the most commercially developed alternative. In this sense a high energy future and a nuclear future tend to be partners. If on the other hand ERR had got it right, then with up to ten times less energy to look for, the world could be much more relaxed about future energy sources. Of course there is a large territory between these views, but it is important to find some way of choosing between them in terms of broad direction.

The first issue is whether or not energy demand can now be separated ('decoupled' in energy jargon) from economic activity. Until the 1970s it was widely believed that there was a kind of iron law binding energy use to economic activity. For every extra 1 per cent of economic output, it was said, there would need to be an extra 1 per cent of energy provided. There was a good deal of post-war experience to back this up, but once energy prices rose, after 1973, economic growth continued in the OECD nations while energy demand *fell*. Between 1978 and 1983 national incomes in those countries grew by 9 per cent, while energy use fell by 7 per cent. But now that economic activity has picked up in the late 1980s energy demand has started to rise again. The question is, was the apparent 'decoupling' a hiccup in the operation of the old iron law, or did it herald a new era of potential choice for the energy future?

It is impossible to give an unqualified answer to this question, but two points can be made in favour of the view that the decoupling was real. The first is irrespective of policy and concerns the nature of technological change, as well as the responses to higher energy prices in the 1970s. There is little doubt that the broad sweep of new technologies which have begun to make an impact in the 1980s, and will do so increasingly in the next decade – information technology, biotechnology and new materials – are inherently energy-saving. This means that the achievement of energy efficiency will no longer be the once-for-all decision to put an extra 50 mm of insulation in the loft, for the technological frontier in energy efficiency is itself moving rapidly, much more rapidly than the frontier in energy supply technology. Particularly if economic growth clusters around these new technologies, then a high degree of decoupling is likely to be built into the fabric of economic activity, completely independent of policy.[9]

To this 'technological trajectory' in favour of improvements in energy efficiency, it is possible to add the increased consciousness of energy efficiency that has been built into the design of *all* technologies since the energy price rises of the 1970s. Thus, to take two important examples, houses and cars are now built to radically higher energy efficiency standards than was the case 20 years ago, largely because this consciousness has fed through to the regulatory and design process. Especially in the case of housing, where it takes a long time for the stock of houses to be renewed, this effect will quietly work away at reducing energy demand for many years, even with no conscious policy and no further technological change.

There are of course contrary trends. In particular, developing countries tend to have very high incremental energy demands as (or if) their economies grow. If the poorest in the world are to become less impoverished they are likely to need more energy – they could hardly use less than the pittance (usually of firewood or charcoal) to which they now have access.

The balance of these conflicting forces is impossible to predict. But if the world were to receive a strong impulse towards much more active conservation *policies* – and this is surely what a shutdown of nuclear power would provoke – there would be a technological impetus towards efficiency and conservation that could be built on. For these reasons we can be hopeful that a strong push towards conservation would almost certainly achieve significant results. The ERR vision of the future seems at least a possibility, while the IIASA vision seems narrow and unnecessary.

Having outlined this general assessment, it is important to be more specific. As was pointed out above, nuclear power is electricity specific, and if we need to find a substitute for nuclear power, conservation and efficiency policy would need to target electricity use. Nor should it be forgotten that much of the new technology mentioned earlier is captive to electricity – most obviously micro-electronics – but fortunately it tends to use micro-*energy* as well. The range of electricity conservation policies is substantial. They would need to aim above all at peak (maximum) electricity demand, because in the absence of significant storage technologies, electricity systems need to have more than sufficient plant to cover peak demand.

The experience in the US utility system of electricity conservation gives some idea of what might be possible. There are two kinds of policies: those which reduce demand by manipulating the operation of the electricity system, and those which concentrate on the use of energy in specific appliances. On the system side there is an excellent example of the way in which generic new technology can have great potential for energy saving. The diffusion of electronic meters, up to now a slow process (and in the UK virtually non-existent), offers enormous potential for interaction between customer and utility. Customers could, for instance, be given a financial incentive to allow their deep freezes or hot water systems to shut down for half an hour at peak time; or simple programming packages, in conjunction with more cost-reflecting prices, might allow them to instruct limited shut-off of certain appliances for specified periods. In addition, existing industrial and commercial load management schemes could be expanded. These policies could not be applied instantly – the meters are not yet installed – but within a few years they could undoubtedly make a major contribution, especially to reducing peak demands.

There are also ways in which the long-term improvement in the energy efficiency of electrical appliances could be speeded up. Best-practice energy efficiency in both industrial and domestic technologies – industrial motors, lighting, refrigeration, etc. – is far ahead of average current efficiency levels. A combination of financial incentives to speed up the replacement of old appliances and to encourage retrofit of energy-saving technology to existing appliances (e.g. electronic load reducers on industrial electric motors) could make a great impact.

Under the increased political and economic pressure which a nuclear shutdown would engender, there is little doubt that new ways to reduce electricity demand – without necessarily increasing inconvenience – would be found. The important point to stress about these kinds of policy is that they are not only technically feasible, they are also in most cases highly cost-effective judged against normal commercial criteria. Electricity conservation would therefore not necessarily impose large economic penalties, and it could, if well handled, conceivably do the reverse.

Long-term Alternatives to Nuclear Power: Renewable and Non-renewable Sources

It is no accident that demand and conservation have been placed before energy supply sources in considering alternatives to nuclear power. To the reasons already given – that energy efficiency is highly compatible with new technology in general, and that the scope for rapid improvement is substantial – another must be added: the environment. There are of course many supply options to replace nuclear power, but all those in wide current use, mainly fossil fuels, carry serious environmental problems with them. Understanding of these problems, and popular awareness of their gravity, are both advancing apace. Consequently replacing nuclear energy with saved energy has enormous environmental attractions.

The conventional 'soft path' reply to this is to encourage the development of environmentally more benign renewable technologies; and in the context of nuclear shutdown, this is of course necessary and desirable. But nuclear shutdown would also put a premium on rapid solutions, and there is no escaping the fact that few renewable technologies are yet ready for such rapid diffusion that they could quickly fill all the supply gaps left by nuclear power – gaps which would certainly remain for a number of years, however successful conservation policies might be. This has two implications. One is that there would be no avoiding an expansion in the use of fossil fuels (especially coal and gas). The second is that those renewable technologies closest to the point of large-scale commercialisation are in some cases those that are environmentally least benign, particularly tidal barrages and possibly wave power. These are large, centralised technologies with serious environmental implications. But because they are geared to renewable resources, this is the sort of technology for which political pressure would probably prove strong in the absence of nuclear power. There are other promising renewables which carry much more limited environmental impact, and wind power is one such. But the general point is important: saving energy is inherently preferable to supplying it, even if much of the new supply would be renewable.

Among the supply sources that could be substituted for nuclear power, increased use of fossil fuel is the most easily implemented as a short- and medium-term option. Oil is a genuinely scarce fuel and little could be expected from it. Gas is somewhat less scarce and there is currently a short-term glut. Together with large new fields in northern Norway and elsewhere, there is a real chance that gas could take a substantial share of increased fuel demand. In terms of sulphur pollution, it offers great advantages over both oil and coal. Nevertheless, growth in gas supplies is unlikely to continue for more than a few years.

No such qualifications about resource adequacy surround coal. If there were no environmental drawbacks, coal could satisfy a nuclear-gap-sized expansion in energy demand for many decades into the future. The last decade has revealed enormous increases in accessible coal reserves, so that physical exhaustion is not even a medium-term worry. The real problems are environmental. At present the most politically sensitive of coal issues is air pollution – particularly acid rain. While nitrous oxide emissions can be reduced without much real difficulty, sulphur remains a problem. There is control technology in the form of 'flue-gas desulphurisation', but it is a big, expensive and primitive technology with an almost unlimited appetite for limestone, thus raising a new set of environmental problems as it cumbersomely solves another. If coal use is to grow significantly, other sulphur-removal technologies will be necessary. Among these, the use of 'pressurised fluidised bed combustion', where fine coal particles are burnt in a turbulent mixture in a strong up-current of air, offers the possibility of sulphur removal in combustion itself. This technology is not yet at the point of commercialisation, however, and renewed research and development efforts would be needed to improve it.

The other technology which would undoubtedly be more widely used in a nuclear shutdown is combined heat and power (CHP), where waste heat from power production is used for space heating, instead of being dissipated to the atmosphere, as commonly happens now. This is a conservation technology as much as a supply technology – the proportion of coal input that is converted into useful energy rises from around 37 per cent to around 70 per cent. CHP is expensive, and heat loads take time to accumulate. It is therefore a technology whose greatest impact would be seen over 20 to 30 years, rather than at once.

Finally, in respect of coal, the spectre at the feast is the 'greenhouse effect' – the global warming caused by the release of carbon dioxide when coal or other fossil fuel is burned. It seems to have been well established that the greenhouse effect could be disastrous if it were allowed to develop. However there now seems more doubt about the extent of coal's complicity in it. Some recent estimates suggest that coal combustion in power plants may make only a 5 per cent contribution to the total warming effect. Were this only approximately true, it would, in the context of nuclear shutdown, be extremely good news; but uncertainty about the greenhouse effect and its causes remains much greater than our knowledge of it. No serious post-nuclear energy policy could rely entirely on coal, because of the greenhouse effect and because of other worries about exhaustion and land dereliction through mining. It is therefore time to turn to the renewable sources.

If nuclear power – representing science, industry, centralisation, control over nature and maleness – is at one extreme of the symbolic spectrum in energy, renewable energies are at the other extreme – representing decentralisation, rural life, harmony with nature and femaleness. Whether or not nuclear always lives up to its symbolic meaning, renewables sometimes do not. As has been said, renewables can be pressed into large-scale, centralised and (for that matter) high-technology forms. Those who want renewables for symbolic and political purposes might not find the thrust of policy in a non-nuclear world much to their taste. Pressure would be strong for the rapid introduction of large chunks of technology – without this, the spread of renewables would probably be slower, and fossil fuel use correspondingly higher.

Renewables have been starved of state research and development support, and this largely accounts for their uneven and sometimes embryonic level of commercial development. In the mid 1980s the OECD countries were spending some US $500 million in research and development annually on all renewables. This may sound substantial, but nuclear technologies were collectively absorbing $4,800 million a year.[10] Even the best supported among the renewables, direct solar energy of all kinds, had less than a third of the expenditure devoted to that most exotic of all nuclear technologies, fusion, which is not expected even by its supporters to be a commercial proposition for at least 50 years (all going well). A non-nuclear world would clearly reorient energy research away from its concentration on nuclear, and the main beneficiaries would be renewables and improved forms of fossil fuel use. This would provide a sounder technical base for some renewables, though not overnight. It is salutary to remember that after 40 years of sustained state support around the world, nuclear power still only contributes 5 per cent of world primary energy. Commercialisation and diffusion of any new technology is necessarily a long process.

The major technical problem involved in the widespread use of renewable energies is that of storage. As mentioned earlier, there are no satisfactory cheap technologies for storing electricity, so that in general it must be generated at the same time as it is needed. Renewable technologies do not necessarily produce their greatest output at the time of greatest demand, and this means that much expanded research into more effective storage technologies would be a high priority, particularly if it became an objective to reduce fossil fuel use in electricity generation to very low levels.

Most research into renewables has concentrated on their use as a source of electricity: this has been much criticised by many supporters of renewables, but in the context of nuclear shutdown, it would appear rather fortunate. Official fashions in renewables have changed in recent years. The story of the British government's espousal of wave power, followed by rejection when it threatened to become reasonably feasible and potentially economic, is one of the most discreditable episodes in recent energy policy.[11]

The most promising of the renewable technologies at present would seem to be wind power and solar photovoltaics. Interestingly, both are essentially offshoots of major high technology industry – the aerospace industry in the case of wind turbines, and the computer materials (semi-conductor) industry in the case of photovoltaics.

Wind power is already a more or less commercial proposition. Many wind turbines, some hundreds per year, have already been sold, and in some countries, notably Denmark, there is a sizeable wind turbine industry. However, it would be premature to say that wind power is yet commercially mature. Recent sales to California, the world's largest market, have substantially slowed because the tax and subsidy regime is no longer as favourable to renewables as it once was. Nevertheless, wind turbines are now beyond the stage of needing large state research and development subsidies. The great bulk of development work is now funded by private companies, and they clearly expect to sell increasing numbers of machines in open competition even without the 'advantage' of nuclear shutdowns. British official figures show land-based turbines as coming within range of commercial viability, with the possibility of much greater offshore potential, currently seen as more expensive. For smaller, crowded countries like the UK, offshore may be an important location, because wind power is relatively land-hungry, though activities such as farming are not necessarily incompatible with it.

In the past it has been widely supposed that the problems of wind variability – and therefore power output availability – might limit the proportion of total electricity that could be managed on an integrated grid. Recent British work suggests, however, that much higher proportions – up to 50 per cent or more of total power – could be managed without serious operational problems.[12] While it would take time, and a lot of land, to reach such levels even if electricity demand were successfully restrained, wind power is perhaps the one renewable technology in which it is possible to have confidence, on the basis of what is technologically clear now, as a large source of fairly cheap power into the long-term future.

There are of course many other possibilities. Of the water-based sources, there is significant scope world-wide for expansion of conventional hydroelectricity. However the environmental difficulties of hydro are becoming increasingly manifest, so that while the technology is mature and fairly unproblematic, large-scale expansion is perhaps unlikely. Tidal power is limited to particular geographical locations with suitable conditions. Britain has several of these, of which the Severn estuary is the largest and most famous. The technology is again fairly straightforward, but environmentally there are potential problems as yet untested. Tidal power could make a contribution, but in global terms it would be a small one. Lastly among the water-based possibilities there is wave power. This is one of the most uncertain of all the renewables. The idea of offshore machinery, subject to severe buffeting, covering tens of miles, and very difficult to maintain cheaply, sounds inherently unpromising. Against this, British research made large strides on low budgets while subject to much official discouragement, and Norway is experimenting with the use of more sheltered locations in fjords. It is one of those technologies on which a non-nuclear age would almost certainly want to spend substantial research resources, without however having any certainty of good commercial results.

This survey of renewables is not comprehensive, but ought not to omit the last of the 'high-tech' options – photovoltaics. This uses various forms of silicon to turn light directly into electricity. Its initial uses were military/exotic (e.g. electricity for space exploration) and its initial costs were very high. As semi-conductor technology has rapidly advanced, so its costs have fallen by orders of magnitude, and while it is still not nearly as cheap as wind power, it is the one renewable technology where continuing real cost falls can be confidently predicted because of its intimate link with the most technologically dynamic of all the world's industries. It is also particularly intriguing because it offers the possibility of rural, small-scale and modular use at costs no higher than in central or concentrated forms. However it is also a prime example of the pressing need for the development of superior energy storage technologies. At the moment a very high proportion of the costs of photovoltaic systems is in the auxiliary equipment, particularly the large battery storage needed if photovoltaics are to be used at night. Unless something more effective than a lead-acid battery can be found for storage, photovoltaics are likely to remain relatively expensive even if the silicon technology eventually comes almost for free (which is not impossible).

Conclusions

While it is not dominant in electric power production, nuclear power technology contributes substantially to world electricity output. This means that although its economic record is modest even on the narrow criteria used by electric utilities, it could not be removed without substantial disruption and cost. These costs would nevertheless be bearable. A non-nuclear future would need to place heavy emphasis on achieving accelerated conservation, largely for environmental reasons. But this would undoubtedly be assisted by the direction of overall technological change. Fossil fuels, especially coal, would necessarily play a large part in the transition. Renewable sources of energy would be strongly encouraged in such a world, but it would be unwise to expect them to make too large a contribution until substantial further research and investment had been made.

Notes

1. Statistics from this section are from standard UN and OECD/IAEA sources and from S. Thomas, *The Realities of Nuclear Power*, Cambridge University Press, 1988.
2. OECD/NEA, *Projected Costs of Generating Electricity from Nuclear- and Coal-Fired Power Stations for Commissioning in 1995*, OECD, Paris, 1986.
3. Cambridge Energy Research Ltd. (N. Evans and W. Bullen), *Nuclear Economics and the Price of Coal*, 10 Jesus Lane, Cambridge, UK 1987.
4. CPRE (Council for the Protection of Rural England), *An Update of the Economics of Sizewell B*, London 1987.
5. CEGB, *Analysis of Generation Costs*, London, 1983, and *Analysis of Generation Costs*, 1983/4 Update, London, 1987.
6. For example, in CEGB, proof of evidence to the Sizewell inquiry (P/9) *The Nuclear Fuel Cycle* by J. K. Wright, November 1982.
7. IIASA, *Energy in a Finite World*, Ballinger, USA, 1981.
8. D. Olivier et al., *Energy Efficient Futures*, ERR, London, 1983.
9. W. Walker, 'Information technology and the use of energy', in *Energy Policy* vol. 13 no. 5, October 1985.

10. IEA, *Energy Policies and Programmes of IEA Countries*, 1985 Review, Paris, 1986.

11. See House of Commons Energy Committee, *Energy Research Development and Demonstration in the UK*, Ninth Report, HMSO, 1984.

12. M. Grubb, 'The Integrated analysis of new energy sources on the British supply system: methods and application': paper presented to Institute of Electrical Engineering's Energy Options Conference, Reading, UK, 7–9 April 1987.

7

Getting Out of the Nuclear Fix: Towards an Alternative Model of Development

PRAFUL BIDWAI

The case for nuclear power has always rested on a number of questionable, or worse, wholly irrational, assumptions, whether explicit or implicit. These are, first, that nuclear fission represents a cheap, safe, abundant and potentially inexhaustible source of energy.[1] Secondly, that there is, at least in the long run, no alternative to atomic energy since fossil fuels, only finite quantities of which exist, are liable to run out. Thirdly, that the environmental costs of nuclear energy are basically affordable; in particular, that however serious the problems of long-term storage and disposal of nuclear waste, they are amenable to technical solutions. Fourthly, that the technology trajectory involved in the so-called nuclear fuel cycle is an acceptable choice from society's point of view. And finally, that there is something universal and global about the appropriateness of nuclear energy, which transcends particular contexts or conditions, whether social, economic, political, cultural or geographic.

Chernobyl, even more powerfully than the 150 or more major nuclear accidents which preceded it world-wide, has all but demolished the critical component in the first assumption. The most ardent advocates of nuclear power can no longer pretend that atomic energy is safe; at best they can plead, rather unconvincingly, that it should and can be made safe. At any rate, the debate since April 1986 has only served to highlight the *generic* problems of nuclear safety, independent of specific designs or combinations of coolants and moderators.[2]

As for the presumed cheapness of nuclear electricity, the experience of the past 30 years should have put paid to this proposition, and not only in the US, still the world's most nuclear nation, with its history of abandoned plants and utility company crashes. Elsewhere, too, the promise of cheap power from nuclear stations has proved delusory, despite massive state subsidies and the concealment of true costs – research and development, fuel, decommissioning and waste storage – which the nuclear industry does not quite acknowledge or even budget for, let alone pay.[3]

The assumption that nuclear power is indispensable rests on a crude Energy Malthusianism which grasps neither the fact of a steady decline in the energy intensity of industry, coupled with the spread of energy-saving techniques since 1973–4, nor the impressive growth recorded in renewable energy development over the past two decades.

If it is impossible for anyone to argue convincingly that there is no alternative in the long run to nuclear power, it is equally difficult to contend that humanity is any closer than it was 30 years ago to solving the problem posed by nuclear wastes.[4] Indeed, even in principle, there may be no solution at all to that problem: it may be impossible to fabricate materials which can confine huge quantities of radioactivity, chemical energy and heat in small volumes for tens of thousands of years, with a reasonably low risk of leakage, breach or corrosion. Nor is it possible to discover geologically stable formations in which such wastes may be safely placed and which are remote and guaranteed to remain bone-dry (so that the debris does not leach into the environment) for prolonged periods of time. [5]

The world's experience with the technology path charted by nuclear power development, in particular the possibilities of nuclear weapons proliferation that it has opened up, has been such as to leave even the enthusiasts of the 'peaceful atom' cold. The most elementary concern for peace and nuclear disarmament cannot be reconciled with an endorsement of the destructive technology trajectories of nuclear energy. In the nuclear weapons states, the strong and numerous connections between the military and peaceful programmes, mediated by the 'plutonium economy', are testimony to the horrific reality of 'vertical proliferation'. The examples of India, Pakistan, Argentina and Brazil, as well as those of Israel and South Africa ('horizontal proliferation') should be constant reminders of the potential threat that nuclear technology poses to human survival.

It is striking that the 'softer' nuclear states, the first four in this list, could not have come as close as they have to the acquisition or use of weapons-grade fissile material without an overtly 'peaceful' nuclear programme which, among other things, provides a cover for the clandestine military one.[6] Underwriting the destructive possibilities contained in the nuclear technology trajectory has no part in any rational conception of the relationship between society and technology, or indeed in any concern for survival itself.

Finally, only a perverse equation of certain peculiarities of industrially developed societies with the conditions in the rest of the world can support the assumption about nuclear power's appropriateness, which is questionable even in the countries of the North. For reasons we shall examine below, the patterns of energy demand and consumption among two-thirds of the globe's people are such that nuclear power could not possibly have any contribution to make to them, even if it were safe, cheap and ecologically benign, which it is not. Far from being universally appropriate, nuclear energy must be seen as globally inappropriate.

Each of the assumptions underlying the argument for atomic power is thus false or grossly irrational. And yet, the case for that technology depends on the proposition that all of them are not only true but *universally* accepted as such. This universal acceptance is indeed an important premise which has underpinned every single nuclear power expansion programme drawn up in any part of the world, as well as the notoriously extravagant – because wildly inaccurate – projections of nuclear capacity growth made by the International Atomic Energy Agency (IAEA), the Organisation for Economic Cooperation and Development (OECD), and by a host of nuclear industry lobbyists.[7]

In the absence of that premise, it is simply inconceivable that governments would have drawn up ambitious nuclear expansion programmes of such proportions that they have had to be pruned by an order of magnitude. The 'universal acceptance' premise involves the assumption that nuclear power development would be conflict-free and would command broad-based consensus. Everything that has happened since the early 1970s, in virtually every country seeking to produce electricity by means of nuclear fission, violates that assumption.

In fact, there are few technologies which have engendered as much popular opposition and social conflict as has nuclear power generation. Almost every aspect of atomic energy projects, from basic design and safety systems to location and emergency management procedures, has come in for public criticism.

Nuclear power has run into conflict with various social institutions which have a role in building a broad consensus or in democratic decision-making. Decisions taken at the top to position nuclear installations at particular sites have often highlighted conflicts between centralisation and local or regional autonomy, and the democratic right of communities to veto national programmes. Secrecy, which always shrouds the procurement, movement and processing of nuclear materials, has tended to generate debates on the adverse consequences of nuclear power development for democratic rights and civil liberties.[8]

The inevitable and routine exposure of specialised groups of workers to radiation and other hazards in nuclear facilities has raised awkward questions of equity and the right not to be discriminated against. The clandestine storage and dumping of nuclear wastes, as in the Nukem/Transnuklear episode in West Germany in January 1988 (and an earlier deal between Western European firms and China, by which the latter agreed to store 4,000 tonnes of reactor wastes in the Gobi desert against the payment of US $6 billion), have raised issues such as national sovereignty, international conflict and the iniquity of existing North–South relations, as well as the ethics of the nuclear industry's practices. Similarly, restrictions on nuclear exports, imposed by the nuclear supplier states and regularly violated by private firms in those countries, have alarmed their own public opinion and engendered hostility in the importing states.

These conflicts and contentions are not mere accidents or aberrations in the history of nuclear energy development. They are central to it. They originate in the very heart of the technology and are inseparable from its development and use. Precisely because nuclear power generation is based on the principle of first bringing into existence, and then attempting to tap, enormous quantities of energy released in a process marked by an extraordinary degree of volatility (or extremely high levels of entropy), its use is necessarily fraught with problems: safety may be jeopardised by fatigue in fragile materials, or by human error in the course of routine operations (which are always unusually hazardous in this technology). At the other extreme, political difficulties and dangers may arise from differential access to sensitive materials and processes, and from the military uses to which nuclear capacity is liable to be put.

The persistence as well as the magnitude of these problems underscores the proposition that the development of nuclear power is inherently incapable of promoting consensus or harmony. It can only generate conflict and suspicion – and repression and violence as a response to them. This much should be evident from the international rivalry that has marked the pursuit of nuclear energy: between Argentina and Brazil, and India and Pakistan in the 1970s and 1980s, between Western Europe and the US in the 1960s over the choice of reactor types,[9] and between Israel and Iraq, the high point of which was the Israeli bombing in 1981 of the Osirak power reactor in blatant violation of Iraqi air space.

Within nation-states too, opposition to nuclear power has always been tackled by force and police methods. Nuclear power development has also been associated with deception, dissimulation and disinformation: witness the recent Thatcher cabinet decision to withhold publication of the full testimony of witnesses in the Windscale accident of 1957 and the suppression of relevant information on its health consequences by the Macmillan government 30 years ago; or the Indian government's persistent refusal to disclose figures for heavy water production, a material it claims to use solely in commercial power reactors; or the French government's extraordinary campaign of lies over the Chernobyl cloud, which mysteriously bypassed France in 1986.

A technology which necessitates such disinformation and the use of the repressive powers of the state, and fuels suspicion and rivalry is, fundamentally, *socially irrational*. Little suprise, then, that nuclear power is increasingly an imposition by the state upon the people. It can only be imposed at the cost of restricting civil liberties and fundamental rights, and through the practice of deception – or if that fails, by outright repression. Without the modern state's support for and commitment to it, nuclear power could not possibly exist.[10]

The state's support for nuclear energy fits snugly with, indeed derives from, its commitment to something larger, namely a particular model of development associated with the North. This model is radically elitist, technicist, conservative, conflict-oriented, consumerist and biased in favour of centralisation. Underlying it is a vision of society as an entity composed of discrete individuals, each separated from his or her living resources and alienated from nature, each committed to advancing his or her 'welfare' at the expense of the rest, each seeking the highest level of pleasure or satisfaction, conceived only in terms of the acquisition of more and more goods and services. In such a society, the criteria for judging progress are the unceasing advancement of the productive forces irrespective of their consequences for society and ecology, and the ability of the state to satisfy the potentially limitless wants of its consumer-citizens.

Within the Northern model of development, technology is predatory upon nature and designed for its conquest and subordination. Given the mass nature of the wants (demands) it is called upon to fulfil, technology tends towards complex and large-scale systems, and is consequently best organised and operated by large, specialised agencies such as transnational corporations, or gigantic state enterprises, which of necessity assume a degree of alienation from society and consequently entail the loss of public control over productive forces. The favoured technology must also produce goods which are designed to suit individual use, and are 'convenient' in accordance with the existing patterns of consumption: cars instead of buses or trains; individual family homes rather than community dwellings; private clinics, not public hospitals.

The energy perspective associated with the Northern model logically assumes the electrification of society as an ideal: electricity, the most refined form of energy, must become the commonest, if not the universal, form of its consumption, although power turbines can only tap a third of the heat that is generated to produce the steam which drives them. Such electricity is ideally produced in large centralised plants. It must be abundant in its availability, in conformity with the prime criterion of progress.

Nuclear power is the ideal, ultimate and complete expression of this energy perspective. It completes the alienation from nature of an important component of the modern productive apparatus, and distances it from the constraints imposed by the finitude of natural resources and the rhythms of nature. For the first time, a technology seems to promise truly limitless possibilities.

Atomic energy thus represents the triumph of science and technology over nature. It is, quintessentially, the most developed expression of the ideology of super-industrialism. It also frees energy generation from such social constraints as trade unions and labour indiscipline. It establishes the technocrat's total and absolute control over the productive process in a crucial area of productive activity.

Nuclear power is therefore an ideal expression of the triumph of what Marx called dead labour over living labour, indeed over society itself. Thus, logically, nuclear power would represent capital's ultimate victory over both nature and human beings. However, atomic energy is at the same time such a concentrated expression of bourgeois irrationality and of technocratic arrogance that its proponents have been unable to ensure that society at large will accept it. This was inevitable, given the way in which the case for nuclear power was, or had to be, presented from the very beginning. Society was asked to believe, without the slightest evidence in support of the claim, that science and technology could be fully trusted to solve, for instance, the problem of nuclear waste disposal. This was in the early 1950s when the precise composition of debris from nuclear power reactors was not even fully understood, and the problems of safe disposal of nuclear wastes and decommissioning nuclear plants had not even been practically posed. The assumption was that the might of science, which after all had made Hiroshima and Nagasaki possible, could always be trusted to find solutions to all problems; presumably it would even make radioactivity go away or, at the very least, somehow render it harmless.

The early celebration of the globe's nuclear future, and the euphoria over 'Atoms for Peace', were thus rooted in nothing less than pure faith. What else could have moved nuclear scientocrats to declare that atomic power would be 'too cheap to meter', before a single convincing computation had been made of the capital costs of atomic energy generation?[11]

Today, these promises stand betrayed. Indeed they were never realisable in the first place. The nuclear establishment is now paying the price of its unfulfillable promises and its technocratic arrogance, in the coin of a growing popular rejection of atomic power. Its social unacceptability has trapped nuclear energy in a grave crisis.

The present crisis of nuclear power is itself symptomatic of the larger crisis of the Northern model of development to which it is bound by a strong nexus.

Like nuclear power, the Northern model finds its highest level of development in the First World where it originated. But its appeal is by no means confined to the industrially developed capitalist countries of the West or the OECD. Despite all their systemic differences with the West, the countries of the East have pursued the same model, with the possible, and in many ways limited, exceptions of China and Albania. The similarities between East and West go far beyond Lenin's formula of 'Soviets plus Electricity'. They are reflected in the patterns of production and consumption that prevail in the socialist states and the people's democracies.

The similarities are rooted in the failure of the East to evolve alternative, less elitist, anti-consumerist and non-technical approaches to development. Its science and technology have not undergone the structural transformation that its society and politics have been through. Its systems of production are in no fundamental way different from the West's in their plant-level organisation or technology. The East, 70 years after the October Revolution, continues to compete with the West on basically Western terms, although it has replaced the role of private capital by the state.

The Northern development model has its strong adherents in the Third World too. These are narrowly-based elites who have set themselves the goal of completing the task that colonialism left unfinished. The goal essentially entails imitating the West in the hope that its trajectory of capitalist development, and in particular industrialisation, can be replicated in the Third World and that the objectives considered desirable in the Northern model can become relevant to the 'backward' and 'less developed' countries.

The Third World elites' project is becoming increasingly unviable, thanks to major changes in the structure of the world economy and in the technological base of production, growing disparities between the North and the South, increasingly adverse terms of trade for the latter, and most important, the failure of the protagonists of the project to institute domestic reforms which alone can furnish the basis for rapid economic growth with a measure of equity. Barring exceptions, indeed negative examples, such as South Korea, Taiwan, Hong Kong and Singapore, the Third World has not made the transition towards an economic 'take-off'. The prospect of such a take-off is looking increasingly bleak for the vast majority of Third World countries.

However, their elites have not abandoned their developmental goals. Instead, they have increasingly resorted to coercion in imposing them upon their subject-peoples. These elites are politically bankrupt. They have no alternative projects of their own. But they have developed a heavy stake in perpetuating the Northern model: their power has come to depend on the ability to dispense patronage through the implementation of development projects in irrigation and water supply, land management, agriculture, forestry, mining, industry and communications. Such programmes account for the bulk of state expenditure and provide an infrastructure for and a crucial input into private business whose leaders are closely allied to the functionaries of the state.

In sharp contrast to the elites with their stake in imitative development strategies, stand the people in the Third World. For them, the Northern model is not just inappropriate, it is actually predatory. Indeed, every development project deriving from that model tends to displace and uproot people, separating them from their living resources, robbing them of the produce of nature to which historically they had had free access, and impoverishing them materially and culturally.[12]

Development projects, whether in mining, industry or agriculture, bring in their wake the timber contractor, the trader, the government official, the property shark and the bootlegger, all of whom have an essentially parasitic relationship with the majority. A new regime of social, juridical and economic relations follows which further marginalises the poor, often driving them off the land and into beggary, crime and prostitution. At the same time, development's depredations upon nature – inevitable in the manner in which irrigation, mining and chemicals-based agriculture are planned and executed – lead to the degradation of the environment, often turning vast tracts of land into deserts. The crippling cooking-energy crisis, the decline of agriculture and the near-famine conditions incessantly reported from different parts of the Third World in the 1980s are direct consequences of the development projects and modernisation plans undertaken in the 1960s and 1970s by elites in pursuit of the Northern model.

Thus, in the most profound sense, the poor in the Third World are the greatest victims of the Northern model. Increasing poverty in the South is inseparable from the consequences of that path of development. However, this is not to argue that the people of the North are its true beneficiaries or that a majority of them have a stake in it. They certainly do not; only the Northern elites do.

The Northern model has run into crisis everywhere. It is increasingly proving ecologically unsustainable, socially undesirable, culturally impoverishing and politically bankrupt in the industrially developed countries too.

This is especially true of the West. The First World is already witnessing the collapse of the 'welfare consensus'. The structural changes that have occurred in the capitalist production process in the past decade or more have transformed the capital–labour relationship retrogressively, making high rates of unemployment a permanent feature of Western society. At the same time, growing numbers of the poor in the West face the real prospect of political disenfranchisement. Political democracy is under a new threat as the substance of politics gets drained from public forms of democratic life and decisions are increasingly taken by bureaucrats unaccountable to the public. Individual freedom is in jeopardy as the state increasingly turns to administrative measures and 'law and order' approaches to the problem of reproducing the existing structure of hegemony. Some of the once-stable institutions and organisations of Western society, such as the trade unions, are facing a steady erosion of their power.

Thus the greatest achievements and promises of the bourgeois revolution themselves face a threat today. The search for individual autonomy and political subjectivity is 'redirected and neutralized as a need to construct individual uniqueness and authenticity out of mass-produced commodities'.[13] And the culture of postmodernism promotes the values of hopelessness and despair as well as a fake notion of subjectivity. The West's citizens, already atomised and greatly alienated from the real, the earthy and the communal, are now increasingly disoriented in a world which they can barely comprehend, let alone regulate or direct.

The contemporary crisis of Western society only highlights the perverse nature of the development model it has followed. The crisis deepens even as new inequalities and new forms of domination emerge in the West's relationship with the rest of the world, to the further disadvantage of the most underprivileged and poorest of the planet's people.

There cannot be the slightest doubt that the dominant Northern model of development is neither viable nor desirable. It has demonstrably failed to create a secure, equitable, prosperous and humane world. It has only reinforced the structures of dominance over the majority by privileged minorities everywhere. It has made profligacy (of the few), greed (of the successful), violence (of the powerful) and power (of the privileged) into virtues. And it has inflicted enormous damage upon the majority, i.e. the weak and the poor; it has misallocated global and national resources; it has jeopardised peace and security; it has poisoned the world's air, water and land, wreaked untold havoc upon the planet's ecology, and destroyed the delicate balances of nature. It thus threatens the survival and wellbeing of billions of people.

But what is the alternative to the dominant Northern model of development? How can we roll back some of the damage and correct our course? What are the central themes and concerns on which such an alternative model must base itself?

A number of efforts have recently been made to formulate a coherent alternative. The more notable of these are to be found in the work of the Club of Rome, Schumacher, Boulding, Hirsch, Kapp, Bahro, the Dag Hammarskjöld Foundation (Sweden), the Intermediate Technology Development Group, the Other Economic Summit (UK), and the Centre for Science and Environment (India).[14] The UN Environment Programme, Habitat, and the Bruntland Commission (World Commission on Environment and Development) have also contributed to these efforts.

There are some common strands in the otherwise disparate orientations and themes that mark this work: the need to impose rational limits on economic growth, conservation of natural resources, concerted global action to protect the world's fragile ecosystem, restructuring of North–South relations, promotion of production systems which are appropriate to local needs, shift from large to small scales of production, emphasis on 'human-scale' economics, decentralisation of production and planning, local self-reliance, ecosystem-based reallocation of resources, local production cooperatives, strengthening local community initiatives, empowerment of the poor and the weak.

All these initiatives share with the green perspective a concern with reversing the misallocation of resources and correcting the perverse priorities on which the Northern development model is based and which it reinforces. While some efforts (e.g. the Dag Hammarskjöld Foundation's 'What Now? Another Development?') tend to emphasise a restructuring of the international economic order, some others (e.g. Schumacher) tend to be concerned with more local issues related to production, distribution and exchange. All of them are critical of the ideology and politics of super-industrialism.

The emerging critique of industrialism and the Northern model of development is part of, and has contributed to, the greatest ferment the world has witnessed since the mid-1970s in the form of popular movements for peace, for environmental protection, for industrial safety and the defence of natural resources. This churning up of society has thrown up thousands of ecology groups and hundreds of issue-based initiatives in virtually every part of the world. The range of problems they are concerned with is itself impressive, spanning as it does health and drugs, chemicals in agriculture, forestry, conservation of seed varieties and plant genetic resources, protection of the oceans, biotechnology, unethical promotional practices of transnational corporations, irradiation of foods and protection against nuclear radiation, informatics, Bhopal ...

Some of these initiatives and collectives have come to play an important role in lobbying and in other ways influencing international organisations such as the World Health Organisation (WHO) and the Food and Agriculture Organisation (FAO) of the United Nations. Indeed, groups such as Health Action International, Pesticides Action Network, International Organisation of Consumer Unions, International Baby Foods Action Network, Seeds Action Network and their national or regional affiliates now command a presence that can no longer be ignored by governments. Their effort in resisting extreme right-wing and isolationist attacks on progressive international organisations, especially from within the US, has been impressive. So have their achievements in compelling some of these organisations to respond to their concerns. At the national policy-making levels in many countries, they are, or are in the process of becoming, a major force.

Some other groups in this spectrum are experimenting with alternatives such as forming cooperatives of self-employed women, artisans and small producers; setting up manufacturing and distribution on a non-commercial basis; building networks that promote traditional or natural agricultural practices; working on the development of renewable energy sources as well as other appropriate or intermediate technologies; and exploring new approaches to culture, language, lifestyles and communications.

Yet others tend to concentrate on local work on soil and water conservation, protective or community-oriented forestry, organic agriculture, banks of plant genetic resources, common property resources, industrial safety, consumer protection, public health, woman and child health care, rational drug therapy, and on a host of issues pertaining to the urban and rural habitat, housing, sanitation and water supply.

Most such groups, coalitions and collectives recognise that the conventional Northern model has failed. They question the assumed infallibility of Western science and technology, and tend to emphasise the equal validity of traditional knowledge. While a few of these tendencies reject all that is modern, scientific, industrial, sophisticated, high-technology and 'advanced' in Western terms, the vast majority are by no means opposed to industrialisation or technology *per se*. As a rule, they are not the Luddites that they are accused of being.

This is not the place to attempt a critique of these alternative currents or to discuss the limitations of their perspectives and activities. However, it is relevant to note that the largest, and the most important, influential and persuasive of such currents do *not* take an absolutist stand which uncritically rejects modernism, industry or science. Rather, they emphasise that what the 'Northern' orientation leaves out, ignores, runs down or denigrates, may be relevant, valuable, useful and valid.

What they are attempting is a fusion of two divergent orientations. They are groping towards a radical redefinition of priorities in social policy and development approaches, to be founded on a critique of conventional Northern wisdom. This furnishes the basis for an altogether new model of development and sets a wholly different agenda.

One basic theme of this agenda, unpleasant as it may sound to many Northern ears, is 'back to nature', or 'back to the earth'. This has many components and spans different cognitive levels and categories, global and local, cultural and economic, political and social. Another theme is socialism, the struggle for an egalitarian order in which the plebeian masses rule.

First of all, a coherent alternative model of development must involve a radical departure from the currently dominant conception of the world. This departure is simply that the South is *the centre of the world*, representing a majority of its people and the bulk of its natural resources, culture, civilisation and traditions. In any definition of the world, the South must be the principal determinant, the main criterion. Representing the majority, the South defines the mainstream. Its cultures and concerns are *globally the most important*. The North is the periphery, the minority, the exception.

This premise is an inversion of the conceptualisation associated with the development of capitalism and the colonisation of the world, which has continued in the contemporary post-war period. It demands a shift from the categories that the Northern model presumes to be universally applicable and valid, to those which are relevant to the South: from urban to rural, industrial to agricultural, high-cost to low-cost, capital-intensive to labour-intensive, mechanical to animal or human, inorganic to organic, modern to traditional, exotic to indigenous, processed to unprocessed, marketed to subsistence, quantitative to qualitative, geometric to irregular, visible and seen to invisible and unseen, tidy to untidy, standardised to vernacular, hard to soft, individual to community, male to female, light-skinned to dark-skinned, temperate to tropical, indoors to outdoors.

This shift in biases is crucial not just to delivering the fruits of development to the people, but to the very *definition* of development. It entails the rectification of a parochial minority perspective which is based on the prejudices of the dominant and the arrogant.

An alternative model must involve a new measure of the human being. That means putting people first. Equally, it must entail judging development on the basis of an entirely different set of indicators of economic progress. The emphasis is no longer on the gross national product and its growth rates but on the performance of the economy – in both its formal, organised and informal, unorganised sectors – in satisfying the broadest range of human needs, in particular the basic requirements of food, shelter, clothing, health, education, transport and culture – improving the quality of work and of life, promoting endogenous growth and self-reliance at the community, local, regional and national levels, integrating social justice with growth, conserving natural resources, and protecting the ecological balance.

The economic criteria of the alternative model are centred on human beings, their health, work, leisure and social wellbeing, and their environment and resources. The criteria must take special note of the economically, socially and culturally vulnerable, the weak, the underprivileged and the poor. Indeed the basic, most definitive criterion must be the progress and wellbeing of the poorest, illiterate woman in the most deprived and resource-poor community – not growth in maldistributed average per capita incomes.

In society and culture, the emphasis must shift from uniformity, standardisation and homogenisation to plurality, diversity and heterogeneity. Uniformity and standardisation invariably mean the subjugation of the vernacular, the local and the dispersed by the dominant, the elitist and the concentrated. And homogenisation, inflicted by the dominant cultures and groups in society, can only impose the hierarchical order of the Brahmin upon the rest of society. It means discounting, delegitimising, downgrading and destroying traditional skills and knowledge or local dialects which in the South tend to be closely related to particular communities, environments and economic-geographic contexts.

Politics in the alternative model is based on socialism and on the principles of mass democracy, pluralism and transparency of decision-making. This means open government, minimal delegation of representative authority to the non-elected, greater devolution of power, full answerability to the electors and acceptance of their right to know. It also entails promotion of local government and decentralisation of power and the involvement of the people in planning the allocation of resources. Full consultation with local communities, indeed with all those liable to be affected by any development programme or activity, is imperative in such a model.

Equally necessary is the fusion of alternative or 'green' concerns with the core of the traditional socialist or 'red' perspectives. This fusion alone can give the socialist vision a truly radical character and content. Socialism, after all, is nothing unless it aims to transform not only society but society's entire relationship with nature.

Such an affirmative model cannot come into existence within the narrow confines of the existing order. It can only be forged on the basis of a struggle that involves the exploited and the oppressed – the sole agents of radical social change. Put differently, a great deal of social ferment will necessarily precede the new order which the alternative perspective seeks to establish. In this ferment, voluntary coalitions of alternative groups can play an important but limited catalytic role. They cannot substitute themselves for the mass of the exploited and the oppressed, who alone can set the agenda for action.

The agenda for an alternative, socialist, human-scale model of development must start with altogether new priorities: satisfying human needs (as distinct from market demand) in an equitable, egalitarian and ecologically sustainable manner. The implications of such a perspective have often been discussed in the context of the countries of the North by the green movement and by ecologically-minded socialists.

Here I wish to place particular emphasis on the broad contours of the appropriate agenda for the South which must remain pivotal to the whole approach.

Land

The most serious problem facing the South is the degradation of this priceless resource. Indeed as much as a third, if not more, of the South's land is turning arid or is well on the way to desertification. Barring the prime watersheds, much of the rest is already moderately to highly degraded after decades of resource mismanagement, soil erosion, deforestation, waterlogging and salinity, excessive use of chemicals and monoculture. The situation is truly alarming: in some Southern countries, farmers lose 20 to 40 kg of topsoil – that almost irreplaceable resource which it takes nature centuries to regenerate – for every kg of grain that they harvest. Balanced, as against overexploitative, agriculture is becoming increasingly unviable in region after region. Typically, the river valleys and the best watersheds, accounting for a quarter or less of the total land area, now tend to produce half or more of the food grown in many countries of the South, while vast swathes of land outside those areas tend to register absolute *decreases* in output or to go out of cultivation altogether and become wastes.

The highest priority is to regenerate land. Putting life back into a field that has for years suffered a *biological* drought – the death of beneficial life-forms which give it its fertility – is a Herculean task. It demands a carefully balanced mix of measures to stop soil erosion, improve water retention, and prevent further loss of fertility caused by grazing animals and chemicals. It means reshaping the contours of the land, building small *bunds* (narrow, slightly raised earthen barriers) round it and planting trees that will enrich the soil. Above all, it means giving the land a rest and allowing it to recover its vitality under protected conditions. Such an effort will involve a tremendous amount of labour, thus creating useful work for large numbers of currently underemployed landless people.

The land regeneration perspective is ideally integrated with programmes to reafforest land on a large scale and under popular control. This will naturally entail a radical alteration of existing land-holding, use and ownership patterns and the transfer of plots from governments and from the rich to the poor. It also means ceding the initiative to local councils of the poor, while subsidising them on a limited scale for a short span of time. There is no alternative to such long-overdue reforms, if land is to be rejuvenated and if the integrated system of agriculture, forestry and husbandry which once existed in large parts of the South is to be recreated. There is no other way to restore the ecological balances which have been destroyed in province after province, country after country.

A precondition for the success of any such programme is the immediate cessation of all commercial forestry and logging, especially where the timber is for export to the North. This might entail a temporary loss of revenue for governments. However, that loss would pale into insignificance beside the potential benefits from the programme, which the poor could start reaping within two or three years: higher food output, valuable trees, assured soil fertility, better water retention and the restoration of that key factor, balance in the local ecosystem.

Another priority whose importance must not be underrated is the dechemicalisation of agriculture. Enough has been written since Rachel Carson's *Silent Spring* (1962) on the ecological destruction that farm chemicals have visited on virtually every country in the world. The alternatives to chemical fertilisers and to toxic pesticides are now well understood. It is established that natural nutrients and non-chemical pest management are more rational, effective and productive means to achieve increases in agricultural output and productivity. More work needs to be done, however, on traditional farming systems which achieved a unique balance between ecological stability and high output with a mix of crops, in combination with grasses, legumes and trees.

It is even more imperative to halt the intrusion of bioengineered hybrid seeds into agriculture. These represent the worst form of capitalist greed and a grave threat to the land and environment. Western biotechnology companies are now aggressively promoting seeds that are designed to be compatible with pesticide overuse. The safety of such products is yet to be established, especially in tropical climates. The alternative approach lies in an altogether different direction: conserving and enriching the natural stock of plant genetic resources of the world, in particular of the South (which is where most of it exists) and tapping it for the genotypes and primitive land races that are most appropriate to particular climates and ecosystems.

Water

After land, water is probably the most misused and irrationally exploited resource in the South. Critical shortages of water have become routine, especially in countries that are dependent on highly seasonal rainfall. These are attributable not to lack of precipitation (which is unusual) but rather to high run-off rates – the result of soil erosion and the absence of effective obstacles to the flow of water.

Since the colonial period, the standard solution to the problem of water has been the large irrigation dam. This involves concentrating water collected from a vast catchment area into a relatively small area. Not only does this entail a high cost in immobilising large bodies of water; it also necessitates the draining of the lower reaches of the catchment area and thus the impoverishment of the bulk of the land in it. And that is not all. This method of surface irrigation directly affects the prime portion of the catchment, usually well forested, where the dam is built, especially if it is a hydroelectric dam.

Large dam irrigation projects can lead to waterlogging, and render large areas uncultivable. It is increasingly accepted that they are also liable to cause seismic disturbances in certain regions and thus raise the likelihood of earthquakes.

Lift irrigation too has its problems, the worst of which is the lowering of the water-table and the disruption of deep aquifers through excessive pumping. In parts of the South, lift irrigation has caused untold havoc by spreading salinity. In overexploited zones, the water-table has sunk to as much as 150 or 200 feet below ground level, raising cultivation costs astronomically.

The principal task is to conserve and tap water precisely where it falls. This is best done through land recontouring, soil erosion prevention measures, and the construction of large numbers of small tanks and reservoirs that will supply a limited area without disrupting its natural hydrology. Simple as this may sound, it is a gigantic task which needs careful local-level planning and substantial renewable and conservable resources. But action must not be postponed any longer. The future of the world's agriculture depends on it.

Energy

Closely related to the problems of land and water is that of energy. There are not one, but two, energy crises: that of the rising costs of non-renewable resources consumed primarily by the affluent or the organised sector, and the other crisis caused by the disappearance or decreased availability of the primary energy sources relevant to the needs of the poorest peoples of the South. While the first is relatively well understood, it is not adequately appreciated that the second is even more grave.

At least 2 billion people in the world do not have secure access to the energy they need to cook their food and to light and heat their homes. Thanks to ruthless deforestation and to the intrusion of the cash economy into the 'periphery' of the South, which has led to the commercialisation of agricultural 'wastes', the poor are compelled to buy firewood (in terms of effective heat productivity, the most expensive fuel there is almost anywhere today) at unaffordable prices. Those who earlier had access to common property resources and paid nothing for the twigs and branches, or stalks and leaves, which they collected from forests and farms are now increasingly being denied that access and forced into the market.

In parts of Asia, sub-Saharan Africa and Latin America, the poor – especially women and children in indigent rural families – are compelled to spend as much as *two to three hours a day* just gathering fuel for cooking.

No alternative perspective on development can possibly have any relevance to the majority in the South if it fails to address itself to this 'other energy crisis'. Its solution demands a whole range of measures, from improving the efficiency of cooking stoves and planting fuel trees on a massive scale, to cultivating species that yield a large quantity of fodder, and using animal dung in biogas plants so as to generate additional fuel for rural homes.

The development of alternative, renewable and ecologically safe energy sources – solar, wind, tidal and biomass – is a high priority. These are particularly amenable to decentralised use and to public control at the local level; they fit snugly into the pattern of energy needs of small communities, both rural and urban. They can no longer be considered immature or 'futuristic' technologies. Rather they are examples of what might be called *arrested technologies*, whose development has tended to be suppressed by interest groups which are closely linked to centralised energy systems, to conventional fossil fuels or to nuclear energy, and which oppose the spread of decentralised energy generation and consumption. A classic case is that of solar photovoltaics (PV) in the United States. Small PV firms, set up by groups of technocrat-entrepreneurs on slender capital bases, were taken over by large transnational corporations in the oil business during the 1980s and quickly lost much of their dynamism.

There is no reason why the development of these energy resources should be left to private firms alone. There are compelling reasons for undertaking a joint multilateral effort, as well as national initiatives in the public sector, to develop these sources as a priority. However, it is important that they are not taken over by large, centralised energy systems (as is possible, for instance, with tidal power or solar-thermal-electrical energy) before the demand of the decentralised, energy-deprived sector has been satisfied. Electricity does remain the most efficient and useful form of energy when it comes to lighting homes – of which a majority in the rural South remain deprived of power.

Health

There are few areas where the misallocation of resources has been as gross as in the field of health. Primary health continues to receive low priority in those very countries which record the highest rates of infant mortality and in which the infectious diseases (wrongly called tropical diseases) steadily take a heavy toll of people's lives and wellbeing. Expensive and inappropriate techniques borrowed from the North tend to be imposed upon the South even as perfectly effective traditional methods are discarded or destroyed.

The current emphasis in the health programmes of the South is on cure, not prevention. Inappropriate or harmful drugs, vigorously promoted by unscrupulous multinational companies, tend to add to the existing imbalance, while large numbers of the poor continue to be deprived of access to a bare minimum of essential drugs. At the same time, there is growing elitism in health-care systems. Public hospitals cede pride of place to private clinics. The system is geared to producing too many doctors and too few primary health-care professionals and nurses. The costs of basic medical care are increasingly beyond the reach of the underprivileged, both rural and urban.

This situation can only be remedied if the emphasis shifts towards primary health care, prevention, essential drugs, rational drug therapy, free public access to medical care, and – most important – towards providing clean, safe drinking water, sanitation, better housing and nourishment.

An important component of such an alternative approach must be the revival of traditional systems of healing, health care and herbal medicine. In many ways, when standardised and rationalised, they are at least as effective as, if not superior to, the modern Western systems; this is true, for example, of herbal medicine. More significantly, ordinary people are either familiar with them or likely to find them more acceptable; they are simpler to deliver and manage; they are cheap and they are based on locally available knowledge.

The best example of such systems is the Indian village midwife, or *dai*, who with some elementary training can manage most pregnancies and can when necessary (in emergencies or problem cases) draft in the expert services of a fully trained doctor. Unfortunately, the institution of rural midwifery has fallen into disuse and been driven underground by the modern Northern medical system. It needs to be resuscitated.

Habitat

It is a commonplace that large cities have become horrors and that megacities – growing mainly in the South – are or will be nightmares. Economically, large urban agglomerations are simply unviable. This is especially so where private ownership of urban land, invariably leading to reckless hoarding and speculation in real estate, combines with mass poverty and a hopelessly inadequate civic infrastructure, as it tends to do in the South. The poverty and appalling standard of life of the urban poor are in many ways worse than the misery of the rural poor. There is no way that the metropolitan sprawl, and the growth of horrifying slums that always accompanies it, can be stopped unless rural and semi-urban areas and smaller towns are allowed to prosper.

Meanwhile, the problems posed by the megalopolises can only be solved if the poor are granted access to land, property ownership by business is abolished, and the rich are taxed in proportion to their parasitical consumption of resources such as land, water and roads. Changes in building by-laws to allow informal housing and the use of locally available materials (often urban waste materials) are as imperative here as the promotion of mass public-transit systems and discouragement of private vehicles.

Even more daunting than such a programme of urban renewal is the problem of shelter for the rural poor. The impoverished in most countries of the South have been reduced to living in dingy, unventilated, and badly built houses which are made of flammable and flimsy materials and often lack a half-way stable and waterproofed roof. A large-scale programme to develop low-cost, airy houses with locally available materials, such as mud, unburnt bricks or specially treated sand–mud combinations, is a high priority.

Several such projects have been undertaken and there are excellent examples of appropriately designed, well-built, elegant and cheap houses. However, these projects have rarely received the state support they deserve. This can only come if there is a popular community-based movement for a better habitat relevant to people's needs, which takes an integrated view of housing, local resources, town and country planning, traditional architecture, sanitation, water supply, municipal infrastructure, transport, energy, education and health.

The time has surely come to promote rururban (rural-urban) centres which combine the best features of both towns and villages, and to establish an altogether different relationship with the environment and with nature.

Industry

Balanced industrialisation, of the endogenous, self-reliant, safe and ecologically sound variety, remains a desirable objective for the world. If the North has recklessly pursued industrialisation as an end in itself – with all the disastrous consequences of pollution, concentration and overcentralisation of industry, and work alienation and decline in the quality of life – the South has so far tried only to imitate it in its worst, socially undesirable and dehumanising aspects. Thus, Southern countries often show a greater imbalance in the concentration of capital and industry, the preponderance of hazardous industries, and the incidence of sweatshops. Worse still is the higher incidence of rapacious exploitation of labour and the absence of a legal code or institutions to protect workers' rights.

Industrialisation, now under increasing pressure from external competition, has not helped the countries of the South to overcome or reduce their dependence on the North for technology, finance capital and export markets. That can only happen as a result of a radical restructuring of the world economy and changes in the pattern of world trade, coupled with the development and growth of appropriate industrial technologies in the South.

Appropriate industrialisation of the South is simply incompatible with an attempt at replicating the North. It demands popular involvement in, and control of, industry and industrial planning, location and pricing. It also requires the phasing out of hazardous processes and products, a ban on polluting industries (often relocated from the North), prevention and control of pollution, and the imposition of a stringent safety-control regime that is responsive to the public. The example of Bhopal is too horrifying to permit anyone to forget what the consequences of inappropriate industrialisation can be.

All this will naturally involve, indeed it presumes, a structural transformation of a magnitude and of a quality that the world has not witnessed even in the past three centuries, the most turbulent period in its history. An alternative perspective on development, however, must see that recent past as only the prelude to even more momentous changes, indeed transformations of a civilisational order.

The possibility of such changes is not grounded in mere hope but premissed upon the dynamic of social movements, the popular awareness and new concerns which have been unleashed by the very forces and processes that have shaped capital's history and the world as it is today. Discontent with capital's betrayal of its own promise of a better society has not gone away, nor have the 'red' and 'green' critiques of the existing order lost their validity and vitality. The same impetus that put the democratic agenda before the world, promoted humanism, egalitarianism and freedom as ideals, inspired the socialist movement, fuelled the process of decolonisation and, more recently, spawned an altogether new consciousness of issues such as equality of the sexes, ecology and peace, is at work in this dynamic too.

There is another way of looking at this movement of history. I am tempted to cite it as a somewhat unusual reinterpretation of Northern concepts through the imagery of the South, in particular the symbolism of a myth from the *Rig-Veda*, so as to stress the universal nature of the idea of liberation.

Hindu mythology explains the emergence of civilisation as the result of an (obviously mythical) conflict between the good and the evil, the Heaven-born and the Impious.

There was a time according to Hindu tradition when the Heaven-born and the Impious forsook their feuding. They joined hands to churn the cream of life from the primeval milky ocean. Their churning stick was a mighty mountain, the axis of the universe. The chieftain of the serpent people lent them his coils to twist the churning stick. Many significant gifts to mankind came out of the ocean during the churning; among them the Magic Tree that grants fulfilment of wishes; the miraculous cow, bestower of bounty; then, a spate of virulent poison. Shiva, the primeval 'Great God', took it upon himself to swallow the poison. Only then did the nectar emerge. Both the Devas, the Heaven-born, and the Asuras, the Impious, wanted it for themselves. After some tension, Vishnu appears on the scene in the shape of a beautiful temptress whose 'mediation' the Asuras accept under her blandishments. She serves the precious nectar to the Heaven-born until there is none left for the 'Impious' Asuras. These naturally feel cheated and create an uproar which renews the ancient feud.[16]

The ablest of scholars[17] interpret the myth in terms of an encounter between two kinds of people or two kinds of cultures: the Devas being semi-nomadic Aryan groups who came from the North, and the Asuras being the autochthonous people of the South, who practised settled cultivation. The Devas strongly favoured male values, and worshipped male deities of the sky and air. The Asuras, by contrast, were closely related to the earth and water, and worshipped female deities.

In today's world, the Devas and the Asuras exist everywhere as opposites: dominant and dominated, exploiter and exploited, white and black, organiser and organised, sophisticated and simple, North and South.

The original conflict between the Asuras and the Devas has been viewed, according to Richard Lannoy,

as one of the great racial encounters of the world, the most dramatic encounter between black and white. If you want a characterization of it, it is like the difference between earth and air. The Aryans worshipped sky gods while the indigenous population were people who were sedentary, deeply rooted as it were, earthbound in the best positive sense of the word.[18]

In the Hindu myth, the Devas emerged as the victors, if only by cheating, but the feud did not end. In history too, capital has, at least for the present, emerged as the victor, the North as the conqueror, the rich as the ruler – within nations and globally, again by cheating.

And the feud has not ended. It will end nowhere, not so long as the Sky-People within countryside and town, in province and nation, in North and South, and in the world as a whole, do not accept the Earth-People as their equals and nature as sacred, not something to be conquered and plundered. That acceptance lies at the very foundation of an alternative model of development which promotes the genuine progress of humanity.

Notes

1. The terms 'nuclear' and 'atomic' in this chapter relate to nuclear fission and exclude fusion. Although a section of the nuclear establishment claims that nuclear fusion is the ultimate solution to the global energy problem, that technology is nowhere near

maturity. Indeed, it is still at the most elementary, experimental stage. Until it is proved viable and safe, research work on fusion must be treated on a par with several non-technological or aesthetic activities of an esoteric nature.

2. All existing designs of nuclear power reactors, most of which were originally developed as power plants for military purposes, are fraught with safety problems which are not amenable to solutions within the given design framework. The deficiencies in safety systems that mark the Chernobyl design are by no means unique to it. No existing nuclear reactor design has eliminated the possibility of a core meltdown. See Gruppe Oekologie, Hannover, *International Nuclear Reactor Hazard Study*, Greenpeace, Vienna, September 1986.

3. See Charles Komanoff, *Power Plant Cost Escalation: Nuclear and Coal Capital Costs, Regulation and Economics*, Komanoff Energy Associates, New York, 1981, republished by Van Nostrand Reinhold, 1983; Colin Sweet, *The Price of Nuclear Power*, Heinemann, London, 1983; Christopher Flavin, *Nuclear Power: the Market Test*, the Worldwatch Institute, Washington DC, 1983; William Mooz, *Cost Analysis of Light Water Reactor Plants*, Rand Corporation, Santa Monica, California, 1978.

4. See Barry Commoner, *Environmental Impacts of Expanded Utilization of Nuclear Energy* (prepared for the UN Environmental Programme), CBNS, Queens College, City University of New York, Flushing, NY, 1985 (mimeo).

5. See Ivan Tolstoy, 'High-level waste: no technical solution', in *The Ecologist*, vol. 16, no. 415 (1986); G.T. Bredehoeft et al., 'Geological disposal of high-level radioactive wastes', US Geological Survey *Circular 779*, 1978; and C. de Marsily et al., 'Nuclear waste disposal: can the geologist guarantee isolation?', in *Science*, vol. 197.

6. A good deal of material has been published on nuclear proliferation in conjunction with the recent Non-Proliferation Treaty review conference. The best work is to be found in successive editions of the SIPRI *World Armaments and Disarmament Yearbook*, Oxford University Press. Of particular interest is the slightly biased but nevertheless useful account in Leonard Spector, *The New Nuclear Nations*, Vintage Books, New York, 1985, and *Going Nuclear*, Ballinger, Cambridge, MA, 1987. Also Mason Willrich and Ted Taylor, *Nuclear Theft: Risks and Safeguards*, Ballinger, Cambridge, MA, 1974.

7. See Commoner, *Environmental Impacts*, and Christopher Flavin, *Reassessing Nuclear Power*, Worldwatch Institute, Washington DC, 1987.

8. See J.A. Camilleri, *The State and Nuclear Power*, Wheatsheaf

Books, Brighton, 1984; Rosalie Bertell, *No Immediate Danger*, Women's Press, London, 1985.

9. See I.C. Bupp and J.C. Derian, *Light Water: How the Nuclear Dream Dissolved*, Basic Books, New York, 1978, and Leonard Spector, *New Nuclear Nations*.

10. See Camilleri, *State and Nuclear Power*; Walter Patterson, *Nuclear Power*, Penguin Books, Harmondsworth, 1976, and *Going Critical*, Paladin Books, London, 1985; Jim Falk, *Global Fission*, Oxford University Press, Melbourne, 1982; Robert Jungk, *The Nuclear State*, John Calder, London, 1979; J.E. Katz and O.S. Marwah (eds), *Nuclear Power in Developing Countries*, Lexington Books, Lexington, MA, 1982. Also Peter Pringle and James Spiegelman, *The Nuclear Barons*, Michael Joseph, London, 1982; Dorothy Nelkin and Michael Pollak, *The Atom Besieged*, MIT Press, Cambridge, MA, 1981.

11. For example, Spencer R. Weart, *Scientists in Power*, Harvard University Press, Cambridge, MA, 1979; Roger Williams, *The Nuclear Power Decisions: British Politics 1953–78*, Croom Helm, London, 1980; Richard R. Lewis, *The Nuclear Power Rebellion: Citizen versus the Atomic Industrial Establishment*, Viking Press, New York, 1972.

12. See Centre for Science and Environment, *The State of India's Environment 1984–5: The Second Citizens' Report*, CSE, New Delhi, 1986; and Bina Agarwal, *Cold Hearths, Barren Slopes*, Allied Publishers, New Delhi, 1986.

13. Zygmunt Bauman, 'Fighting the wrong shadow' in the *New Statesman*, London, 25 September 1987; Perry Anderson, 'Figures of descent', in *New Left Review*, 161, January–February 1987.

14. Reasons of space make it impossible to append an adequate bibliography here. But especially noteworthy are: Paul Elkins (ed.), *The Living Economy: A New Economics in the Making*, RKP, London, 1986; Dag Hammarskjöld Foundation, *What Now?: Another Development*, DHF, Uppsala, 1975; Rudolf Bahro, *Socialism and Survival*, Heretic Books, London, 1982, *From Red to Green*, Verso, London, 1984, *Building the Green Movement*, Heretic Books, London, 1986; K. Boulding, *Beyond Economics*, University of Michigan Press, Ann Arbor, 1968; Robert Chambers, *Rural Development: Putting the Last First*, Longmans, Harlow, 1983; K.W. Kapp, *The Social Costs of Private Enterprise*, Harvard University Press, Cambridge, MA, 1950; M. Muller, *The Health of Nations: North–South Investigation*, Faber & Faber, London, 1982; Amory Lovins, *Soft Energy Paths*, Penguin Books, Harmondsworth, 1977; Centre for Science and Environment, *India's Environment 1984–5* and the 'Second Statement of Shared Concern'.

15. Derived from Robert Chambers, in Paul Elkins, *Living Economy*, pp. 305–22.

16. From Alexandra George, *Social Ferment in India*, Orient Longman, Hyderabad, 1986, p. 1.

17. See, for instance, the remarkable Indian Marxist scholar, D.D. Kosambi, *Culture and Civilization of Ancient India in Historical Outline*, Vikas Publishing House, New Delhi, 1977.

18. Quoted in Alexandra George, *Social Ferment in India*, pp. 23–4. See also Lannoy's *The Speaking Tree*, Oxford University Press, 1975.

8

Alternative Détente

KATE SOPER and MARTIN RYLE

The most immediate official reaction in the West to the news of the Chernobyl meltdown was that 'it couldn't happen here.' But as the dust of the disaster began to settle both literally and metaphorically, this ideological reflex response ceded to a more collusive rhetoric. We began to hear rather less of the evils specific to Soviet administration and technology and rather more of what we could 'all' hope to learn from the Russian misfortune in our continuing and common struggle against the perils of nuclear fission.

The prevalence of this more complicit and pragmatic approach among official circles highlights one of the most politically significant and paradoxical aspects of the tragedy: that it forced a trans-bloc 'establishment' consensus around the virtues of technocratism out into the open. As the accident, not of a Soviet institution, but of a technology much favoured in the West and commonly defended as an essential adjunct of its particular style of civilisation, Chernobyl revealed a certain vulnerability in traditional Cold War posturings. The 'oppositional' systems were after all not so different in certain key respects: in their common commitment to industrialisation, their common belief in the overriding value of improved material prosperity, their common excitement in the technologies necessary to promote those goals, and their common interest in surmounting the challenges they pose.

It can be argued, moreover, that the Soviet reforms and the attempted economic *perestroika* have significantly enhanced this collusiveness. For while any democratisation in the USSR is incontrovertibly welcome, and the economic reforms are likely to have some benefits even in environmental terms in curbing wasteful use of resources, the overall inspiration of the Soviet restructuring is very much in line with the growth-directed economic policies of the capitalist nations. When placed, in fact, in the context of the more relaxed pattern of East–West relations that has followed on Mr Gorbachev's ascent to power, we may say that Chernobyl came at the beginning of a transitional period in Cold War politics and may even have played a certain part in advancing it. It would be premature to speak of a post-Cold War situation emerging, but the signs of a new rapprochement are clearly discernible in the forms of East–West cooperation now being canvassed and in the similarity of pronouncements on social and economic policy at official levels 'across the blocs'.

All this is undoubtedly welcome in so far as it reduces tension and assists in confidence building. It may even (though current signs are not at all encouraging) issue in further measures of disarmament and an unprecedented degree of liberalisation in the Soviet bloc. That would be even more welcome. But the fact remains that it would be possible to make quite considerable headway with the disarmament and civil liberties agendas which have tended to preoccupy the peace movement hitherto, without breaking definitively with patterns of production and consumption which are profoundly inimical to global peace and wellbeing in the long term. A 'détente' built around a commitment to the goals of economic growth and prosperity as currently defined in the industrialised nations will accentuate rather than alleviate suffering and exploitation in the poorer countries. It will do little to defuse tensions in those areas where military conflagration is most likely, since these are in many instances sites of the most anxious and intensive competition to defend the flow of resources essential to the pursuit of affluence; it will not protect those resources themselves from the squandering and attrition which annually denies the barest essentials to millions of people, and is now threatening the long-term viability of the human species; and it will not stem the pollution which is already beginning to poison the atmosphere of affluence itself and has immeasurably compounded the deprivations of all those who have never breathed in that more prosperous ambience.

It is for these reasons that the disarmament movement, which has already done so much to foster the idea of the indissolubility of peace and human rights, is now beginning to accept that ecological issues must form an equally integral part of its concerns. In encouraging this idea, the impact of Chernobyl at the 'unofficial' level has been of equal – if antithetical – significance to that at the 'official'. For it has allowed anti-nuclearism to emerge as the central plank of a trans-bloc ecological platform of opposition to the pro-nuclear trans-bloc technocratist consensus.

The reasons for this have been discussed elsewhere in this book at greater length. Suffice it to mention here two factors of some importance. In the first place, the accident served to direct attention to some common conditions of existence at a point where trans-national peace movement dialogue had been focusing around divisions of experience. And this was so in a double sense: not only were we all subject to nuclear accidents and radiation, but we were all in thrall to the secrecy of the nuclear industry. The anti-nuclear preoccupations of the Western movements, which in a sense had been previously contrasted to the civil liberties emphasis of Eastern groups, could now be viewed as complementary: they too were about democracy and its preconditions. This did not mean that forms of repression exclusive to totalitarian regimes were forgotten, but it did allow a deeper analysis of the peace–liberties nexus and more sympathy for Western complaints about the particular forms of unaccountability to be found in market societies.

In the second place, the Chernobyl disaster – so manifest and terrifying an example of the fragility of our control over our own technologies – lent force to the fundamentalist aspect of the ecological critique and gave it a more respectful hearing. It allowed the overcoming of the political division of the blocs to be associated more closely with the green demand for a radical rethinking of the instrumentalist approach to nature and the forms of reliance on technology that go with it.

Some may want to question the suggestion that Chernobyl has proved a more 'educative' experience in the East than in the West. But given the predominantly anti-nuclear focus of the Western peace movements, the disaster was bound to be received by them more in the way of confirmation than enlightenment. Western peace activists, after all, had long been insisting on the dangers of nuclear power, which they already viewed as the ultimate symbol of environmental degradation – as the worst pollutant, and the wrong of the greatest magnitude we were inflicting upon nature and ourselves in the name of progress.

In contrast to this Western nuclear 'fixation', Eastern groups had previously been much more absorbed in campaigning on human rights and in so far as they viewed themselves as peace movements it was primarily in terms of their opposition to conscription and the militaristic regulation of their societies. Nor was nuclear power a primary target of ecological protest, which was directed for the most part against the appalling chemical and dust pollution afflicting extensive areas of Eastern Europe, and to alerting the public to the environmental consequences of such ill-considered gargantuan schemes as the diversion of Siberian rivers or the Gorskaya dam project in the Bay of Finland. A measure of the formerly rather sanguine attitude of environmentalists to nuclear power is given in the fact that ecological awareness was first raised in Hungary through the campaign to replace the hydroelectric barrage across the Danube, at Nagymaros, by a less ecologically disruptive nuclear power plant.

However, when we take account of the actual levels of pollution affecting Eastern Europe, these campaigning priorities appear less surprising. It is against this background (which has been sketched in Chapter 4) that we must assess the impact of Chernobyl as a crisis not only in physical terms but for environmental thinking in Eastern Europe. It has certainly heightened nuclear awareness and thus served to generate more sympathy and support for the anti-nuclear stance of the Western peace and ecology movements. But it has also served to expose more fully the nature of the dilemmas facing the Eastern bloc. An ecological alarm that prior to Chernobyl might have looked to nuclear power as a cleaner alternative to the particularly contaminating emissions of low-grade coal-fired stations, has now been alerted to the potentially even more disastrous dangers of that option. Moreover, this ecological Hobson's Choice has revealed itself in a context where the supply of electricity is by no means plentiful, and in some areas so meagre as to justify speaking of extreme deprivation by Western standards.

Even, then, as trans-bloc dialogue draws strength from the growing acknowledgement of common dilemmas, it will need to remain sensitive to asymmetries of experience and situation. While the green movement in the industrialised West has sharpened the edge of its ecological protest to the point where protection of the environment is now seen as secondary to the more fundamental assault upon the politics of affluence, environmentalism remains the predominant concern in Eastern Europe, although its scope has now been enlarged to include the issue of nuclear pollution. These differences of priority themselves reflect differences of lifestyle: those who have never enjoyed the luxuries of mass consumption in the West cannot be expected to be so alarmist about the squandering of resources they incur. On the other hand, greens in the West whose lives are less dominated by the immediate evils of pollution may find themselves impatient with the more parochial targeting of ecological activity elsewhere.

In the last analysis, however, these differences of emphasis indicate the complexity of the area in which we are searching for a common politics rather than any fundamental incompatibility of outlook. The most serious pollution may indeed be found in areas of greatest material deprivation, but this is itself the by-product of the quest for improved 'living standards'. To question the human value and ecological viability of the pursuit of Western models of affluence is thus also to engage in environmental protection. Equally, those whose immediate protest is against the disease and premature mortality caused by industrial expansion are also questioning the coherence of prevailing definitions of happiness. In this sense, 'lifestyle' and 'environmental' campaigning proceed from a shared philosophy: a philosophy which places the issue of human needs and their integration with the needs of nature at the top of any responsible, life-enhancing political agenda.

The existing demands of the peace movement – for disarmament and democratisation – are perfectly consistent with this philosophy and provide its essential campaigning framework: a framework in which 'peaceful coexistence' is freed of its traditional conservatism and viewed as a dynamic process of reconciliation evolving through transformation of the existing political and economic structures of both Western and Eastern blocs. By extending this framework to include the demand for an equitable, sustainable and non-polluting use of resources, the peace movement will only be pursuing the campaign for this reconciliation to its logical conclusion. For just as there can be no peaceful coexistence in a divided Europe, so there can be no peaceful coexistence while the industrially developed nations remain ecologically divided against the rest of the world.

All this suggests the need for a programme which redefines 'détente' in a way that allows it to encompass the construction of a new and ecologically responsible order in Europe as a first step to global peace. As we have said, there is a good deal of potential for a convergence of East–West activity around such a 'new détente' programme. The question now is how far it can be realised in concrete policies for economic and social change.

Eco-protest, Green Politics, Economics

The first moment in the founding of this new politics might seem to be, as with the peace movement, a moment of *protest*. East *and* West, we are against something, or rather (and here already the real complexities start to appear) against a range of practices: atmospheric pollution, spillage or dumping of toxic chemicals, destruction of areas of beautiful or ecologically valuable countryside ... The importance of Chernobyl here, as we have indicated, has been the effect the disaster had in alerting environmental campaigners in the Soviet bloc to the perils of nuclear power, which had for many years been a major focus of campaigning for Western ecological groups.

Chernobyl has indeed opened up a new possibility of developing trans-bloc ecological protest. More generally, in conjunction with the campaigns for disarmament and democracy, it encourages the possibility of forming what some people in the West have called a 'league of opposition',[1] bringing together activists and movements whose common identity would lie above all in an uncompromising attitude of refusal: refusal of the constituted authorities, refusal of incorporation in the networks of power. This idea appears to have some currency in the more fundamentalist and anarchistic wings of peace and green movements, and in green parties too. 'Antipolitics' – the title of the Hungarian George Konrád's famous book – is a crucial term for many East European dissenters; and the 'anti-political' orientation of some greens, the 'proclaimed non-ideological stance' which Václav Havel finds, and welcomes, in the green movement, the rejection he expresses of 'abstract political visions' an notions of 'systemic change': this suggests that the Western green/ecology movement, playing the part of a marginal but uncompromising critic, has a particular affinity with some important strands of dissent in communist states.[2]

Even where the greens have established a footing within formal politics, as in the West German *Bundestag*, they have used the opportunity as much for counter-cultural protest as for intervention in law-making. And even this non-establishment stance has not prevented many members of *die Grünen* from feeling that the party is now compromised. The long and divisive debate between 'fundamentalists' and 'realists' in the party is symptomatic of a tension bound to afflict all movements which combine attitudes of fundamental opposition with attempts to exert power or deal with those who exert it. The tensions that have arisen, the continuing force of the 'fundamentalist' critique, and the fact that Rudolf Bahro – best known of the *Fundis* – quit the party declaring that no more progress was to be made along that road might be taken as evidence that opposition is the right stance, and that the decision to intervene in formal legislative/electoral activity was mistaken.

It is impossible, however, to think seriously about ecological questions without realising that an attitude of protest is insufficient and ultimately self-indulgent. We have already mentioned protests against three different forms of electricity generation: hydroelectric power (the Danube barrage), coal- or lignite-fired stations, and nuclear plants. Simply to oppose a series of projects (though of course the specific rejection of the Nagymaros scheme implies no rejection of hydro power as such) is easy in principle, and easy enough in practice too, in Western Europe. But if we are concerned, as all environmentalists now are, both about acid rain and about nuclear leaks and risks, then at the very least we have to develop arguments about alternative energy sources. We may also have to consider whether the total energy demand of a modern industrialised society is not excessive. If, bearing in mind the cumulative effects of carbon dioxide emission (the 'greenhouse effect') as well as of chemical and dust pollution, we argue that wind, wave, tidal and solar energy offer the best prospects for a sustainable future, we have to recognise the strength of the economic and bureaucratic interests vested in the status quo, and the political upheaval that change would entail. So even if we start from the 'single issue' of energy, we find ourselves drawn into a discussion of alternatives, of institutional obstacles and political and economic dimensions. After all, if the movements are not developing and arguing for their own positive programmes (as, increasingly, they in fact are), then they are effectively inviting the state – the much-reviled state – to make the decision on their behalf.

It is in recognition of this need to develop positive alternative programmes that the green parties which now exist in many Western European states have come into being, developing from environmental protest groups, grassroots initiatives, and lifestyle-directed movements. Now active in about 15 countries (Italy and Austria being two recent additions where green representatives have been elected to national parliaments), the parties are small but their influence and importance are considerable. The influence is a matter of the extent to which, by raising public concern and also, in countries with proportional representation systems (which means all the other European Community members except the UK, for a start), by exerting direct electoral pressure, they have obliged mainstream opposition parties, and indeed governments, to take action on urgent environmental issues.

Their importance lies in the fact that they are trying to formulate programmes which integrate 'ecology' with social and economic policy at large. Eco-protest encompasses many 'single issues': to the campaigns already mentioned in this essay, we might add those against nitrate pollution of groundwater by agro-chemicals, against the destruction of tropical rainforest, against intensive rearing (with regular dosages of hormones and antibiotics) of battery 'farm' animals ... and many more. To be against so much is, one realises, to be against an entire model of progress, a definition of economic rationality, a consensus about needs – and also to be against the institutions that promote and benefit from that. Again, one has to take the next step and be *for* an alternative, one which not only addresses the economic and cultural causes of environmental crisis, but also calls in question the continued 'right' of Europeans (above all, of Western Europeans) to enjoy such an unequal share of the world's finite resources.

There is no space here to say more about this alternative, except in one particular area, that of economic policy, where the East–West dimension and the possibilities for fruitful dialogue in the framework of 'détente from below' are especially interesting.

There is a good deal of ambiguity in the stated economic policy of both the UK Greens and *die Grünen* (one German Green described the economics section of their 1983 manifesto as a 'mosaic'). There is a clearly anti-capitalist tone to such general statements as 'real wealth is not stocks and shares and money in vaults'; there is a commitment to the redressing of inequalities, but there is at the same time – just, of course, as in the social democratic parties – an underlying dependence on market mechanisms. It is not our intention to criticise this reliance on markets in the name of socialist orthodoxy: and today, plenty of socialists – Mr Gorbachev to name but one – seem to regard the introduction of market incentives as more than compatible with socialist objectives. Ecologically, however, the inherent expansiveness of the market (the very 'productivity' which makes it an element of *perestroika*) is in principle a liability rather than an asset, certainly for already-rich countries. And if our problems, social as well as ecological, are those of indiscriminate production, and of plainly inequitable distribution, so that within societies immensely wealthy by any historical and almost any geographical comparison, there s still poverty and deprivation and an ecologically, historically, and ulturally absurd belief that we can solve our crisis by producing more – if his is the case, as we believe (and as most greens would agree), then the eed for democratic political control of the economy, rather than an ltimate reliance on profitability as the basis of investment and roduction, is clear.

This is obviously not a majority position, as the Labour Party seemingly repares to shed the last vestiges of its anti-market rhetoric (having in act promoted the market as the basis of its economic policy almost from he beginning). But it is a position that can and should be on the political genda. The ecological arguments against markets, by no means expressed nly by socialists, will be of increasing importance over the next decades.[3]

But all this will give pause to those in the East who will be our partners n dialogue. There are countries, they may want to point out, where there as been rather a lot of planning and rather a scarcity of free markets. here are, after all, economic and consumer benefits which arise from an nlarged market sector (and we for our part have already admitted that it s all too easy for Western eco-activists to bash out denunciations of consumerism' on their word-processors). There are also the incalculable enefits of pluralism and self-organising activity to be derived from the mergence – within societies where political power is indissolubly ssociated with economic power and both are unaccountable – of utonomous commercial activity. It is all too easy to imagine an eco-socialist' regime which would resemble rather closely what some eople in Eastern Europe already have to put up with. 'An economy lanned in accordance with ecological limits', 'democratic control of roduction': behind those fine slogans, what *actual* political forms are eing advocated?

Ve will not pursue any further these questions, which seem to have led us ar from Chernobyl but which are part of any attempt to develop an co-alternative. It is clear that their exploration will gain immeasurably rom an exchange of views between independent thinkers from socialist nd capitalist countries, working within a shared commitment to peace, lemocracy and ecological sustainability. This, as well as the support we an hopefully give each other in protest actions and expressions of dissent, nust be part of our political responsibility and activity in the ambiguous eriod of the new détente.

The Politics of Minority Protest and the Green Alternative

n considering the common forms which might be given to such protests and xpressions of dissent, we must begin with the obvious fact of the livergence of national political systems and its effects on the campaigning options open to minority movements.

In the West, where government is periodically answerable to the electorate, the peace movement has devoted a good deal of its energy to formal politics: in the first instance by persuading voters of the wisdom of its programme, and secondly by pressurising political parties to adopt it – which in effect has meant working within or in close association with them. In Britain, for example, the adoption of a non-nuclear defence policy by the Labour Party has much to do with the very strong support for CND within its own ranks. Elsewhere in Western Europe a similar pattern obtains, whereby specific parties are linked with the aims in whole or part of their national peace movements. Ecological protest has likewise, as we have indicated, found representation on the official political spectrum through the formation of the green parties.

In Eastern Europe, by contrast, where 'peace' and 'ecological' campaigning is supposedly taken care of by the state and fully tolerated only under its aegis, the situation is rather different. Not only is any challenge to the state's particular construction of these issues regarded as inherently subversive, but there are no recognised means for challenging its interpretations. There is, in other words, a huge and hitherto almost unbridgeable gap between what might be called the 'formal' political process (the state machinery) and minority protest ('dissidence').

It is hardly surprising therefore if groups like Charta 77 in Czechoslovakia and Wolnosc i Pokoj (Freedom and Peace) in Poland have seen their role as essentially 'anti-political': as contributing to the construction and diffusion of an alternative political culture. In the absence of 'civil society' (where society is saturated by the state and all accommodation with its institutions proceeds at the risk of compromise and cooption), radical opposition is necessarily forced to adopt a strategy of 'informal' subversion.

It would, of course, be mistaken to imply that peace and ecological protest in the West is exhausted in conventional political campaigning. In an important sense, it too is a way of life, and many who support its aims do so only in the sense that they subscribe as private citizens to its general philosophy. Indeed, if one can speak of a counter-cultural movement in Western Europe, it is in virtue of the extensive but loosely-knit network of groups and individuals who share an 'eco-peace' perspective which they despair of finding reflected in the argument and vocabulary of their official political representatives. It should be recognised, moreover, that a good part of the symbolism and protest of the peace movement (as manifested in the peace camps and marches, and in the innumerable local events) is neither political in any formal sense, nor tied to any precise agenda, but rather expresses a yearning for a more general shift of cultural values and an attempt to provide some positive exemplar of where that shift might take us.

To this we may add that there is now a growing scepticism even in the more politically engaged circles about the extent to which the peace and ecology programmes can be advanced through pressure on the normal political institutions. Many activists have been saddened by the electoral evidence of the unpopularity of these programmes. But they have been in some ways even more demoralised by the pragmatic response of professional politicians to that evidence. In Britain, for example, the Labour Party leadership – which during the recent electoral campaign appeared signally reluctant to offer the public any of the more cogent arguments for a non-nuclear defence policy – is now taking the latest Conservative general election victory as proof that anti-nuclearism is an electoral liability to which the party should probably accommodate in its future policies. There is a feeling, in short, that politicians will inevitably seek to adjust to what they perceive are public wishes, rather than engage in the harder and less personally rewarding task of popular conversion. There is a growing sense, too, that the economic and ideological forces ranged against any significant changes of direction are such as to make it unlikely that what is pledged by political parties in opposition will ever be fully translated into practice in government. And in any case, as far as the green programme is concerned, there is little to bring comfort in the economic policies of any of the mainstream parties.

Hence the suggestion that energies might now be better spent in assembling some sort of coalition to unite common-minded, oppositional groups across the blocs, outside the forum of officialdom in the East or party politics in the West. Without prejudicing the exact interpretation to be put on this idea, which remains in fact somewhat unclear and under-discussed, we would argue that if it is construed in the larger sense of an anti-statist politics in the West which would meet and reinforce antipolitical' impulses of dissent in Eastern Europe, then there are several grounds on which to question its wisdom.

Admittedly, even the more sympathetic politicians have proved rather resistant to the scale of conversion which the peace and ecology movements are now insisting is necessary. But despite this, some headway has certainly been made. After all, the word 'green' scarcely figured in the vocabulary of politics before the beginning of the 1980s, nor was there anything like the same public awareness then of the dangers of the nuclear industry. This progress, minimal as it may seem, has arguably only been achieved because of the extent to which the various peace and green lobbies have engaged in debate with all levels of the political process and addressed themselves directly to parties and the institutions of the state. There is a real risk that in making any moves which tend to confine discussion to the likeminded, we alienate and exclude those elements most in need of further education and thus sacrifice what gains have already been made.

Besides, it would be paradoxical for those in the West who have so persistently denounced the absence of political pluralism in the East now to advocate a politics which in effect proclaimed the futility of the formal procedures and institutions of Western democracy. Nor can an unqualified anti-statism or anarchistic politics be in any sense an adequate response where right-wing libertarianism is in the ascendancy.

But there are also a number of features of the East European situation which suggest the inadvisability of pursuing too univocal and oppositional a strategy. In the first place, it should be said – and Western sympathisers should note – that groups such as Charta 77, Wolnosc i Pokoj or the Hungarian 'Blues' are by no means motivated by any simple spirit of anti-statist rebellion, and in many cases have engaged in direct appeals to their own governments on environmental issues – sometimes with notable success. One might argue that some of this success and the measure of tolerance accorded such groups, despite their technically illegal and unwelcome activities, reflect their own resistance to a more cloak-and-dagger style of politics; for 'antipolitical' groups in the East are not labouring to create their own subcultural enclaves but rather to expand civil society 'from below'. Important too has been the credibility they gain from Western contacts whose comportment has made it difficult to dismiss them as mere 'oppositionists'.

To this we might add that ecological activity is no more confined to 'dissident' circles in the East than it is the exclusive province of left-wing activism in the West. Relative to civil liberties, ecology is a relatively 'safe' campaigning issue, which is already the focus of a number of official clubs, and a topic on which many scientists, cultural figures and members of the administrative bureaucracy have voiced their particular protests and felt able to expose the folly of official policy. Rather than react to the relative 'respectability' of this style of ecological campaigning as an automatic index of its deference to the state or of the anodyne quality of its demands, it may be better to think how best it might be exploited in order to extend the sympathy and audience for the sharper political argument of the independent groups which have now linked issues of ecology into their demands for civil liberties and democratisation.

There would seem all the more reason to pursue such a policy at a point where the space for autonomous and semi-autonomous activity is being enlarged as a result of the Gorbachev reforms. We should also take note of the fact that there are many different forms of 'opposition' now seizing the opportunity of *glasnost* to promote themselves, and not all of them are obviously progressive. The semi-spontaneous group known around Moscow as the 'Lyubers' is inspired, according to Boris Kagarlitsky, by nostalgia for Stalin, and there are distinct nationalistic or anti-semitic tendencies discernible in groups such as Pamiat (USSR), Grunewald (Poland) and the Populists (Hungary). Moreover, 'opposition' even of the kind which might be sympathetic to Western movements, and which Western movements might want to engage with, is more factional and divergent in outlook than is sometimes assumed – and there is some suggestion now that this divergence includes differences of opinion regarding the strategy of dissent itself in the new *glasnost* context. Writing, for example, of the current left opposition in the USSR, Kagarlitsky maintains that the problem was not whether to participate in the changes but '*how* to participate ... The trouble with the liberal intelligentsia was that it showed itself quite incapable of any constructive initiative of its own, preferring just to applaud Gorbachev's decisions ... However, an acute need for new ideas, a new culture, had arisen in society; what was wanted was criticism not so much of the past as of the present, not so much of others as of ourselves, and a rejection of liberal dogmas no less resolute than our rejection of any others.'[4] In a situation where such discrimination around the notion of 'opposition' is in evidence in Eastern Europe, the Western peace movement will need to develop an equally nuanced political language.

This brings us in conclusion to some more general considerations regarding the nature and scope of support for an 'eco-peace' politics. Is it being suggested by the 'league of opposition' approach that this support is as limited at present in the East as it is in the West – and to be found essentially only among a minority of informed activists? Given the absence in Eastern Europe of any electoral channels for the public to voice its feelings on this issue, it is impossible to assess the level of support it might command. On the other hand, such indices of public opinion as are available – for example, the popularity of cultural works dealing with ecological themes – give the impression that there is a deeper and more pervasive concern with the social and natural consequences of industrialisation than is to be found in Western Europe at present. Much of this concern may be rather unfocused and nostalgic in character: an unease at the disruptive incursions of 'progress' upon traditional ways of doing things, rather than a prescription for alternatives. But it remains the case that a Vosnesensky can command an audience in the USSR for his sombre poems on the themes of war and environmental damage which only a rock singer or star comedian could hope to expect in the West.

This brings us to a further question: given that ecology has had such little success with the electorate in the pluralist and democratic West, how far should we assume that democratisation will automatically advance its cause in Eastern Europe? In a sense the question is ill-formulated: we want to respond that it all depends on what is meant by 'democracy'. But it is probably important to raise it even in this crude form, if only to alert ourselves to some of the more paradoxical and disturbing aspects of the context in which we are strategically planning for the promotion of the 'green alternative'. To put the matter bluntly, then:

popular sympathy for the ecological argument may be more extensive where it has least means to express itself, and come easiest where consumerism is least rampant. The evidence certainly suggests that the market-dominated, liberal, pluralist societies of the West provide rather infertile terrain for the emergence of the 'spirituality' and general asceticism in material consumption which are ultimately indispensable to the furtherance of green politics. Soviet propaganda has not been slow to exploit this difference of disposition: capitalist society, as we are tired of being told, is a hotbed of decadent consumerism. Of course, Gorbachevian liberalisation is designed to introduce precisely those forms of 'efficiency' and market accountability whose logic has ultimately given us capitalism – and capitalist consumption. If this were only a matter of Soviet propaganda getting muddled, it would hardly be of much import. But to anyone alarmed by the ecological consequences of this form of economic revisionism, the problems lie much deeper.

Much of the argument of this book has tended to the idea that ecology must now be linked into the peace–democracy nexus to form an inseparable triad of peace movement concerns. As a banner or rallying point, 'peace-democracy-ecology' can hardly be faulted. But it should be recognised that the addition of ecology, if it is to prove more than a ritual piety of peace movement discussion, involves a commitment. Ecology is not a politics in itself but a demand in the first instance that the natural limitation of resources be accommodated in the way we organise our economy. (It means much more as well, justice in the distribution of resources being a major consideration, but it is the acknowledgement of natural constraints on human productivity which is distinctive and fundamental to the ecological argument.) Now if, as we have suggested, a capitalist economy is inherently anti-ecological, this has some implications for the 'democracy' element in the green–peace–democracy nexus. It will mean, for example, taking some care to differentiate between the different levels and forms of freedom which have historically coexisted within democratic societies. The Western capitalist societies *are* democratic relative to those of the Eastern bloc, but they are so in virtue of the various political freedoms associated with civil society rather than in virtue of their market economy (whose 'free forces' are to be found asserting themselves in many politically repressive and autocratic regimes elsewhere in the world). Or, if it is insisted that democratic 'freedoms' include the entrepreneurial and consumer freedoms which only the uncontrolled market permits, then one will have to contest the compatibility of that form of freedom with respect for the needs of ecology.

We are suggesting, then, that discussion and clarification of these distinctions will be essential to the furtherance of any serious campaigning around this broadened agenda. Many activists in the West have long been uneasy with the tendency of dissenting opinion in the East to associate democracy in an unqualified way with the general pattern of Western society. Ecology provides a trans-bloc focus of common concern around which these over-simple conceptions can be challenged and redefined.

The introduction of ecology onto its agenda also suggests that the peace movement might now think of extending its 'utopian' imaginings of alternatives to our current nuclear impoverishment, to encompass the pleasures of a world converted to more peaceful and egalitarian patterns of consumption. For the grindstone of commodity production has deprived us of many delights in which we could otherwise have indulged.

Much of the foregoing argument suggests that 'needs' are to a significant degree formed under the impact of what is available for consumption. (Were this not the case, for example, anxieties about the 'mindless consumerism' encouraged by the market would be out of place.) But it would be mistaken all the same to assume that they are entirely moulded by the commodities thrown upon the market, or that there is no element of desire in people which would respond to alternative hedonist images to those projected by the advertisers and political 'realists'. There is some evidence, in fact, of its presence in the conflictual nature of current desires – for whatever their consumer habits, there is no doubt that many people are in some sense mentally torn these days between their desire for more motor or air transport and their desire for unpolluted air and uncongested cities; between their desire for everything which is speedier and their desire for a more leisurely pace of life; between their workaholic obsessions and their yearnings to be free of the rat race, and so on. Moreover, there are arguably many symptoms of dissatisfaction with contemporary existence which are discernible only in the negative forms of drug addiction, clinical depression, domestic violence, vandalism and other prevalent pathologies of our times.

One is not suggesting that nihilism of this kind is only waiting for a compelling image of a greed-free, uncorrupted world for it to convert to a heady affirmation of the joys of life. One is suggesting only that affluent society has also bred extensive malaise, not all of which is accountable simply to economic deprivation; and that where there is no acknowledgement in political discourse of these less tangible sources of discontent, and no expression of the less material gratifications it may be hankering after, sensibility itself becomes dulled: people begin to lose sight of what it is they may be missing, and in the end they cease to care. We are also implying that to date there has been practically nothing in the argument of the mainstream political parties to suggest they are even aware of these complexities of need; amd certainly no attempt – and here it was surely the parties of the left which had the duty – to portray some vision of society, in which the more buried but les materialist aspirations felt by many people could have found a clearer reflection and more positive encouragement.

Let us begin then to correct this deficiency, and to be bolder in speaking of a more sober material consumption as the condition of the good life – as the condition indeed of a much more riotous enjoyment of certain pleasures: of the pleasure of clean and junk-free environments; of natural landscape; of cities reclaimed from the snarling dictatorship of the motor car; of days restored to us from the nine-to-five tyranny of producing more labour-saving things; and not least of the pleasure of knowing that we are no longer lending ourselves either as producers or consumers to those trends which have caused such misery and deprivation in other parts of the globe, and made a mockery of the idea of building a better and safer future for our children. And since we are speaking of indulgence, let us not hesitate either to permit ourselves the pleasure of dismantling those pulsating nuclear monstrosities squatting on our beaches or in the remoter reaches of our countryside and threatening irremediable damage to the most elemental sources of joy. We do it first in the imagination – then in reality.

Notes

1. This phrase was used in the preparatory meetings for the 1987 European Nuclear Disarmament Convention. See Lynne Jones's article in *END Journal*, Summer 1987.
2. George Konrád, *Antipolitics*, translated by Richard E. Allen, Quartet Books, London, 1984. Jan Vladislav (ed), *Václav Havel, or Living in Truth*, Faber & Faber, London, 1987, p. 92.
3. See, for instance, William Ophuls's dispassionate and scholarly work, *Ecology and the Politics of Scarcity*, W.H. Freeman, San Francisco, USA, 1977.
4. Boris Kagarlitsky, *New Left Review*, 164, p. 25.

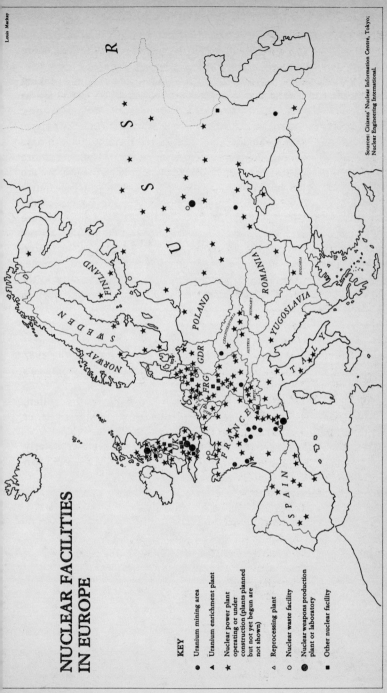

NUCLEAR FACILITIES
IN EUROPE

KEY

● Uranium mining area

▲ Uranium enrichment plant

★ Nuclear power plant
operating or under
construction (plants planned
but not yet begun are
not shown)

△ Reprocessing plant

○ Nuclear waste facility

◉ Nuclear weapons production
plant or laboratory

■ Other nuclear facility

Louis Mackay

Sources: Citizens' Nuclear Information Centre, Tokyo;
Nuclear Engineering International.

NUCLEAR FACILITIES IN THE WORLD
(Excluding Europe and the USA)

★ REACTORS NOT SHOWN

Many of the nuclear power plants whose approximate positions are shown on these maps consists of several reactor units. Small research reactors, which exist in many countries, are also not shown. In addition to the world's 400 or so power plant reactors on land, some 500 more are currently operating at sea as propulsion units in submarines and other naval vessels.

Louis Mackay

Sources: Citizens' Nuclear Information Centre, Tokyo; Nuclear Engineering International.

KEY

●   Uranium mining area

▲   Uranium enrichment plant

★   Nuclear power plant operating or under construction (plants planned but not yet begun are not shown).

△   Reprocessing plant (civil or military use)

○   Nuclear waste facility

◉   Nuclear weapons production plant or laboratory

■   Other nuclear facility

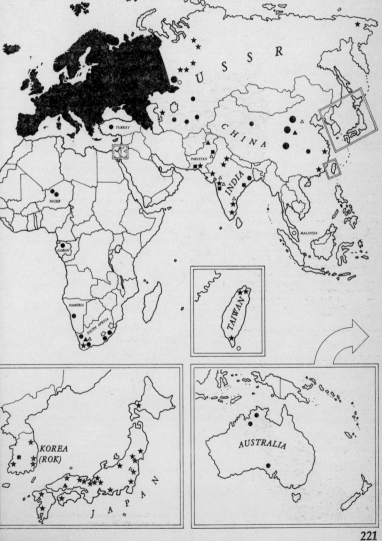

NUCLEAR FACILITIES IN THE USA

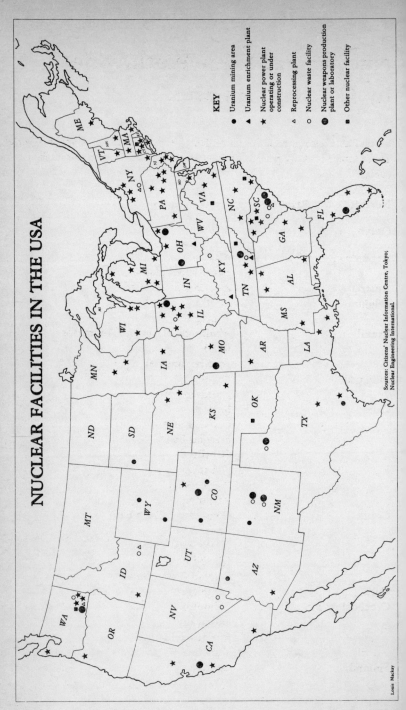

KEY

- ● Uranium mining area
- ▲ Uranium enrichment plant
- ★ Nuclear power plant operating or under construction
- △ Reprocessing plant
- ○ Nuclear waste facility
- ◉ Nuclear weapons production plant or laboratory
- ■ Other nuclear facility

Sources: Citizens' Nuclear Information Centre, Tokyo; Nuclear Engineering International.

Louis Mackay

Nuclear Facilities Worldwide, by Country and Site

Latest figures from the IAEA show 416 working nuclear plants world-wide. These tables identify power stations and other facilities in the nuclear cycle.

Nuclear Power Stations

Country	Site
Country	*Site*
Argentina	Atucha
	Embalse (Cordoba)
Austria	Zwentendorf (unused)
Belgium	Doel
	Tihange
Brazil	Almirante A. Alberto (Angra dos Reis)
	Peruibe (Iguape)
Bulgaria	Belene
	Kozluduy
Canada	Bruce
	Darlington
	Douglas Point
	Gentilly
	Pickering
	Pint Lepreau
	Rolphton
China	Guangdong (Daya Bay)
	Jinshan
	North-east China
	Qinshan
	Su Nan (East China)
Cuba	Cienfuegos
Czechoslovakia	Bohunice
	Dukovany
	Mochovce (Levice)
	Temelin
Finland	Loviisa

Country	Site
Finland (continued)	Olkiluoto
France	Belleville
	Bugey
	Cattenom
	Chinon
	Chooz
	Civaux
	Creys Malville
	Cruas
	Dampierre
	Fessenheim
	Flamanville
	Golfech
	Gravelines
	Le Blayais
	Marcoule
	Monts d'Arrée
	Nogent
	Paluel
	Penly
	Phénix
	Rapsodie
	St Alban
	St Laurent des Eaux
	Tricastin
German Democratic Republic	Magdeburg (Stendal)
	Nord
	Rheinsberg
German Federal Republic	Biblis
	Borken
	Brokdorf
	Brunsbüttel
	Emsland
	Grafenrheinfeld
	Grohnde
	Gundremmingen
	Hamm
	Isar (Ohu)
	Jülich
	Kahl
	Kalkar
	Karlsruhe

Country	Site
German Federal Republic Republic (continued)	Krümmel
	Lingen
	Mülheim-Kärlich
	Neckarwestheim
	Neupotz
	Niederaichbach
	Obrigheim
	Pfaffenhofen
	Phillipsburg
	Stade
	THTR 300 (Schmehausen)
	Unterweser (Esenshamm)
	Vahnum
	Würgassen
	Wyhl (Süd)
Hungary	Paks
India	FBTR (Fast Breeder Test Reactor)
	Kakrapar
	Madras (Kalpakkam)
	Narora
	Rajasthan
	Tarapur
Italy	Alto Lazio (Montalto di Castro)
	Apulia
	Caorso
	Cirene
	Garigliano
	Latina
	Lombardy
	PEC (Brasimone)
	Piedmont
	Trino Vercellese
Japan	Fugen
	Fukushima
	Genkai
	Hamaoka
	Ikata
	Joyo
	Kashiwazaki-Kariwa
	Maki
	Mihama
	Monju

Country	Site
Japan (continued)	Ohi
	Onagawa
	Sendai
	Shimane
	Takahama
	Tokai
	Tomari
	Tsuruga
Mexico	Laguna Verde
Netherlands	Borssele
	Dodewaard
Norway	Halden
Pakistan	Chashma
	Kanupp
Philippines	Napot Point (unused)
Poland	Zarnowiec
Romania	Cernavoda
	Olt
South Africa	Koeberg
South Korea	Kori
	Uljin
	Wolsung
	Yeonggwang
Spain	Almaraz
	Asco
	Cofrentes
	Jose Cabrera (Zorita)
	Lemoniz
	Regodola
	Santa Maria de Garona
	Sayago
	Trillo
	Valdecaballeros
	Vandellos
Sweden	Barsebäck
	Forsmark
	Oskarshamn
	Ringhals
Switzerland	Beznau
	Gösgen-Däniken
	Graben
	Kaiseraugst
	Leibstadt

Country	Site
Switzerland (continued)	Mühleberg
Taiwan	Chinshan
	Kuosheng
	Maanshan
	Yenliao
UK	Berkeley
	Bradwell
	Calder Hall
	Chapel Cross
	Dounreay
	Dungeness
	Hartlepool
	Heysham
	Hinkley Point
	Hunterston
	Oldbury
	Sizewell
	Torness
	Trawsfynydd
	Windscale
	Winfrith
	Wylfa
USA	Arkansas
	Beaver Valley
	Bellefonte
	Big Rock Point
	Braidwood
	Browns Ferry
	Brunswick
	Byron
	Callaway
	Calvert Cliffs
	Carroll County
	Catawba
	Clinton
	Comanche Peak
	Donald C. Cook
	Cooper
	Crystal River
	Davis Besse
	Diablo Canyon
	Dresden

Country	Site
USA (continued)	Duane Arnold
	EBR 2
	Joseph M. Farley
	Fermi
	James A. Fitzpatrick
	FFTF (Fast Flux Test Facility)
	Fort Calhoun
	Fort St Vrain
	Robert E. Ginna
	Grand Gulf
	Haddam Neck (Connecticut Yankee)
	Hanford
	Edwin I. Hatch
	Hope Creek
	Humboldt Bay
	Indian Point
	Kewaunee
	La Crosse
	La Salle
	Limerick
	Maine Yankee
	William B. McGuire
	Midland
	Millstone
	Monticello
	Nine Mile Point
	North Anna
	Oconee
	Oyster Creek
	Palisades
	Palo Verde
	Peach Bottom
	Perry
	Pilgrim
	Point Beach
	Prairie Island
	Quad Cities
	Rancho Secco
	River Bend
	H.B. Robinson
	St Lucie
	Salem

Country	Site
USA (continued)	San Onofre
	Seabrook
	Sequoyah
	Shearon Harris
	Shippingport
	Shoreham
	South Texas
	Virgil C. Summer
	Surry
	Susquehanna
	Three Mile Island
	Trojan
	Turkey Point
	Vermont Yankee
	Alvin W. Vogtle
	Waterford
	Watts Bar
	Wolf Creek
	WNP (Washington Nuclear Plant)
	Yankee Rowe
	Zion
USSR	Aktash (Crimea)
	Armenia (Oktembryan)
	Balakovo (Nizhinekamsk)
	Bashkir (Nefyekamsk)
	BN 350 (Shevchenko)
	BN 600 (Beloyarsk)
	Beloyarsk
	Bilibino
	Chernobyl
	Gorky
	Ignalina (Druksja)
	Kalinin
	Kharkov
	Khmelnitski
	Kola
	Kostroma
	Kursk
	Leningrad
	Melekess (Ulyanovsk)
	Nikolaiev (South Ukraine)
	Novovoronezh
	Obninsk

Country	Site
USSR (continued)	Odessa
	Privolzhskaya (Saratov)
	Rostov
	Rovno (West Ukraine)
	Smolensk
	Tatar
	Troitsk (Siberia)
	Tsimlyansk (Volgodonsk)
	Voronezh
	Zaporozhe
Yugoslavia	Krsko

Uranium Mining Areas

Country	Place
Argentina	Los Gigantes
	Malargue
	Sierra Pintada
Australia	Nabarlek
	Ranger
	Roxby Downs
Brazil	Pocos de Caldas
Canada	Cluff Lake
	Elliot Lake
	Key Lake
	Rabbit Lake
China	Hunan
	Xinjiang
Czechoslovakia	Jáchymov
France	Cerilly
	Commanderie, Hardon, Escarpière
	Coutras
	Fanay, Margnac, Bellezane
	Le Bernardan
	Le Cellier, Pierres Plantées
	Lodève
	St Pierre Cantal
Gabon	Oklo
German Federal Republic	Menzenschwand
India	Jaduguda

Country	Place
Namibia	Rossing
Niger	Akouta
	Arlit
South Africa	Karoo Basin
	Palabora
	Witwatersrand Basin
Turkey	Salihli
USA	Black Hills, South Dakota
	Front Range, Marshall Pass,
	Tallahassee Creek, Colorado
	Grants mineral belt, New Mexico
	Gulf coastal plain, Texas
	Northern Arizona
	Paradox Basin, Colorado
	Washake, Wyoming
	Wyoming Basin, Wyoming
USSR	Alma Ata
	Bukhara
	Fergana–Tashkent
	Krivoi Rog
	Northern Caucasus
	Northern Kazakh

Uranium Enrichment Plants

Country	Facility
Brazil	Belo Horizonte
China	Lanzhou
France	Pierrelatte
	Tricastin
German Federal Republic	Gronau
Japan	Ningyo-toge
Netherlands	Almelo
Pakistan	Kahuta
South Africa	Valindaba
UK	Capenhurst
USA	Oak Ridge Y12 plant, Tennessee
	Paduca, Kentucky
	Portsmouth, Ohio

Reprocessing Plant

Country	Facility
Argentina	Ezeiza
Belgium	Mol
China	Beijing
France	Cap la Hague
	Marcoule
German Federal Republic	Karlsruhe
India	Kalpakkan
	Tarapur
	Trombay
Israel	Dimona
Japan	Tokai
Pakistan	Rawalpindi
South Africa	Pelindaba
UK	Dounreay
	Sellafield
USA	Hanford, Washington
	Idaho National Engineering, Idaho
	Savannah River, South Carolina (military use)

Nuclear Waste Facilities

France	La Manche
German Federal Republic	Asse
	Gorleben
Malaysia	Papan
Taiwan	Lan-yu Island
UK	Drigg
USA	Barnwell, South Carolina
	Beatty, Nevada
	Hanford, Washington
	Idaho Falls, Idaho
	Los Alamos, New Mexico
	Nevada Test Site, Nevada
	Oak Ridge, Tennessee
	Pentex, Texas
	Sandia, New Mexico
	Savannah River, South Carolina
	West Valley, New York
USSR	Chelyabinsk
	Kurchatov near Tallinn, Estonia

Nuclear Weapons Production Plant

China	Baotou
	Chongqing
	Xian
France	Celestin
Israel	Dimona
UK	Aldermaston
	Burghfield
	Chapelcross
USA	Argonne Laboratory, New Brunswick, Illinois
	Ashtabula fabrication plant, Ohio
	Hanford, Washington
	Kansas City Plant, Missouri
	Lawrence Livermore Laboratory, California
	Los Alamos, New Mexico
	Miamisburg mound facility, Ohio
	Oak Ridge Y12 plant, Tennessee
	Pentex, Albuquerque, New Mexico
	Pinellas plant, St Petersburg, Florida
	Rocky Flats, Colorado
	Sandia, Albuquerque, New Mexico
	Savannah River, South Carolina
USSR	Chelyabinsk
	Kurchatov

Other Facilities

Country	Name and Function
Argentina	Cordoba (conversion)
	Ezeiza (fuel fabrication)
Brazil	São Paolo (conversion)
Canada	Chalk River Institute Moncton (fuel fabrication)
	Petersborough (fuel fabrication)
	Pickering (H-3 production)
	Port Hope (fuel fabrication and conversion)
	Toronto (fuel fabrication)
France	Annecy (fuel assemblies)

Country	Name and Function
German Federal Republic	Emsland (fuel assemblies)
	Grossauheim (fuel assemblies)
	Grosswelzsheim (fuel assemblies)
	Hanau (fuel assemblies)
India	Hyderabad (fuel fabrication)
	Trombay (fuel fabrication)
Israel	Dimona (fuel fabrication)
Pakistan	Chasma (fuel fabrication)
	Multan (conversion)
South Korea	Daejon (fuel fabrication)
UK	Amersham International (radio isotope production)
	Culham (UKAEA Institute)
	Harwell (UKAEA Institute)
	Risley (UKAEA Institute)
	Springfields (nuclear fuel production)
	Windscale (UKAEA Institute)
	Winfrith (UKAEA Institute)
USA	Cimarron, Oklahoma (assemblies)
	Columbia, South Carolina (fuel assemblies)
	Erwin, Tennessee (fuel assemblies)
	Hanford, Washington (fuel assemblies)
	Lynchburg, Virginia (fuel assemblies)
	Wilmington, North Carolina (fuel assemblies)
	Windsor, Connecticut (fuel assemblies)
USSR	Atommash (nuclear industry complex)

Glossary

AEC: Atomic Energy Commission (US).

AES (Russian acronym): 'Atomic Energy Station'.

AGR: Advanced Gas-Cooled Reactor.

Alpha Radiation: the emission of alpha particles (high-energy helium nuclei, containing two protons and two neutrons). Alpha radiation is the least penetrating form (a sheet of paper will stop most of it), but alpha-emitters (such as plutonium-239) are extremely dangerous if they become absorbed into the human body, where they can cause cancer.

Atom: The smallest possible part of a given element, characterised by a particular relationship between the number of neutrons, protons and electrons it contains.

Becquerel (Bq): unit of radioactivity representing one radioactive emission per second.

Beta Radiation: the emission of beta particles (high-energy electrons). Beta radiation, which may penetrate a thin sheet of metal, is more penetrating than alpha radiation, but much less so than gamma rays.

BNFL: British Nuclear Fuels Ltd.

BWR: Boiling Water Reactor.

CANDU: Canadian Uranium Deuterium reactor.

CEGB: Central Electricity Generating Board (UK).

Chain Reaction: self-sustaining reaction in a critical mass of fissile material, produced by free neutrons striking nuclei and releasing more neutrons in greater numbers.

CHP: combined heat and power fossil-fuel power station.

Cladding: sheath in which nuclear fuel elements are sealed.

Comecon: Council for Mutual Economic Assistance – economic organisation comprising the USSR, Bulgaria, Cuba, Czechoslovakia, German Democratic Republic, Hungary, Mongolian People's Republic, Poland and Romania.

Containment: the structure which surrounds a reactor and prevents radioactivity escaping into the environment.

Control Rods: rods of neutron-absorbing material which can be inserted into the core of a reactor in order to slow or stop the chain reaction.

Coolant: liquid (water or metal) or gas used to cool the core of a reactor and convey the heat used to generate steam to power turbine generators.

Core: the central part of a reactor, containing the fuel elements, moderator, etc.

Critical: state in which the number of free neutrons is neither increasing nor decreasing, and a self-sustained chain reaction can occur.

Critical Mass: the mass of fissile material required to sustain a chain reaction.

Curie (Ci): = 37,000,000,000 Bq (the radioactivity of one gram of radium).

DoE: Department of Energy (UK).

Dose: the amount of energy delivered to a given mass of material by radiation passing through or into it.

Electron: negatively charged particle inhabiting the outer part of an atom.

Enrichment: the process of increasing the proportion of the fissile uranium-235 isotope in a given quantity of uranium above the natural 0.7 per cent.

ERR: Earth Resources Research (UK).

Fallout: airborne radioactive material (from a nuclear weapon or reactor accident) falling on the earth.

FBR: Fast Breeder Reactor.

Fissile: capable of undergoing fission.

Fission: the disintegration of an atom's nucleus into lighter fragments and free neutrons

Fission Products: atoms created from the rupture of another atom's nucleus.

Fuel Temperature Coefficient: positive or negative correlation between the temperature of the fuel in a reactor and the rate of fission in the reaction.

Fusion: the joining of two nuclei to form a single, heavier nucleus.

Gamma Radiation: high-energy (very short wavelength) electromagnetic radiation, able to penetrate a metre of concrete.

GEC: General Electric Co. (UK)

Gigawatt (GW): 1,000,000,000 watts.

Gray (Gy): unit of radiation dose, equivalent to the absorption of one Joule of energy into one kilogram of matter, and equal to 100 rads.

Half-life: the time taken for the radioactivity of a given quantity of a particular element to decline by half.

Heat Exchanger: boiler in which steam to drive the generator turbines is produced with the heat conducted in the reactor coolant.

Heavy Water (Deuterium Oxide): water (hydrogen oxide) in which the hydrogen (deuterium) atoms have a neutron lacking in ordinary hydrogen.

High-level Waste: highly radioactive waste containing substances with medium and long half-lives.

IAEA: International Atomic Energy Agency.

IIASA: International Institute of Applied Systems Analysis.

INF: Intermediate-range Nuclear Forces.

INSAG: International Nuclear Safety Advisory Group.

Ion: an atom with one or more electrons missing (but the nucleus intact).

Isotope: one form of an element which exists in several, each characterised by the number of neutrons in the nucleus (the number of protons is the same in all isotopes of the same element).

Krypton: a chemically inert but radioactive gas.

Light Water: ordinary water.

LMFBR: Liquid Metal Fast Breeder Reactor.

Low-level Waste: nuclear waste including material of low radioactivity and shorter half-life.

LWR: Light Water Reactor (includes non-PHWR PWRs).

Magnox: a magnesium alloy used as cladding in early British gas-cooled reactors.

Megawatt (MW): unit of power – 1,000,000 watts.

Meltdown: overheating of solid fuel in a reactor core to the point where the fuel cladding, the fuel itself, or even the surrounding structure melts.

Moderator: material such as water, heavy water or graphite, used to slow down the neutrons in a reactor core in order to improve their chances of striking the nucleus of a fuel atom and causing fission.

MWe: Megawatts of electric power.

MWt: Megawatts of thermal power.

Neutron: uncharged particle in an atom's nucleus, released in fission, capable of being absorbed into the nucleus of another atom, and of causing further fission.

NPT: Non-Proliferation Treaty (1963).

Nuclear Fuel: fissile material such as natural or enriched uranium, or plutonium dioxide, suitably prepared for use in a reactor.

Nuclear Reaction: reaction involving the rupture of atomic nuclei.

Nucleus: The kernel of an atom consisting of protons and neutrons (except in the hydrogen atom which has a proton but no neutron).

OECD: Organisation for Economic Cooperation and Development.

PHWR: Pressurised Heavy Water Reactor.

Plutonium: plutonium-239 is an artificial element; it is produced by bombarding uranium with neutrons.

Power Density: the heat output (in kilowatts) from each litre of volume in a reactor core.

Proton: positively charged particle in an atom's nucleus.

PWR: Pressurised Water Reactor.

RAD: 'Radiation Absorbed Dose' unit. 1 rad = 0.01 Grays.

Radiation (Nuclear): the emission from radioactive substances in the form of gamma rays, alpha or beta particles, or neutrons.

Radioactivity: the rate at which a substance is emitting radiation.

Radionuclide: radioactive isotope nucleus.

RBMK (Russian acronym): 'High Power, Channel-Type Reactor'.

Reactivity: the degree to which the fissile materials in a reactor are able to support a chain reaction.

REM: unit of 'effective dose' taking into account (unlike rads and Grays) the different 'quality' of different types of radiation. 1 rem = 0.01 Sieverts.

Reprocessing: the treatment of used fuel, or nuclear waste, in order to recover fissile material.

Scram (verb or noun): emergency shutdown of a reactor.

SDI: Strategic Defense Initiative ('Star Wars').

Sievert (Sv): unit of 'effective dose'. 1 Sv = 100 rems.

TMI: Three Mile Island (Harrisburg, Pennsylvania).

Tritium: 'hydrogen-3' (with two neutrons – normal hydrogen has none, deuterium, one).

UKAEA: UK Atomic Energy Authority.

Uranium Hexafluoride ('hex'): easily vapourised uranium compound used in enrichment processes.

Void Coefficient: positive or negative correlation between the amount of gas (steam) present in a liquid cooling system and the rate of fission in the reaction.

Watt: unit of power (or rate of transfer of energy: 1 watt = 1 Joule per second).

WHO: World Health Authority.

Wigner Energy: energy stored in irradiated graphite (moderator).

Xenon: chemically inert, but radioactive and neutron-absorbing gas.

Yellowcake: mixed uranium oxides produced in refinement process.

Zircalloy: zirconium alloy used in fuel cladding because of low neutron absorption.

Notes on Contributors

Praful Bidwai is Senior Assistant Editor on *The Times of India*, New Delhi. He has written extensively on developmental, nuclear and peace issues, contributing critical analyses of the Indian nuclear programme and official development plans. He is associated with numerous environmental, anti-nuclear and peace initiatives in South Asia.

Richard Erskine has a PhD in molecular physics, and is a member of SANA (Scientists Against Nuclear Arms). He has contributed to several SANA briefings on subjects such as deterrence and Chernobyl, and is employed as a computer software analyst in computer-aided design.

Martin Ince is Features Editor on *The Engineer* magazine, and the author of books on British energy and science policies, and space policy.

Mary Kaldor is a Fellow of the Transnational Institute in Amsterdam and a Senior Fellow of SPRU (the Science Policy Research Unit) at Sussex University. She was among the founders of the European Nuclear Disarmament organisation, and has been Editor of the *END Journal* for several years. Her publications include *The Disintegrating West* (1978) and *The Baroque Arsenal* (1982).

Louis Mackay is a freelance writer and a member of the *END Journal* editorial collective. He is the author of *China: a power for Peace?* (Merlin Press, 1986) and co-editor of *Nuclear-Free Defence* (Heretic Books, 1983).

Gordon MacKerron is an economist who has researched in energy policy for ten years. An adviser to the Monopolies and Mergers Commission in its investigation of the CEGB in 1980/81, he was also a witness at the Sizewell Inquiry for the Electricity Consumers Council. He is a Senior Fellow on the Energy Programme at SPRU. The Energy Programme is part of the ESRC (Economic and Social Research Council) Designated Research Centre in industrial innovation and energy policy. He is co-author of *The Economics of Nuclear Power* (forthcoming).

Zhores A. Medvedev was born in Tbilisi in the Georgian SSR, and has worked at the National Institute for Medical Research in London since 1973. As well as specialist medical books, he has written many landmark political and scientific studies on Soviet subjects, including *Khrushchev – The Years in Power* (with Roy Medvedev, 1976); *Nuclear Disaster in the Urals* (1979); *Andropov* (1983) and *Gorbachev* (1986, updated edition forthcoming); and Soviet Agriculture (1987).

Martin Ryle is a writer and teacher. His *The Politics of Nuclear Disarmament* was published by Pluto in 1982, and he is currently preparing a book on socialism and ecology.

Kate Soper is a philosopher and writer. She teaches part-time at the Polytechnic of North London, and is the author of *On Human Needs* (1981) and *Humanism and Anti-Humanism* (1986). She was Chair of END in 1986/7.

Mark Thompson is a freelance writer and translator. He is also a Deputy Editor of *END Journal*.

Philip Webber co-authored *London After the Bomb* (1982) and *Crisis over Cruise* (1983), and contributed to *The Militarisation of Space* (1987). He has a PhD in physics, researched for over 12 years at the Imperial College of Science and Technology, and is a member of SANA. He is employed as an Emergency Planner in South Yorkshire.